W9-ACG-920

South of the Moon

Blaine Littell

South of the Moon

On Stanley's Trail through the Dark Continent

HARPER & ROW, PUBLISHERS, NEW YORK

The heading for Chapter 1 is an excerpt from H. M. Stanley's *Notebook*. All other excerpts from Stanley's writings are from his two-volume work, *Through the Dark Continent*, which describes his expedition across Africa.

The quoted lines on pp. viii and 292 are from Robert Ardrey's *African Genesis*, published by Atheneum Publishers in 1961.

FIRST EDITION

LIBRARY OF CONGRESS CATALOG CARD NUMBER: 66-11477

for
R. L.

CONTENTS

South of the moon, where man was born,
all values and all symbols seem upside down.

ROBERT ARDREY,
African Genesis

South of the Moon

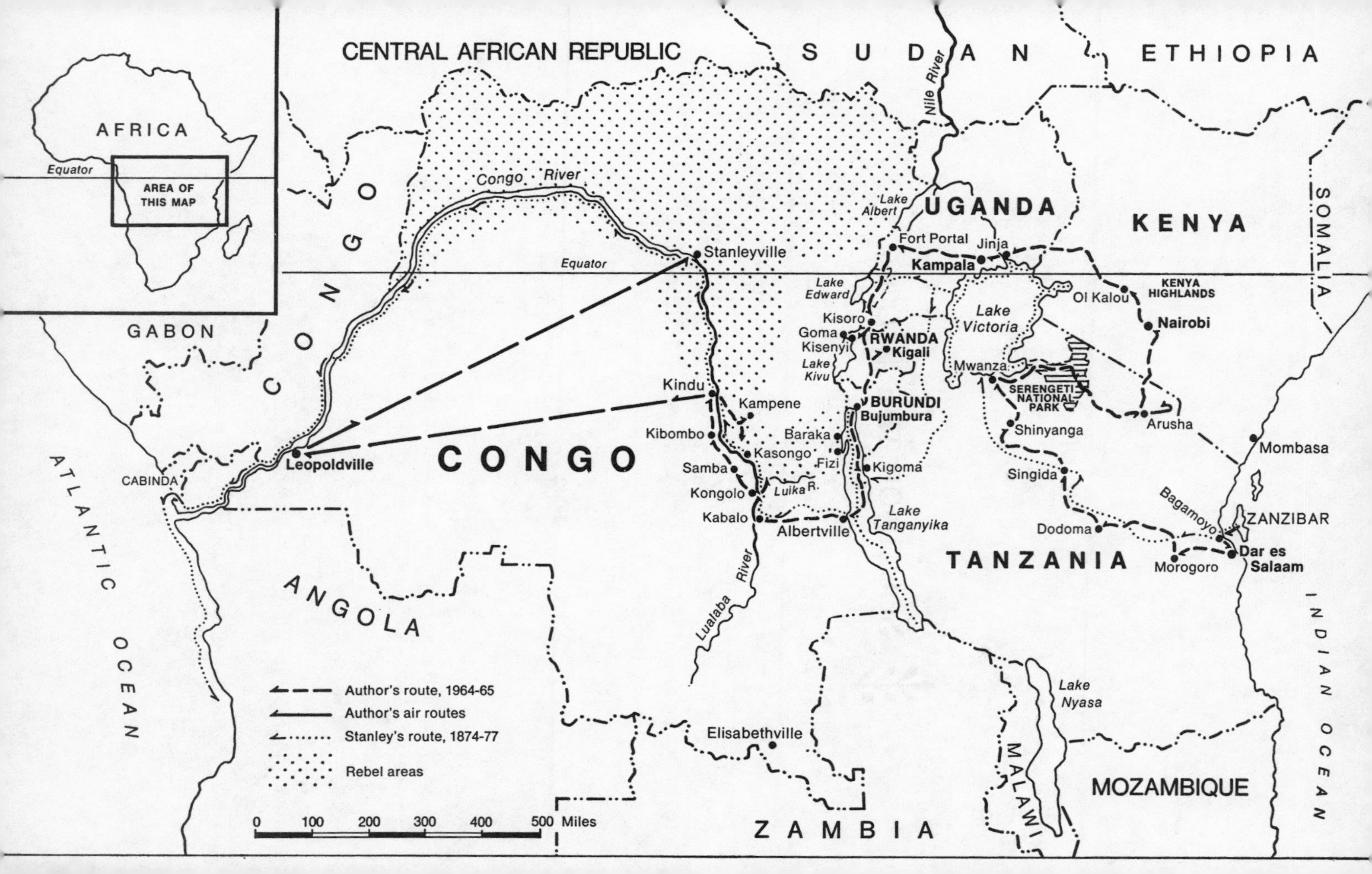
AFRICA
Equator
AREA OF THIS MAP
CENTRAL AFRICAN REPUBLIC
SUDAN
ETHIOPIA
SOMALIA
KENYA
UGANDA
Nile River
Lake Albert
Fort Portal
Jinja
Kampala
Ol Kalou
KENYA HIGHLANDS
Nairobi
Lake Victoria
Lake Edward
Kisoro
Goma
Kisenyi
RWANDA
Kigali
Lake Kivu
Mwanza
SERENGETI NATIONAL PARK
Arusha
Mombasa
BURUNDI
Bujumbura
Shinyanga
Kigoma
Singida
Lake Tanganyika
Dodoma
Bagamoyo
ZANZIBAR
Dar es Salaam
Morogoro
TANZANIA
INDIAN OCEAN
Congo River
Stanleyville
Equator
CONGO
GABON
Kindu
Kampene
Kibombo
Baraka
Kasongo
Fizi
Samba
Kongolo
Luika R.
Kabalo
Albertville
Leopoldville
CABINDA
ANGOLA
Lualaba River
Elisabethville
Lake Nyasa
MALAWI
MOZAMBIQUE
ZAMBIA
ATLANTIC OCEAN
Author's route, 1964-65
Author's air routes
Stanley's route, 1874-77
Rebel areas
0
100
200
300
400
500 Miles

CHAPTER I

CLOSE UP, BOYS!

Dear Livingstone! another sacrifice to Africa! His mission, however, must not be allowed to cease; others must go forward and fill the gap. "Close up boys! Close up!"

—HENRY MORTON STANLEY

THE winds of change blow softly through the Personal columns of *The Times* of London, if indeed they blow at all. There, amidst uniform beds of type, retired gentlewomen requiring part-time employment walk arm in arm with ex-cavalry officers seeking suitable positions. The gravel crunches under the measured tread of nannies who can no longer climb stairs and aged and distressed widows listen for the reassuring warble of ornithologists calling to other ornithologists. It is a place for the discreet cough, not the raised voice; a haven of repose for placid passions and domesticated dreams.

The custodians at the outer gates of this inner sanctum do not suffer fools or foreigners gladly especially when they appear as I did without proper credentials. Unless accompanied by a letter of recommendation from my clergyman, the advertisement I had brought with me could not and would not be considered for inclusion within the sacred precincts. I had never known a clergyman I could call my own and the idea of striking up an acquaintance with one now solely for his help in placing an item in the Personal columns of *The Times* seemed not only deceitful but time-consuming as well. I asked if a publisher or an editor would do. They would not, said the man from *The Times*, and neither would a literary agent, journalist or anyone in the American embassy below the rank of ambassador. But, he added, helpfully, a letter from my doctor might serve instead.

My doctor was delighted when I told him that he ranked above publishers and only just below clergymen and wrote me a one-sentence letter which I will use on my headstone if nothing better turns up in the meantime.

"The bearer," he wrote, "is a suitable candidate for an advert in *The Times*."

I submitted this appraisal to the Classified Advertisement Department together with the following suggested announcement:

> Adventurous, eccentric young Englishman, handy with fists, firearms, fotography, French, fourwheel drives wanted share some expenses with chance return on investment, hazardous 4-month trip Zanzibar points West, leaving immediately.

The following morning I received a letter from the manager of the Classified Advertisement Department regretting to advise me that "we would prefer not to accept this announcement for insertion in our columns and ask you please to accept our apology that this information was not given when you called."

The English are chary about revealing their identity. Consequently, I still do not know who it was I talked to when I called the Classified Advertisement Department and asked to speak to the manager. (The signature on the letter was purposely indecipherable.) Whoever it was, his voice was distant and disembodied. After I had read back the advertisement in question, there was dead silence at the other end of the line.

"I see," he said at length. The matter was obviously highly distasteful. But what had given offense? Where had I erred? There was another pause.

"Well, what," he asked, "what exactly did you mean by the word 'eccentric'?"

So that was it! A double meaning. A code word used by the Third Sex. Close up, boys! Close up! I felt the color rise in my cheeks as I stuttered out an explanation. No, I said, I had meant it straight. England, I had always heard, was the home of eccentrics—the bold, devil-may-care, I-do-what-I-damn-well-please-and-to-hell-with-what-*they*-think sort. *The Times* began to sound mollified. But there were other questions. Why, for instance, had I stressed the need for somone proficient with his fists and in the use of firearms? He had a point there. This was the period when the Congo rebellion was reaching its peak and the newspapers were full of stories about white mercenaries. I promised the anonymous voice that I was not recruiting paid gunmen. We talked, and we compromised. "Fists" and "firearms" came out and with them my attempt at alliteration; "fotography" was changed to "photography," which gave *The Times* the last laff. But I managed to hang on to Zanzibar even though the voice felt that "the island isn't exactly what you might call stable."

My pasteurized appeal ran eventually just under "EXPERIENCED NANNY" and drew a response that can only be described as pathetic. All in all, I received eight letters. None were from photographers and none of the writers (this surprised and disheartened me) seemed particularly keen on going. They were just asking—vaguely. One applicant, who signed himself "your obedient Servant," listed among his qualifications an adventurous spirit and a "clean" driving license. A day later, his uncle wrote to inform me that his nephew was only eighteen and that I would be "legally" taking him away from his guardian. He was not, however, suggesting I assume the boy's guardianship.

"He is a most unstable boy and not very well educated," the uncle continued. "I appeal to your good sense not to consider him for your trip as I am sure it could only end in disaster for you and for him."

Both quantitatively and qualitatively, the reaction to my advertisement was depressing, all the more so when compared with the outpouring of enthusiasm that greeted the announcement ninety years before that Henry Morton Stanley, the journalist and explorer, was about to embark on another African adventure and needed traveling companions. His first trip, during which he tracked down the hermitic Dr. Livingstone, had made him famous.

Now, more than twelve hundred applicants besieged Stanley for a place on his second expedition, among them cooks, waiters, hotel clerks, army officers, spiritual mediums and "magnetizers." Twelve hundred to eight, and of my eight the most promising was an unstable youth with a "clean" driving license. Obviously either times had changed or Stanley had something which I did not. Although I did not know it then, I was to be reminded of this latter fact many times as I tried to retrace his route of march through Africa.

As outlined in the *Daily Telegraph* of London, Stanley's mission was "to complete the work left unfinished by the lamentable death of Dr. Livingstone; to solve, if possible, the remaining problems of the geography of central Africa; and to investigate and report upon the haunts of the slave traders. . . ."

It was then and remains today the most ambitious and successful voyage of discovery ever undertaken on the Dark Continent. Starting on the island of Zanzibar, he moved westward. Nine hundred and ninety-nine days later he emerged at the mouth of the Congo River, a gray-haired old man of thirty-seven. In between he had circumnavigated and charted Lake Victoria and Lake Tanganyika, both hazy and conjectural blurs on the maps until he arrived. More important was that he found out what the Congo River was all about. Until Stanley paddled, forded and fought his way down its length, no one knew whether the brown waters of the Lualaba (Stanley tried to call it the Livingstone but the name didn't stick) flowed into the Nile, the Niger or the Congo. All this and more Stanley accomplished on his epic expedition, losing along the way his three white companions and 277 of the 359 Africans who started with him in the coastal town of Bagamoyo.

There is no question that Stanley set events moving in Africa. As if on his signal the European powers rushed into black Africa with a speed not to be equaled until the time came for them to rush out again less than a century later. The only question that springs to mind as the traveler drinks his beer at the long bar of the New Stanley Hotel in Nairobi, watches the haze rise over Stanley Falls near Stanleyville or follows the eyes of Stanley's statue as they stare blindly across the Stanley Pool at Leopoldville is whether he would have done the same thing if he had known how it would all turn out.

"For me," wrote Stanley of his porters and his scouts, "they are heroes, these poor ignorant children of Africa." He does not sound like the sort of man who could respond enthusiastically to the spirit of *Uhuru* or take kindly to being called a tool of the imperialist colonialists. For that was what he was and that is what he would be called today.

My reasons for deciding to follow his footsteps originated with the simple, even simpleminded notion that it might be fun one day to try. That was some years ago and for a long time the idea lay dormant while I worked on other things. Then, after two and a half years of covering Africa as a reporter, I was assigned to Paris and discovered almost immediately that I missed the open spaces, the pale sun and the sound of drums at night. I had been told that Africa had this effect on people and I was not entirely surprised when it happened to me. It was at this time that the idea of retracing Stanley's second voyage through Africa began to take root and flower.

Stanley's route, when placed over a modern map of Africa, steers through seven newly-independent nations–Zanzibar and Tanganyika (now collectively known as Tanzania), Kenya, Uganda, Rwanda, Burundi and the Congo Republic. Each was different and yet each would have something to say about black Africa as a whole. Zanzibar seemed to have become a potential launching pad for a major Chinese Communist penetration of Africa. Tanzania, which started off so well under one of the most moderate and thoughtful of African leaders, had come dangerously close to collapse during a short-lived army mutiny. Kenya might possibly wade through the thickets of tribalism, just as Uganda appeared to be nullifying the power of its ancient kings. Of Rwandi and Burundi I had heard little since independence except that the medium-sized Hutus had been killing off the long-stemmed Tutsis. The Congo, of course, remained the most explosive, bloody-minded and unpredictable country of them all.

That was the journalist's Africa, but there was much else that I wanted and expected out of my trip–none of it having much to do with the practice of journalism. I had been a reporter among other reporters in Africa, and I had failed. I think we all failed in one way or another not through any fault of our own but because Africa today is at best an elusive target and we were shooting at it with weapons designed for more conventional coverage. The fact of the matter is that much of what is going on in Africa defies description. The novelists and the poets have tried, and some have succeeded, but what is a newspaper editor or a headline writer to make of a war in which no one is killed; of a power struggle in which the participants remain the best of friends, and of a coup d'état which takes place without the knowledge of its architect? The result was that we journalists tended to leave out the little things that might confuse or bewilder. Occasionally we tried to explain what we thought had really happened, but all too often we found that these were stories which weren't used.

This is not to say that the reporting out of Africa was stereotyped. On the contrary, it was—especially during the journalistic heyday of the Congo immediately after independence—incredibly varied. We brought to Leopoldville and Katanga our passions and our prejudices (some preconceived and some conceived on the spot), and who, even now, is to say who was right? There were those who viewed the whole business as a colossal joke. The liberals among us insisted that there *was* hope and spent their time seeking events that would buttress their contention. The racists saw the Congo as still another example of the black man's incompetence and inability to progress, and there were those who felt that the preservation of the United Nations was more important than what happened to the Congo itself. And vice versa. As a consequence, the diligent reader could pay his money and take his choice. But I am afraid that most readers decided fairly early in the game that it wasn't worth the effort and determined then and there to ignore the Congo—and Africa.

I am not sure whose fault this was—the readers', the Africans' or our own—but I am quite certain that the journalists must share in the blame. For some reason we came to consider fatuous (or impossible to answer) the question we were all asked when we came home:

"What is Africa really like?"

Well, what was Africa like anyway? I had seen some airports and housing schemes and government buildings and bars and fighting and I had met some cabinet ministers and waiters, but what of the people in between? I didn't know them and seldom even noticed them unless they appeared as a crowd rioting, or dancing, or listening to a politician's speech. What was Africa to me? Thinking about it, it became a kaleidoscope, not of important events but of smaller things; not of thoughts so much as emotions; a sadness; a feeling that there was too much I did not understand; the weird but not entirely fearsome sensation of being watched by eyes I could not see; the remembrance of laughter in a market place and of children who never seemed to cry. Africa to me was the unexpected, brittle squish of locusts underfoot as I arose from my bed in a Nairobi hotel room. It was watching a jeep filled with policemen cut a corner too sharply on a Leopoldville street and knock a rider off his bicycle, and seeing the jeep pull to a halt, the policemen jump out and then, instead of helping the fallen bicyclist to his feet, beat him unmercifully with their fists. Africa was the story Henry Tanner of the *New York Times* told me of his hotel room boy coming upon Tanner while he was packing his bags. In answer to his question, Tanner explained that he was returning to Europe to help his mother celebrate her birthday. She was, I think, in her fifties at the time.

"Oh," said the room boy, his face reflecting both wonder and admiration. "We do not live that long here."

Africa was all of these things and each raised nagging questions in my mind which I could not answer. The jigsaw puzzle lay scattered at my feet. If I tried to put it together, would all the pieces be there and would they all fit? Stanley had mapped the contours of lakes, measured the heights of mountains and traced the rivers, but who had mapped the African mind? What were the terrain features of the "African personality"?

There were so many questions, and some of them were so large that there was a danger of bogging down, of becoming involved in one to the exclusion of the others. Besides, time and money were limited. Where Stanley had taken almost three years to cross Africa,

I would of necessity have to try to cover the same distance in three months. Following Stanley within a fixed period of time would give me a goal to shoot for, a sense of mission. What also intrigued me about the Stanley route was that it led not through the big cities and down the main highways but across country. It would be like that game we played as children in which a line is established that must be followed no matter what the obstacles. The game took us through hedges, up and down trees, into bathroom windows, out along rooftops, down drainpipes and into all sorts of places we would not have ordinarily seen. The Stanley route would serve the same purpose and show me the hidden, unnoticed places of Africa. Perhaps the answers were there.

Stanley walked across Africa, but modern man, short on time and stamina, must fly or ride. Having flown all over Africa before and having missed almost everything that way, I chose this time to ride. On the advice of the Land-Rover company, I bought a second-hand example of their product and drove it up to their plant in Solihull just outside Birmingham. The Land-Rover people looked at my vehicle and decided that it needed a reconditioned engine and a hard top in place of the canvas one it carried. They also declared, after one look at me, that it would be sheer folly for me to set out for Africa without taking their three-day course in Land-Rover maintenance and repair.

The three days I spent in that classroom were nerve-shattering. They taught me not only that I knew nothing about the internal combustion engine but also that I would never learn. There were fourteen of us and an instructor dressed in a white surgical coat. It was obvious immediately that my classmates knew more at the start than I could possibly hope to pick up by the end of the course. They were an interesting group, numbering among them a missionary, a wildlife photographer and a mechanic—all on their way to assignments in Africa. With them the instructor was helpful and informative. With me he was kind. At one point he took me aside and explained to me the principle of the Venturi tube. To this day I do not understand the principle involved nor do I have the slightest idea what it has to do with a Land-Rover.

For three days we hovered over engines on blocks, examined pistons and cylinders that had been cut in half, traced wires from battery to spark plugs, and assembled and disassembled small parts. I never quite knew what it was I was taking apart or putting back together but I marveled at the way every piece seemed to depend on the others. One loose nut, one disconnected wire and the whole Land-Rover would sink to its knees and expire. Behind at the start, I fell further behind as the lessons continued until at the end my only hope was that I would not be called on to recite. At the conclusion of the course, the instructor handed us Land-Rover lapel pins and it was only then that I realized nobody had taught me how to change a tire. I didn't dare ask my instructor. It was too late, and besides he would have taken my pin away.

If the Land-Rover course taught me anything it was that I could not possibly follow Stanley without a companion. Listening to the conversation of my fellow students, it soon became apparent that driving was a full-time occupation. Many of them had been to fascinating places; they had traveled widely in exotic lands. But their talk was not of the countryside they had seen or the people they had talked to but of their Land-Rovers and how they had behaved. How was the Sahara? Well, it was best to equip the Land-Rover with special sand tires. In the rocky hills of Afghanistan you had to watch the oil pressure, and never forget to take at least ten extra gallons of gasoline into the Kabylia. They had bought a new generator in Fez, needed an oil change in Timbuctu and had had a one-and-one-quarter-inch Wittworth box hub spanner stolen in front of the Taj Mahal. With one eye on the oil-temperature gauge and another on the road, what would I see of Africa?

September became October. The weather turned cold and wet. A pink-handed nurse gave me a yellow fever shot. A conservative MP on a television panel show said he thought colored people made really excellent bus conductors. Friends appeared startled when I met them on the street, saying they thought I had already gone. I put my Land-Rover on a boat bound for Dar es Salaam, and waited. My telephone had ceased to ring. There were no further letters in response to my advertisement in *The Times*. I waited a little longer, hoping for the perfect Man Friday. But he did not appear.

I was still unprepared, still certain I had forgotten to do something essential. But one day, even more certain that if I waited any longer my dream would leave my side and disappear forever into the London fog, I left for Africa.

CHAPTER 2

HELP! HELP! I AM A PRISONER IN A KIKUYU WHOREHOUSE!

We offered several kinds of beads for the potatoes they had offered to sell, but with a gesture of contempt they refused everything. . . .

—H. M. STANLEY

THE BOAC VC-10 bound for Tripoli, Khartoum and Nairobi left the tarmac at London airport with a sudden whoosh, depositing a lingering ball of pain just under the bridge of my nose. The plane was almost full and I sat next to two women who had never flown before. Somebody, however, must have given them a good briefing because they ordered two double brandies the moment the safety-belt sign went off. They had left Kenya eleven months before in a lemming-like reaction to independence but were returning now not because of any love for Kenya, but because "we couldn't stand the life in England."

I searched the entrails of my own drink for omens and portents. They were mixed. I took as a good sign the fact that I had not been asked to pay any excess baggage charges. The baggage allowance was forty-four pounds; but I had managed to walk on board with a suitcase weighing fifty, and three pieces of hand luggage, including a typewriter and a leather case containing three cameras. That was good. But I still had no traveling companion. That was bad. Perhaps Nairobi, where I had friends, would yield one. I would stop there first before going on to Dar es Salaam and Zanzibar, where Stanley began.

We drank our way across most of France, dined over the Mediterranean and touched down at the Tripoli airport just as my companions finished their after-dinner brandies. The weather was almost as damp and cold as it had been when we left London, but the atmosphere was different. I remembered Libya as the place where Arab leaders went when they didn't want to be followed by the press. The stewardess led us into the transit lounge, a cement block enclosure built under the vaulted roof of a World War II hangar. Our passports were collected and checked slowly by a uniformed security man who stood behind the bar under a Coca-Cola sign written in Arabic. The bartender, a young man who spoke little English, had trouble with the foreign currency offered by the passengers. From time to time the security man would abandon his passports and help the bartender make change. There was an inch of water in the men's room and the passengers, most of whom had left their overcoats in the plane, paced the waiting-room floor to keep warm.

A surprising number of passengers disembarked at Tripoli and the plane was less than half full on the next leg of the flight south. I found three empty seats, folded back the armrests and stretched out. I was asleep two and a half hours later when the time came to fasten seat belts for the descent to Khartoum.

It was still night and the wind, hot and filled with sand in the daytime, had died down. Unlike the Libyans, the Sudanese have made some concessions to the nature of postwar travel and the transit lounge was lined with glass cases containing souvenirs. In the Sudan, things do not decay but turn to dust, and the junk jewelry, the mummified baby crocodiles and the snakeskin wallets in the glass cases were uniformly gray. So was the man from the *Daily Express* whom I found standing at the bar. His face fell when he saw me, but he cheered up considerably after I had explained that I was not on a story but doing a book.

"Then I have this one to myself," he said. What he had to himself was a revolt in Khartoum. Students, he said, had staged an uprising, and the military government had resigned. Perhaps there were eighty dead in the streets. The man from the *Express* said he had managed to talk to a few people before he himself had been arrested, charged with illegal entry and ordered to take the next plane out of the country. But he had his story. As a matter of fact he had filed it the day before from Beirut. Now all his editors would have to do was add a Khartoum dateline. He was under armed guard at the present moment but, this being Africa, the guard was watching his luggage outside instead of the prisoner at the bar. There would be baksheesh for the guard later of course. That was understood. The waiters in the passenger lounge, their eyes searching the table tops for tips, gave no indication that a revolution was underway in their capital city. The passengers, either asleep in chairs or sleepwalking among the cases of souvenirs, would not learn about the revolution until they read about it in the Nairobi papers.

At dawn, the plane headed south again over a sea of tight-packed clouds. I tried to recall whether this was the season of the short rains or the long rains but could not remember. Shortly before our arrival at Nairobi, the captain turned on the loud-speaker and told us that the peak of Mount Kenya was now visible through the clouds on our left. I was sitting on the right and did not get up to see it. The long night had eroded my curiosity, and my thoughts, such as they were, now centered on the problem of getting into Kenya. I had no visa. That was one of the things I had forgotten to do.

The Nairobi airport, like Nairobi itself, was built by and for white men. It is at once modern and nostalgic. It looks to the future but clings to the past. In the room where passengers are asked to wait before filing through immigration and customs, the walls are dominated by animal skins—Burchell's zebra, East Africa's contribution to Op art, on one wall; and, on the other, Grevy's zebra with its narrower black and white stripes. In between there are head-shot photographs of various Kenya tribesmen in their traditional costume—Masai, Kikuyu, Luo, Turkana, Waliangulu—all looking noble and pre-independence. They were obviously taken by a white photographer who loved them for their simplicity and savagery.

There were three immigration officials standing behind three pulpitlike pieces of furniture in the next room. One was white, the second an Indian Sikh in a turban, and the third an African. All three wore white shirts, short trousers and white knee-length stockings. I was steered to the white official, who asked why I hadn't taken the trouble to obtain a Kenya visa. I explained that there hadn't been time and apologized. He stamped a fourteen-day visitor's visa into my passport and let me through. In the customs section I was asked whether I was carrying firearms or ammunition, but my baggage was not searched. The driver of the airport bus waited until each of his passengers had complained about the slow service before he sank into his seat, switched on the engine and drove us into town.

Nairobi never was and never will be Africa to me. But for those who are coming to Africa for the first time it serves as the perfect decompression chamber. The plane from London covers the forty-three hundred miles too quickly for travelers to experience any sense of the distance involved. Without Nairobi, the change would be too abrupt and the traveler, plunged suddenly into the heart of Africa, might easily come down with a case of psychological bends. Nairobi, however, stands between the maiden voyager and all that is new and strange; it is green lawns, clipped hedges, and clipped mustaches which emerge from pints of beer speaking clipped English sentences. It is steel-and-glass shopping-center modern, with parking meters and traffic circling the roundabouts clockwise in the British manner. Whatever *is* foreign and strange about Nairobi is not African but Indian—the minarets and the mosques, the Indian names over the arcaded shops, and the women in their saris.

In the daytime, the streets are filled with Africans but, somehow, they do not belong. They are in transit, much as is the traveler just off the airplane. Strangers here themselves, this is not their part of town, and when the neon signs go on at night they disappear. All except the old *askaris*, the guards in their wide-brimmed campaign hats and ankle-length army overcoats, who build small fires on the sidewalks and sleep on newspapers in the doorways of the shops. Only they remain . . . and the beggars. The beggars of Nairobi are as much part of the local scenery as the Mercedeses and the Land-Rovers, the white hunters in their faded khaki bush jackets and the American tourists with their dark glasses, their cameras and their light meters. They are a walking, limping, crawling sideshow of disease in all its variety. No two are alike. Their limbs are thin and twisted like the gnarled trees in a Japanese garden—almost as if they had been assembled from separate parts in some fiendish morgue. (Consequently, when I was told that an Indian Fagin did indeed preside over the beggars, taking them to and from work in his truck, I was not surprised.) One of them, never more than a few feet from the entrance of the New Stanley Hotel, crawls sideways along the sidewalk like a land crab. Another, with one leg dangling uselessly, carries a long stave and poles himself across the street like a punter on an asphalt Thames. Those with leprosy and those who are blind do not move about but sit along the sides of buildings. "Jambo!" they cry, cupping their hands together in the traditional way of beggars.

Disease and poverty are part of Africa, but in Nairobi the beggars and their ailments do not seem real. It is more as if they had been trotted out for show along with the zebra-skin handbags in the shop windows and the souvenir drums in the lobbies of the hotels. Everything about Nairobi seemed unreal. And, when I read in the morning papers that an American missionary doctor in the Congo named Paul Carlson had been captured by the rebels and would be tried by a military tribunal, that too seemed unreal. It was happening in Africa, but Nairobi was not Africa. Almost immediately after my arrival, I began to feel uneasy, wondering whether the rest of the trip would be like this. It is all too easy to remain isolated and detached in Africa. I had felt this way before but then it hadn't mattered so much because in those days, as a journalist, I was part of a pack. By daylight we foraged and hunted, often separately, but at night we gathered together, sharing our kill and howling in unison. Now I was no longer part of that pack. The journalists had their Africa, but where was mine?

I did not have much time to spend in Nairobi. Zanzibar would be the start of my trip across Africa and I was in a hurry to get to Dar es Salaam, where, I had heard, I stood the best chance of picking up a visa to the island. My only reason for stopping off in Nairobi was to see what could be done about a companion. I had by this time developed the idea that it would be best if that companion was an African. Who better to explain the African mind than a black African himself? He would act as my guide and interpreter and lead me, hopefully, into places and situations denied to most white men. An African, it became increasingly clear to me, would almost automatically give the trip an added dimension. The fact that the thought had occurred to me so late in the game appalled me. Habit, custom, talk and time have a way of freezing instead of thawing the mind. Could I be comfortable only with my own kind? I hoped not.

The immediate problem in acquiring an African companion was that I could not offer him a salary. I was prepared to assume his expenses and guarantee his return passage from Leopoldville to Nairobi—if, that is, we managed to get as far as Leopoldville in the first place. If he was a photographer, and a good one, he could make some money on the trip—or at least so I thought. I would, I decided, try to find an embryonic journalist. In this way I might be able to even the score. In return for his guidance, and the information he would give me about Africa and the Africans, I would teach him what I knew about the practice of journalism.

I spent three days in Nairobi looking for the man I had in mind. I tried the newspapers, the United States Information Service, the International Press Institute, which teaches journalism to students from all parts of Africa, and I talked to friends. All were helpful, and pessimistic.

"We have a lot of them come in here applying for jobs and saying they're journalists," said the man from the USIS. "I don't know what they are but they're not journalists."

My friends, many of whom were reporters themselves, were more direct. They said I would be a fool to take an African along on a trip like this. You cannot trust them, they said. They just don't see things the same way we do. I said this was the whole point and that I was counting on my companion to give me a different perspective. I also talked to several African reporters. They listened politely and expressed interest but none felt he could manage the trip. African journalists are scarce in Kenya, and those who were worth anything already had jobs and could not afford to give them up for a trip of this nature.

But there was one possibility. Frank Barton, who teaches at the International Press Institute, found him for me. His name was Saïd Kadhi, a slim, dapper young man with a thin wisp of a goatee which he appeared to have grown carefully, hair by hair. He hailed from the coastal area of Kenya, which explained his Arab name. He was a city boy and I could not quite see his pointed shoes plunging down on the mud-caked brake pedal of the Land-Rover, but he seemed to know everything and everybody. We met for the first time at the bar of my hotel, and it was all I could do to keep him in his seat. His eyes roved the room constantly as we talked, and every time a new guest appeared at the entrance Kadhi would jump up, greet the visitor and walk hand in hand with him to the bar. For the first few times, I rose when Kadhi did and followed him to the bar. But it happened too often, and eventually I just sat in my chair and waited for him to return. He was like a friendly dog off his leash and out for an airing. He had to investigate everything, dashing here and there, but always coming back, tail wagging, to the man with the leash. Not that I was in any way Kadhi's master. I doubt whether anyone was. But I did hold the pencil which signed the beer chits.

"Oh my," he said after returning to the table for another refill. "You are making me drunk."

During one of his brief return visits to our table, I managed to hold his attention long enough to explain my mission. In reply, he said he was most interested, and that he was certain, as Frank Barton had told him, that the trip would increase his experience. Since he was jobless at the moment, there was no reason why he could not leave immediately. We met again under similar circumstances and in similar bars (he had friends in every bar in Nairobi) and he agreed finally to give me his answer at ten o'clock the following morning.

He did not call. I waited until noon and telephoned Barton. Barton knew where Kadhi lived and promised to drive out to his home during the lunch hour. He did, and found Kadhi there in his underwear. Barton said Kadhi had been most apologetic, but had decided not to accompany me because he had been offered another job. Why hadn't he had the courtesy to call me and tell me this himself?

"I know," Barton replied wearily. "It's very African."

The evening before my scheduled departure for Dar es Salaam I had dinner with two former colleagues and their wives. In Nairobi, restaurants tend to be pretentious, and expensive. Candles in bottles and a menu written in French make it a French restaurant. Candles in bottles and a menu written in Italian make it an Italian restaurant. The cuisine, however, remains defrocked Howard Johnson. We chose a "French" restaurant and had the usual trouble first in reading the menu in the flickering candlelight and then in passing our order on to the African waiter. At one point we hailed the maître d'hôtel and asked him to intercede on our behalf. Soon afterward, the waiter reappeared, again bearing the wrong drinks.

"How else," said the white maître d'hôtel with considerable exasperation, "would you say 'Tuborg' lager in Swahili?"

After dinner (because this was my last night in Nairobi and because we had already had a good deal to drink) it became imperative that we have some more. The wives left us without regret and we walked the few short blocks to the Equator Club. The woman at the downstairs reception desk turned the large guest book around so that it faced us.

"If you sign here," she said, "that will be fifteen shillings each."

One of the reporters, the shorter and perhaps for this reason the more aggressive of the two, shook his head.

"We never pay," he said. The woman at the desk seemed startled. There was something here she did not understand. Maybe she had misunderstood.

"Well," she said, "if you are regular members . . . if you have a regular membership."

"No," said my friend, cutting her off. "We're not members. We just never pay."

He started up the stairs and we followed. The voice of the receptionist, angry and alarmed, trailed after us. "If you're not members you must pay. Fifteen shillings. Those are the club rules. I must insist . . ." By now her voice was drowned by the sound of music from the interior of the club. At the head of the stairs a man in a dark blue dinner jacket stood in front of the doors that led into the club. He made no move to let us through. I took him to be the manager.

"We're journalists," said our leader. "We never pay."

The expression on the manager's face shifted, with some clashing of emotional gears, from frown to smile.

"Of course. This way, gentlemen." He held open one side of the swinging doors and bowed us into the club. The club was almost empty. On the dance floor a white girl was taking lessons in the hully-gully from a lanky, well-dressed African while his friends watched in silence from a table at the edge of the dance floor. At the bar, my aggressive friend found a man from the United States Information Service in Bujumbura. The USIS man was a Chinese-American on his way back to the States for a home leave before taking up his new post in Saigon. He looked like the kind of man who could sit peacefully at a bar all night, drinking without getting drunk and listening. In the morning he would wake up sober and remember everything. I asked him what his specialty was, whether his duties were political.

"Not me," he said. "Strictly ad-min."

There was, in addition to the three of us and our new Chinese-American friend, another customer at the bar, and it soon became apparent that he was listening to our conversation. He was a young man in his early thirties but bald, and he wore a blue blazer and a green, red and black striped tie. My aggressive friend disliked him immediately.

"What's that tie you're wearing?" he asked. The stranger seemed delighted to be included in the conversation.

"It's the Kenya tie," he said. Eager to talk, to become part of the group, he continued. "I'm really a Kenyan, you see. I was born here. I've spent the last sixteen months in England, having a nervous breakdown you might call it, but that's over with now. Now I'm back in Kenya, where I belong."

"You're an Englishman?" my friend asked.

"Well, technically I suppose I am. I carry a British passport."

"And you've come back here to work for the blacks?" My friend liked the stranger less and less.

"You might say that," the man replied, all smiles.

"Would you work for a black bastard? You, a white man?" The stranger refused to take offense.

"Certainly I would," he said. "Wouldn't you?"

My friend snorted. "You can bet your sweet ass I wouldn't," he said. Turning to me, he added, "This guy is queer." There was a fight brewing here, an unnecessary and pointless one. I suggested another round of drinks and started talking to the Englishman.

"Where would you say she comes from?" he asked me, pointing to one of the blown-up photographs of tribal women behind the bar. The one he indicated was handsome, even beautiful. I said I thought she was a mixture, probably part Kikuyu and part Masai. The Englishman was pleased.

"Not bad," he said. "It's difficult to tell. I know most of the tribes of East Africa well. I would agree that she was definitely part Kikuyu and there may be Nilotic blood. But more likely one of her parents was a Somali. You can usually tell by the set of the eyes, and the cheekbones."

We went on talking that way about African tribes, their differences and their similarities. He seemed to know what he was talking about and I was interested in what he said. The waiters around us turned out more lights in the already dark interior of the club. It was closing time and we fished into our pockets and contributed money to the bill, which by now was substantial. I noticed that the Englishman threw a ten-shilling note into the pile on the bar. It was too little but I said nothing and was glad that my aggressive friend hadn't noticed.

On the way down the stairs to the street, the Englishman asked me whether I was interested in going to another club. He said he knew of one still open where there were many girls from different tribes. The two journalists and the Chinese-American said they would turn in. At three o'clock in the morning, I did not find it difficult to convince myself that I was pursuing a course in comparative East African anthropology. If my friends chose to cut classes, that was their business. The Englishman had trouble remembering where he had parked his car but we found it eventually. He drove indecisively in what seemed like a gradually narrowing circle through the dark and empty streets of Nairobi and he pulled up finally under the glow of a neon sign.

The bar to which the Englishman took me was on the second floor. Unlike the Equator Club, however, it was crowded. The male customers, Africans mostly, were without jackets but they wore shirts and ties.

The women were spectacularly varied, the color of their skins ranging from yellow to ink black. Some wore sandals, others spike heels. Some had hair that was blond or red, which confused me until I realized that they were wearing wigs. Others wore bandanas, but most had rejected wigs and bandanas and their hair was either short and kinky, in the traditional manner, or tightly braided, so that their scalps were divided into neat squares like the grid marks on a map.

"I know this place well," said the Englishman as he guided me to a table and ordered beer. "We'll ask for some real Kikuyu girls to sit down with us."

On a signal from the Englishman two girls arrived at our table. In what I thought was an excessively gallant motion, he rose, bowed deeply, and introduced the girls to me. One was called Mary. I did not catch the other one's name. The Englishman spoke in Swahili, his hands suddenly on the move as men's often are when they are speaking a foreign language. The girls answered in monosyllables, lapsing occasionally into peals of laughter, and it occurred to me that the girls laughed more because they thought it was expected of them than because they were having a good time. Mary wore her hair plaited into dozens of spikelike protuberances, which gave her the appearance of a wartime mine. Her friend's was hidden under a blond wig.

"Now these girls are both pure Kikuyu," the Englishman said. As he spoke, the girl in the blond wig moved her chair closer to his and started rubbing his knee with her hand. It was a kneading motion, done almost absent-mindedly, as if she were making dough. The Englishman appeared not to notice. "They're the largest tribe in

Kenya and many people think they are the hardest working and the most intelligent. Bantu stock." He crossed his legs and the girl in the wig started working on his other knee. Either the girls' English was limited or they were bored, because neither paid any attention to what he said.

"I understand the Kikuyu," the Englishman added. "They know this. They're friends of mine."

"I think I'll go home," I said. The clock on the wall behind the bar read 4 A.M. The bar had closed and I was suddenly tired.

"Hope you don't mind if we drop the ladies off first," he said. "They're old friends and they have no transport."

"Do they live far?" I asked.

"No, not far."

I dozed in the back seat, vaguely conscious of an occasional overhead street lamp, each naked lamp bulb surrounded by its carrousel of moths. Then we were off the pavement, bouncing along a rutted track which led for about half a mile to a cluster of buildings. As we got out of the car, the dim outline of trees against the sky and the smell of flowers told me I was in a garden. I followed the group up a set of stairs and waited while Mary produced some keys. The door she opened led into a room furnished with a bed, two armchairs, and an old radio-victrola combination resting on a bureau. The Englishman asked me for some change and gave it to the girl in the blond wig. She disappeared through another door at the far end of the room and reappeared a moment later with two large bottles of Pilsner beer and four glasses. Mary placed a rock 'n' roll record on the machine and began to twist. I lay back on the bed and watched her. She was really quite wonderful. Her shoulders, her arms and her head remained absolutely motionless but from the waist down everything moved. It was a trembling motion and so rapid that her hips and legs blurred.

"She is the only one who can do it that way," said the girl in the wig.

"Extraordinary," said the Englishman. "Absolutely extraordinary. That's an authentic movement—a tribal movement. There are very few girls nowadays, except those in the reserves, who can dance in that manner."

Mary put on some more records and the Englishman and the girl in the wig danced together, the Englishman holding her at a decorous distance.

"I think the time has come to go," I said. The Englishman said I was quite right and that he wouldn't be a minute. He would walk the girl in the wig to her home, which was right next door, and return in a moment.

"How long?" I asked.

"I'll be back in exactly half an hour," he said. I had the feeling that I was being taken in, but there was nothing I could do about it. He had the car.

Mary locked the door behind them. I sat on the edge of the bed, bone weary.

"What shall we do until they get back?" I asked.

Mary, still standing, looked down at me and snorted with impatience. "You are a man," she said. "What do a man and a woman do?"

I noticed now, as she stood in the light of the lamp which hung from the ceiling, that a small scar ran down the length of her short, flat nose. She may have been authentic Kikuyu but she was also not pretty.

"We could talk," I said. She turned away angrily.

"You are a white man," she said, "and you are drunk."

"You are not far off," I said.

"You think because I am a black girl . . ." I saw which way the conversation was going.

"Hold everything," I said. "That's not it at all." But Mary was not to be mollified. Stepping to the other side of the room, she opened a cupboard, reached into the upper shelf and extracted a handful of blue envelopes.

"I am a black girl," she said, flinging the envelopes onto the bed. "But I will marry a British soldier."

"Is he a white man?" I asked.

"Of course he is white," Mary snapped. "Read. Go on. Read the letters."

I opened the first of the envelopes. The handwriting was neat and legible. "Dear Wairimo," the first letter began.

"I thought your name was Mary," I said.

"Yes. My name Mary. My other name Wairimo."

"Is that Kikuyu?"

"It is my name," she replied, again impatient and irritated. "Read more." It was a command rather than a suggestion and I began again.

"Dear Wairimo," it read. "Well, it is time for me to write you another letter. I am in Germany now and miss you very much. I have tried to leave the army but my commanding officer says I must serve another two years although I would like to return quickly to my darling wife in Kenya. . . ."

I looked at Mary.

"I didn't know you were married," I said.

"We *shall* be married," she answered. "We live married in Kenya and we shall be married again."

"You mean a regular marriage with a license?"

"Of course with license," she snapped.

"Will you live in England?"

"We live where he live. In Kenya, in England, in America." She was opening more letters, and as she extracted them from their envelopes she threw them on the bed. I picked up another and read on, my eyes heavy with sleep. Unmindful of me, Mary stopped pacing the floor and removed her dress. Underneath she wore a brassière and a half slip. Her feet were bare.

"I have given up smoking," the next letter began, "and I do not drink any longer with my mates because I do not have much money but do not worry my darling Wairimo I will send you every week twenty shillings."

"He must love you very much," I said.

"Yes, he love me," Mary said. "He is my husband." Then, abruptly, she climbed into bed, pulling the covers over her shoulders.

"We sleep," she announced, pulling the light cord by her bed. For a brief moment the room was totally dark, but then I could see the first gray light of dawn framed in the single window. I groped my way to one of the armchairs. The Englishman would be coming back at any moment. There was nothing else to do but wait for him here.

The room was very light when I awoke. I looked at my watch and it said 7:40. Angrily I heaved myself out of the armchair and stood in the middle of the room, feeling groggy. I had a bad headache. Mary—or Wairimo—was still asleep. I tried the door through which we had entered the room. It was locked. The second door, at the other side of the room, was open. It led into a rectangular courtyard flanked by doors similar to the one I had just opened. A woman was washing a small, naked child by a faucet at the other end of the courtyard. The lather of the soap stood out white and clean against the child's dark skin. The woman smiled.

"Jambo, bwana," she said. I mumbled something and nodded at her, tasting undigested beer at the back of my mouth. Returning to Mary's room, I walked over to her bed and shook her by the shoulders, gently at first and then less gently until she opened her eyes.

"Mary," I said. "I must go. My friend is late. I must go but the door is locked."

Mary rose sleepily from the bed. She stumbled over to the front door, tried it and found it locked. She stood looking at the door, puzzled. I remembered then that she had locked it behind the Englishman and the girl with the blond wig.

"The key, Mary," I said. "Where is the key?" She walked over to the cupboard and began searching her clothes. She was saying something and repeating it but in a language I could not understand. She went through the dress she had worn the night before. I lifted the victrola for her while she looked underneath but the key was not there.

"Where is the key, Mary?" I asked again. "Can you remember where you put it?" A sudden change came over Mary, a disconcerting swing from petulance to anger.

"I want money," she said. "You sleep here last night. I want money for you use my bed."

My hands were in my pockets and I could feel some change and several bills with my fingers.

"Mary," I said, hearing my voice become terribly controlled, violently patient. "You know I did not sleep here last night. You know I was only waiting here for my friend."

Even as I spoke the words sounded ridiculous to me. They must have sounded downright inflammatory to Mary.

"What you mean? What you talkin' about? You sleep here. You pay me money." Mary was snarling. The white brassière and half slip looked like armor against her dark skin.

"I don't have any money," I said. I do not know why I lied at this point. Having lied, however, I could not now admit it. "My friend has the money. If you let me out of here, we'll find my friend and he will give you money."

Craft. That was it. Mary turned away from me and began once again to search for the key among the pile of records.

"How much do you want for the use of your room?" I asked. If she could be reasonable, so could I.

"Two shillings fifty," she replied. It was not much money. As a matter of fact it was very little. At seven shillings to the dollar that was . . . let me see . . . two and a half goes into seven how many times? No, that wasn't the way to work it out. I gave it up. Besides, the mission now was to get out of Mary's room and back to my hotel.

"If you get the door open," I said, "we'll both go and find my friend and I'll see that you get your money." Mary had carried the search for the key back to the cupboard. Somewhat frantically she was going through the pockets of her clothes.

"Can't we ask one of your neighbors to let us out through his door?" I asked.

We were standing now at the open door leading from the room into the courtyard. It was well after eight o'clock and from where I stood I could see several women, their faces expressionless as they listened to our conversation. There was also a young man, bare to the waist, with a checkered piece of cotton cloth wrapped sarong-fashion around his middle. I smiled at him and he smiled back.

"Sir," I called to him. The appellation did not seem to fit the young man but I could think of nothing better to say. "Sir, would you explain to our friend here that I would like to leave this place to find my friend."

The young man smiled. I wondered whether he had understood what I had said and was momentarily grateful to Mary when she burst into her native language. I hoped she was translating. At length Mary came to the end of her speech.

"What did she say?" I asked the man in the sarong.

"She say she want money," he replied.

One of the women in the courtyard appeared with a bottle of beer. Mary reached out and put the bottle to her lips, then handed the bottle to the young man, who also drank deeply. He offered me what was left but I refused. The time had come for decision. For a moment I thought of paying Mary and having done with the stupid business, but pride overcame logic. There had to be another way out of this—a face-saving way—especially since it was my face that needed saving. I noticed that the courtyard door to the room next to Mary's was open. Inside, a house boy in white shorts and jacket was sweeping the floor with a twig broom. Just beyond I could see the door to the outside world. I drew myself up, walked into the adjacent flat and started toward the door at the far end. The house boy who had been sweeping the floor jumped up and flung himself, arms spread-eagle, against the door. Simultaneously a white man emerged from another room inside the flat.

"Get out," the white man shouted.

"I want the police," I said.

"Get out!" The white man's upper lip was covered with a large black mustache. Holding his right arm stiffly, he started to push me toward the courtyard door. He was very strong. "Get out! Get out! You're trouble. You're nothing but trouble!"

"But I'm trying to get out of trouble," I shouted back at him.

"Out! Out! Out!" Alternately pushing and bellowing, the white man propelled me back into the sunlight of the courtyard. The door slammed in my face. Mary stood at the entrance to her room, her arms folded. She seemed unsurprised, almost as if she had expected this. From the flat I had just left I could hear the voice of the white man. He was talking to somebody on the telephone—something about parts for an automobile. The fact that he was actually communicating with someone in the outside world, in a language I could understand, was reassuring. Somewhere—not here; no, certainly not here—there was sanity. I paced the sunny courtyard slowly. The walls were high but over the tiled roofs I could see the tops of several eucalyptus trees silver-green against the blue of the sky. I was still pacing the courtyard and had almost reached the point of capitulation when one of the courtyard doors opened and the Englishman appeared. He was followed by the young man in the checkered sarong and an African girl I did not recognize until she spoke to Mary. Then I remembered that she was the blonde of the night before, wigless now and barefoot. The Englishman blinked his eyes in the sunlight. His clothes were rumpled and he needed a shave.

"Well, well," he said to me. "What seems to be the trouble?"

With considerable irritation I told him what the trouble was.

"But my dear chap," he said, "why didn't you come to fetch me?"

"Because," I said, "your pure-blooded Kikuyu friends won't let me out of here."

"Incredible," he said. "Simply incredible. I'll have a talk with them." The Englishman walked over to Mary and started speaking to her in Swahili. His voice was low and caressing and as he spoke he stroked her arm. His approach seemed to be working because Mary answered him quietly. At length he patted her on the shoulder and turned to face me.

"It's all very simple," he said. "She wants money."

"I know that," I shouted. "She wants two shillings and fifty cents and that isn't much but now that she's locked me up it's become a matter of principle. I know it sounds silly but I said you had the money. For God's sake pay her and let's get out of here."

The Englishman turned back to Mary and again they talked. This time, when the Englishman faced me, his expression was perturbed.

"The situation seems to have changed a little," he said. "Now she wants a hundred shillings."

"Brother!" I said.

"Have you got it?" he asked.

"No," I lied. This began to have the earmarks of a conspiracy. A con game. Even if it wasn't, the Englishman had got me into this mess and it was clearly up to him to get me out. I felt both righteous and stupid.

"We'll have to pay," the Englishman said.

"I'll be damned if I'll pay. I sat up in a chair all night waiting for you. I don't know how you made out and I don't care, but thanks to you I spent a damned uncomfortable night."

"He sleep in my bed," said Mary, glowering at me.

"I don't have a hundred shillings," the Englishman said.

"Me neither," I said. "But I'll tell you one thing. I can't wait around here all day. Tell Mary we'll take her to the police and straighten the whole thing out. Let the police decide."

It was a decision worthy of Solomon and the Englishman nodded.

"Very well," he said. "How do we get out of here?"

"The same way you came in."

We started walking toward the doorway through which the Englishman had entered the courtyard. Quickly, the young man in the sarong darted ahead, opened the door, banged it shut behind him and started to lock it. The Englishman, with me just behind, ran after him and wedged the toe of his shoe in the door. Together we pushed. The door began to give under our combined weight and I could hear the African panting behind it. Suddenly, without warning, the African stepped back. The door swung open. We were off balance. The young man in the sarong seized the Englishman by the shoulders, twisted him and flung him to the ground. The Englishman lay on the cement floor of the courtyard, curled up like a fetus to protect himself. We were surrounded by women and the houseboy in the white shorts and jacket. None of them was smiling. Mary had her hands on her hips and she was rocking back and forth on the heels of her feet. I tried to think of something to do, but nothing came to mind. Slowly the Englishman picked himself off the concrete.

"Incredible," he said.

"I thought they were friends of yours."

"I thought so too," he said, giving me a flabby look. He dusted himself off and disappeared into Mary's room. Not much later he stepped back into the courtyard.

"It's all arranged," the Englishman said. "I've written her a check." I asked him whether that meant we could leave.

"I'm afraid not," he replied. "The young chap over there will have to go into town and cash it to see if it's good." The young man had by this time exchanged his sarong for a pair of robin's-egg-blue trousers and a red sports shirt.

"How far is town?" I asked.

"About five miles."

"Oh God." Now was the time to pull the bills from my pocket and end this farce. But I didn't or couldn't. There was no turning back. Together the Englishman and I, like two passengers on the deck of an ocean liner, paced the courtyard, from one end to the other and back again. One of the women offered me what was left of a cigarette. I accepted gratefully. There was no longer any animosity. Not even curiosity. It seemed almost as if the Englishman and I had been pacing the courtyard like this forever.

"I'll pay you back when we get into town," I told him, breaking the silence.

The Englishman shook his head. "My show, old man," he said. "My bloody fault all the way. This one is on me."

Our somnambulistic walk ended with the return of the young man. In my dreamlike state time had passed quickly and I was surprised when I looked at my wristwatch to find it was past eleven.

"Okay?" I asked the African.

"Okay," he replied. The Englishman, the young man and I entered Mary's room and found her asleep on her bed. The Englishman woke her. Silently the money changed hands and with mysterious speed the missing key was produced and the front door to Mary's room opened. The Englishman's car was in the garden. Children were playing in the road beyond and there was washing hanging from the branches of the trees. It was good to be free. Mary, having pulled a dress over her half slip and brassière, stood on the steps leading to her room with the young man and the girl who had worn the blond wig, watching the Englishman fuss with the door keys of his car.

"Well," I said. "Goodbye, Mary."

"Goodbye," she said.

"That was quite an experience." I shook my head, pretending disapproval. The patient teacher had tried but the patient teacher had failed. Now the patient teacher would have to flunk his student. He was sorry. Mary's hands hung at her sides. Her arrogance, her anger had evaporated.

"I think," she said at length. "I think that when you go back to your country you will say that Kenya is bad."

I smiled patronizingly, rubbing it in. "Yes. Very bad."

"I am sorry," she said. She did not return my smile. "I am very sorry. Because, for us, Kenya is not bad."

CHAPTER 3

THE ALL-AMERICAN BIG BRASS PLOT

If kindly treated, do not know more docile and good-natured creatures.

—H. M. STANLEY

OF all the Americans who passed through Dar es Salaam during the five weeks of my stay, only two emerged untroubled and unscathed. It is a pity that Paul Taubman and Maurice Gusman never met (Taubman was well on his way to Uganda when Gusman arrived) for they shared a common experience. Without so much as a by-your-leave, both were flung into the front lines of the psychological war then raging between the governments of the United States of America and the United Republic of Tanzania. Both acquitted themselves well. Their detractors will say that this was because they did not realize where they were or what was going on around them, but it is my belief that they came out of the battle with flying colors because neither of them believed for a minute that what was happening was really true; and, if it was true, it certainly did not concern them.

Dar es Salaam, as the guidebooks are fond of pointing out, means "Haven of Peace" in Arabic. In one of his speeches while I was there, Dr. Julius K. Nyerere, President of Tanzania, referred to it as "Rumourville." He was closer to it than the Arabs. Most of its residents call the capital city "Dar," which, in these days, covers a multitude of havens. I tried, shortly after my arrival, to make a comprehensive list of the so-called liberation groups that had sought shelter in the city but gave up because no one in Dar seemed to have the slightest idea. Each day there seemed to be more—the Mozambique Liberation Front (Frelimo); the African National Congress (ANC); the South-West African National Union (SWANU); the Basutoland Congress Party; the Ngwane National Liberation Congress; the Zimbabwe African People's Union (ZAPU) and its mortal enemy the Zimbabwe African National Union (ZANU). The list was endless and ever-changing. My favorite was a group bent on the liberation of the Comores Islands. I had no idea there were any Comores Islands until I ran across the sign erected over a store in the Asian quarter of the city. The two French-speaking occupants within rose politely when I entered their headquarters. The taller of the two, an African with a voice that whispered like palm fronds in a gentle breeze, seemed embarrassed when I asked them how the movement was going. They had, he said, been writing to General de Gaulle in Paris.

"Mais il n'a pas répondu."

"Jamais?" I asked.

"Jamais."

I met the Comores liberators several times after that, at various parades and public rallies, and they never failed to recognize me, smile and shake my hand. I think they were also grateful to me for not asking them again for a progress report. There are some subjects that are too painful to discuss. Gentle, quiet and perhaps overly civilized, they were totally unlike their brother liberators, who, in comparison, were frantic, strident and bellicose. With these, the sound was always turned up. I always had the feeling that they had either just broken something and were running away or were running toward something in order to break it. Therefore, it did not surprise me when the Comores group failed to join the others in the bellow of rage that went up when Oscar Kambona, Tanzania's Minister for External Affairs, announced the discovery of a plot against the Republic and its President.

The announcement was carried under appropriately large headlines in *The Nationalist* ("Registered at the Post Office as a Newspaper") and jolted Dar es Salaam out of its customary torpor. *The Nationalist* quoted Kambona as saying that the government was in possession of information that "certain Western Powers were making deliberate moves to bring about disunity in the Government and people of the United Republic of Tanzania, and were ready to commit acts of subversion and aggression against Tanzania and the Nationalist Movements which are based here." Furthermore, there was evidence that the "big powers" involved would use Portuguese and white South African mercenaries.

"I must warn these powers and their duped fascist Portugal," Kambona declared. "No attempts at subversion and aggression against the Republic will succeed. The United Republic believes, as do all true brother African States, that Africa must and will be free."

The Pied Piper had called the tune and his followers (Comores contingent excepted) almost fell over themselves in their haste to supply an anvil chorus of abuse for the plotters.

"We are," said Noel Mukono, secretary for public affairs for the Zimbabwe African National Union, "terribly disgusted by these bastardly acts."

Sam Jujoma, president of the South-West African People's Organization, rose to new heights to deplore the depths to which the imperialists would sink, saying: "To the stooges who linger among us, we say, a day will come when we shall bury them all in an eternal hole." On the following morning, *The Nationalist* carried the story further. Under a headline which read "Documentary Evidence," the newspaper reproduced three letters written in French together with its own not entirely accurate translation into English. In the first, any doubt that "L'Ambassade des XX" (the original typewritten words had been obliterated and X's substituted) was anything other than the American Embassy, or that the "Ministère des Affaires Etrangères" was that of the formerly-Belgian Congo were eliminated in the final paragraph, which said in part that "United States counts on the support of the Congo Government in such affairs. . : ." The letter noted that the presence of Chinese subversion against the Republic of Congo-Léo had been confirmed in the territory of Tanganyika and that, in view of the serious danger to the free world and to peace in Africa represented by this presence, the "XX" had decided to put an end to it.

"As a first measure," the translation continued (for some reason substituting "XX's" of its own where "États Unies" existed in the original), "the XXX will support to bombard all the strategic points being used by Communist China in Tanganyika to take advantage of the minor frontier incidents to bring troubles between the Portuguese territory of Mozambique on the one part and Tanganyika on the other.

"As a second measure and after having introduced intrigues and American influence, to make special arrangements to overthrow the Government of Mr. Julius Nyerere to one still being studied by the Department of State."

The second letter was similar to the first. The third, ostensibly addressed to the American ambassador in Leopoldville, came from an unidentified expert in subversion confirming "my acceptance to carry out the delicate mission for Tanganyika" and asking for an advance of $25,000 to cover the salaries, hotel and restaurant charges of arms specialists the writer said he would recruit in South Africa.

I studied the letters carefully. All three gave me the impression that they had been written by a man intent on giving himself away. It was as if a forger had carefully obliterated the smile on his copy of the Mona Lisa with a bushy mustache. Why else would he have referred to Tanganyika instead of Tanzania? Hadn't he heard of the merger of Tanganyika and Zanzibar the spring before? In addition, the letters contained several typographical errors and grammatical mistakes, all of which gave them an awkward, schoolboyish quality.

The American embassy consulted with itself and with Washington and then issued the following statement: "The Department of State categorically states that references to the United States in these statements are without any foundation whatever. They appear to be based on clumsy forgeries, similar to others which have come to light in recent years intended by those who propagated them to damage the friendly relations existing between the United States and the new nations of Africa."

The *Tanganyika Standard*, which makes a stab at being an independent newspaper by clucking disapproval instead of bellowing it, ran the American denial. But *The Nationalist* did not—possibly because the American embassy had not seen fit to inform the newspaper that it was available.

"If they'd sent somebody over for it we would have given it to them," said an embassy official. "But they didn't so we didn't."

Among Tanzanians, cutting Americans dead had always been considered a socially acceptable practice. After the plot announcement, it became the rage. The Americans I talked to reminded me of the mystified victims in the mouthwash advertisements whose best friends won't tell them. What had they done to deserve this?

In the eyes of the Tanzanians, it was Halloween and America had embarked on a Machiavellian game of trick or treat. According to one letter-to-the-editor in the *Standard*, "The African is becoming aware that when you invite a white man with an open heart, he in turn tries to make mischief and subversive plans, thinking that the African will be foolish enough not to understand what is going on around him." If the plot was the trick it was obviously time now for the treat.

The treat came in the form of Paul Taubman and his All American Big Brass Band. Even *The Nationalist*, carrying stories and pictures of the band's tour of Africa, joined in the general flurry of anticipation that preceded his arrival. In one of the handsome brochures made available to the readers in the USIS library, I learned in both French and English that Taubman had been awarded New York City's highest musical honor—the Handel Medallion—and that he was also "Mayor of Fifth Avenue."

"Home to Paul Taubman is a spacious estate in Old Westbury, New York," the brochure noted. "There with his wife, Emelie, a former opera singer, he entertains the greats from all walks of life."

Unhappily, the citizens of Dar would have to wait for Taubman's arrival, and while they waited relations between Tanzania and the United States deteriorated steadily. Several pre-plot appointments I had made with Tanzanians evaporated without explanation. Waiting in bars for guests who failed to show up took the better part of my days. Those who did appear were in most cases white, or Africans from Nigeria or Ghana. Invariably, we conducted our conversations in low voices, interrupting them entirely whenever the waiters approached with more drinks. Whispered conversations appealed to my sense of the dramatic and gave the words spoken a (usually spurious) importance. For this reason my favorite meeting place became the restaurant run by the Chinese Communists. The food was terrible but I found that diplomats, especially American diplomats, told me more there than they did in their own offices. The conspiratorial atmosphere made conspirators of us all.

This was also true of the Tanzanians and it was only by conspiring with mutual friends that I managed to secure an audience with Bibi Titi, one of the founding fathers (mother in this case) of Tanzania's monolithic and all-powerful political party, the Tanganyika African National Union—TANU. She was then, as I am sure she is now, holding down an important government post. What struck me first about Bibi Titi when I met her in her office was that she was fat. Enormously fat. But it was not the kind of fat that envelopes people in folds of lethargy. Bibi Titi wore hers like extra fuel tanks strapped to a bomber—for greater distance. I am sure Bibi Titi's fat was made of pure adrenalin. The second thing I noticed about Bibi Titi was that she was not alone.

"This is my interpreter," she said in perfect English, introducing an unsmiling man in an open-neck white shirt. It became clear immediately that he was a good deal more than that.

"Would you tell me why you wish to see Bibi Titi?" he asked. I replied that I had been told that no visit to Tanzania was complete without a conversation with Bibi Titi. From behind her desk, Bibi Titi nodded agreement.

"You have the permission of the Ministry of Information for this interview?" It just so happened that I had been to the ministry the day before and had mentioned my forthcoming meeting with Bibi Titi. I told this to the interpreter.

"That is not sufficient," he snapped. "The Ministry of Information has nothing to do with these things. You should have asked permission from the Ministry of External Affairs." It seemed he wanted me to squirm so I did. I apologized for my oversight, admitted that I should have known better, and added that I hoped he would let me by this time because I wasn't really a reporter and was not seeking an interview but had come merely for a chat. Reluctantly and only after a fairly heated exchange with Bibi Titi in Swahili, in which she appeared to be takng my side, the interpreter allowed me to stay. I asked a few questions: Bibi Titi replied with gusto in Swahili and the interpreter translated into English. We were getting along fine until I asked Bibi Titi whether she believed Oscar Kambona's charge that America was plotting the downfall of the Nyerere regime. Bibi Titi's brows furrowed and for the first time in the interview she asked the interpreter to translate the question. This done she answered at length and with growing fervor until the room shook with the sound of her voice. When it was over, I shifted in my chair and settled back again for what I thought would be a correspondingly long translation. Instead, what I got was this:

"Bibi Titi says someone is plotting against Tanzania. If it is not America, who else?"

I waited until I was certain that this was all the interpreter was going to say and then rose to thank all concerned for their courtesy. Bibi Titi was not smiling as I said goodbye. As far as I could gather, Bibi Titi accurately reflected the post-plot climate in government circles. Added confirmation came from the Regional Commissioners who govern (some of them, I was told, with a free hand) the outlying provinces of Tanzania. One of them, as quoted in the *Tanganyika Standard*, warned a crowd in the town of Mbeya, "to be alert, saying that Tanzania had enemies who worked in disguise and that careless talk was playing into the hands of spies."

The Regional Commissioner for Morogoro, Kasian Kapilima, was one of the first to organize a public demonstration against the plot. Apparently the turnout was not up to his expectations and his anger landed him on the front page of *The Nationalist*.

"The Regional Commissioner for Morogoro," said the newspaper, "has ordered all Indian shops in Morogoro to close tomorrow because Indians did not take part in the anti-plot demonstrations here today.

"Mr. Kapalima said the failure of the Indians to support the demonstration against the Western plot to overthrow the Tanzania Government meant that even if Tanzania was attacked with bombs, the Indians would not defend her. . . . If no proper explanation is obtained the Indian shops will be closed indefinitely."

At the time of the plot announcement, President Nyerere was in the interior, on one of his periodic "nation-building" campaigns, and for a period the American embassy entertained the hope that he would dissociate himself from the entire business when he returned to the capital. There was a theory among embassy officials that some form of power play was afoot within the regime. The left-wing extremists led by Kambona and the wild men of the Zanzibar Revolutionary Council were fighting it out behind the scenes with the moderate pro-Westerners led by Nyerere. Or so it seemed. But Nyerere was in no hurry to return to Dar and, when he did, the Americans found him remote and unhelpful.

It was at this low point in Tanzanian-American relations that a chartered plane bearing the thirty-five members of the All American Big Brass Band and their leader touched down at the Dar es Salaam airport.

The United States Information Service, which was sponsoring the tour, installed the musicians in the Agip Hotel. That evening I met several band members, including their leader, at a party given for them on the lawn of Ambassador Leonhart's residence in Oyster Bay, a suburb of Dar occupied almost exclusively by foreign diplomats and the wealthier members of Nyerere's government. It was a good party. Colored lanterns hung from the trees. Several members of the band detached themselves from the bar long enough to play some brisk Dixieland. Couples danced and twisted and even Ambassador Leonhart did not seem unusually perturbed by the fact that there were only a handful of Tanzanians present—and none of these of much importance.

The fact that there were some Tanzanians brave or foolhardy enough to appear made them interesting to me and I stood for a while with an Englishwoman who had offered to identify them for me. She had lived most of her life in Dar and she swayed back and forth as she faced me, drink in hand, making conversation. I tried to weave with her but could not adjust to her rhythm. As a consequence a good deal of her drink spilled down my shirt front. She spotted a Tanzanian woman, at that moment shaking hands with the American ambassador in the receiving line.

"Look at her," said my companion. "Just look at her. Can you believe it? Everybody knows about her. She ran a house until they made her a junior minister. Now all she wants is a white man. Every day a different white man? Can you believe it?"

With that my companion, overcome with incredulity and drink, fell heavily to the ground in a flurry of crinoline and spilled ice cubes. I tried to help her back to her feet but she resisted. Her husband smiled gently.

"I wouldn't bother," he said. "She's quite happy down there."

I was not happy where I was and wandered toward the bar.

"Wonderful. Thank you. Thank you. Wonderful to be here. Thank you." The voice of Paul Taubman rose from the center of a group of admirers and I joined the conversation.

"We've just come up from Lusaka. That's right, isn't it? Lusaka? Capital of Zambia? We had a wonderful reception there. Wonderful. We played in the stadium and President Kaunda loved us. He actually waved his fly whisk at me. Can you imagine? I was told afterward that he had never done anything like that before. Isn't that great?" Several of us in the group agreed that it was great and Taubman went on to say that he had been playing concerts down the west coast of Africa and was now working his way up the eastern side of the continent. He reached into his pocket and produced a ball-point pen.

"I've been giving these away. Great idea. Look at it. See the brass band around the middle? Get it? Brass band? All American big brass band? Great little gimmick. Of course they're not quite so popular in the French-speaking parts of Africa because there we're known as 'Paul Taubman et sa Grande Fanfare Américaine.' The brass band on the pen doesn't mean anything. See what I mean?" Ruminatively, he replaced the pen in his pocket and then, after consulting with a USIS man, announced that the time had come to move to the Dar es Salaam Club, where the band was scheduled to play at a dance sponsored by the Tanganyika Girl Guides.

"We're here to do our bit," said Taubman.

"Great, Paul, great," said the man from the USIS.

I arrived at the Dar es Salaam Club late and found the dance well on its way. The club, a rambling structure built in the days when Tanganyika was a German colony and subsequently occupied by an army of British colonial officials, had recently been nationalized and was now officially multiracial. But it had yet to become a popular gathering place for Tanzania's Africans, and on the occasion of the Taubman concert (either because the Girl Guides were charging ten shillings for admission or because of the American plot, or a combination of the two) there were few Africans present. The audience, which spilled out of the ballroom and onto the club's wide verandas, was made up largely of whites and Asians.

Taubman and his band were going full blast. The band, playing with spirit and precision, came to the end of a number and there was polite applause. Taubman cupped a hand to his ear.

"Let's hear a little applause. Can't hear it. Louder. Still can't hear it. Louder! Tha-a-a-at's better."

The band members, most of whom were white, stared at the audience impassively and shook spit out of their instruments.

"And now, ladies and gentlemen," Taubman announced, "I want to tell you a little story. Before I came to Africa, I wrote a song which I called the 'African Blues.' Tonight, because you've been such a wonderful audience, I'm going to rechristen my song. Tonight, ladies and gentlemen, I'm calling it the 'Dar es Salaam Blues.' "

The concert ended with the "Dar es Salaam Blues" and the band members departed, leaving behind a mountainous pile of musical instruments, collapsible music stands, microphones, amplifiers, chairs and a harried man in shirt sleeves.

"I'm Mr. Shapiro," he told me with sweat streaming down his face. "Got to get all this equipment into the truck, then into the plane. Playing tomorrow in Zanzibar. This is my band. I organized it. Then I got Paul to lead it. But it's my band. You with the embassy?"

I said I was not with the embassy and then, using the conspiratorial whisper so much in vogue in Dar, told him that I was a reporter and that I hoped I could join the band on its flight to Zanzibar.

"Can't hear a word you're saying. Why you whispering?" A local electric guitar group called the Blue Shadows had taken over from the All American Big Brass Band. The dance floor was filling up and becoming anything but a place for this kind of conversation. I shouted a final question at Shapiro and he yelled back that the band would be leaving for the airport at 5 A.M. the following morning.

Ever since my arrival in Dar, I had been trying to get onto the island of Zanzibar. There were two reasons for this. To begin with, Zanzibar was where it all began for Stanley. It was there that he mounted his expedition, drew his supplies and recruited his men. Secondly, I wanted to visit Zanzibar out of simple curiosity. I had not seen the island since its independence in December of 1963 and its revolution a month later. So much of what was happening in Dar might be explained by a trip to the island. But the revolution, which toppled the Sultan and assured the supremacy of the island's 250,000 black Africans over its 50,000 Arabs and Indians, also carried into power a group of gun-toting, slogan-shouting, anti-Western toughs to whom the words "press" and "journalism" were synonymous with sabotage and espionage. Things had changed on the island since my time. Zanzibar now had a Lenin Hospital. The Seyyid Abdulla School had been renamed the Fidel Castro School, and Abeid Karume, the revolutionary leader and First Vice-President of the United Republic of Tanzania, had announced his determination to make Swahili the official language on the grounds that "China has its own language and has progressed a long way and has the atom bomb."

I think I tried everything in my efforts to get to Zanzibar. Knowing of the islanders' aversion to reporters, I had calling cards printed identifying myself as a "travel writer," but the immigration officials saw through this one and turned me down. Official channels turned into dry creeks and unofficial avenues of approach into cul-de-sacs. Spotting an East African Airways brochure advertising three-day excursions into Zanzibar, I applied for passage at a Dar tourist agency, an abortive charade which resulted in the following conversation:

Traveler: "You are advertising excursions to Zanzibar. I am a tourist and would like to go."

Travel Agent: "Do you have your permit?"

Traveler: "No. Where do I get one?"

Travel Agent: "In Zanzibar."

Traveler: "Can I go to Zanzibar to get one?"

Travel Agent: "No."

Traveler: "Then just how do I get one of these permits?"

Travel Agent: "I don't know."

I mulled over the possibility of sneaking onto the island under the cover of darkness in an Arab dhow. I was sure I could hire one but, on reflection, I was also certain that I would be picked up and jailed instantly. Then there would be a period in jail followed most likely by expulsion not only from Zanzibar but from the rest of East Africa as well. My trip would be over before it began and I simply could not afford to let that happen.

I arrived at the Agip Hotel an hour before dawn and found Taubman and his entourage drinking coffee in the lobby. "Great day for a throat cutting," said a member of the band. None of his companions voiced any disagreement. Taubman and Shapiro said it was all right with them if I came along but explained that this trip was neither their idea nor was I their responsibility. They were willing, however, to let me masquerade as a cymbal player.

"It's State Department all the way," said Taubman. "We just do what we're told."

Taubman rode to the airport in a cab. The band followed in a bus and I traveled after them in a car I had rented pending the arrival of my Land-Rover. The sun, red and noticeably larger than it is in northern climes, pushed over the horizon and my spirits rose with it. Maybe the Trojan Horse approach would work after all. I began to picture myself, cymbals in hand, providing shattering climaxes to the Zanzibar Blues. In the airport waiting room, I stuck close to Taubman, trying to look like a cymbal player. Taubman was warming to the idea and telling me at some length how little space his

African tour was getting in the American newspapers when we were interrupted by a young man with crew-cut hair.

"I'm awfully sorry, Mac," he said to me, putting on a smile that would have soured fresh milk. "This is our baby, our plane. No freeloaders." I asked him who he represented and he said the embassy. I told him I would be delighted to pay.

"Sorry, Mac. Awfully sorry."

Taubman, who had been following the conversation with interest, wrapped his arm around my shoulder.

"Look at it this way," he said as the members of his band trailed out onto the tarmac and toward the waiting plane. "This is the first time an American cultural thing has been permitted on Zanzibar since the revolution. File that. It's a first. You got it alone!"

Not much cheered by Taubman's parting words, I drove back to town amidst a stream of early-morning bicyclists on their way to work and bought a copy of *The Nationalist* from a boy on a corner. I was startled to learn what I had missed at the Taubman concert the night before:

"Attempts to restrain Dar es Salaam residents from acts of open hostility failed on Wednesday night, when a number of people boycotted the American national anthem at a ball-room dance in the New Dar es Salaam Club. . . . Before dancing began, the American band played the Tanzania National Anthem and immediately after, the American anthem, during which some people sat down while others stood but engaged in conversation. Among those who refused to stand was a white girl who told a reporter: "I can't stand. I am not American. I am an African." She refused to disclose her identity. . . .

Mrs. B. N. Kunambi, Chief Commissioner for Tanganyika Girl Guides, said in an interview that after Tuesday's revelations by Mr. Oscar Kambona, that certain Western powers were plotting to attack Tanzania, she feared that the dance would flop since an American band was scheduled to play.

"But thank heavens, it was a great success. Many people turned out for the occasion," she added. She said the success of the dance at such a gloomy hour was something very remarkable.

The American embassy muffled whatever irritation it might have felt during the days that followed the plot accusation. The policy was one of restraint—a restraint so restrained that when, at long last, someone decided that the time had come to stand up and be counted on the side of the Americans, an almost perceptible shudder went through the ranks of the embassy staff. American diplomats were conspicuously absent at the Dar airport when a British schoolteacher named Peter Butchard boarded a plane for England at the end of a long day, most of which he had spent in a cell in the Central Police Station, alternately hunger striking and asking to see the British High Commissioner. His offense, according to Job Lusinde, the Minister for Home Affairs, was "political." He had been brought to Dar from the coastal town of Lindi, locked up "for his own safety," and then asked to leave the country.

Lusinde explained that Butchard had been teaching at the Lindi Government Secondary School. The week before, some four hundred tons of food, a gift from America, had arrived in Lindi, destined for Mozambique refugees housed on Tanzanian soil in two nearby camps. On Monday afternoon (it was now Wednesday) the citizens of Lindi held a march to protest the American plot to overthrow the government of Tanzania. Young Butchard, said Lusinde, had taken his Land-Rover to a point where the demonstrators passed and had hung two placards on his vehicle. The signs were written in Swahili and read: "A gift from America, food weighing 560,000 pounds, worth 360,000 shillings, arrived in Lindi yesterday." Lusinde added that Butchard had been lucky the demonstrators had not attacked him.

My impression was that there were several Americans in the embassy who would have cheerfully attacked Butchard themselves for "rocking the boat," an expression one of them used in a conversation with me.

"We've got to give this thing time to work itself out," he explained. "Julius is in a jam. If we make noises now we'll just be hurting him."

"You're sure he's on our side?" I asked.

"Of course he is," the embassy man said and then added reflectively. "If he isn't, who is?"

I think that the embassy man's feeling about Nyerere's allegiance was based neither on wishful thinking nor an informed insight into

Nyerere's mind but on a rumor then current that Nyerere would use his next scheduled public appearance (a "massive demonstration" at the Jangwani Playing Grounds the following week) to accept America's denial, chastise Kambona for having let himself be duped, and perhaps even announce the dismissal of the editor of *The Nationalist*. No, it would not do to rock the boat on the eve of such events.

Paul Taubman and the All American Big Brass Band's round-trip day excursion to Zanzibar ended without incident and they returned to Dar for a final concert before continuing north to Kenya. I asked one of the members for his impressions of the island.

"Nothing, man," he said. "I bought a Swiss watch and some of the boys bought, you know, ivory and stuff. But, man, there's *nothing* there. Dragsville."

Taubman's farewell concert took place on a plot of open ground in the center of the city. There had been talk of canceling the performance because a meeting of Moslem women was taking place in a nearby building which (or so some members of the embassy had heard) would concern itself with the plot. It was feared the women might end their meeting by attacking the band. But the Moslem women, their faces swathed in black shawls and their eyes devoutly downcast, discussed only religious matters and, at the end of their meeting, surrounded the band not as an angry mob but as appreciative listeners. Taubman wore a red jacket and a white sombrero and was his usual buoyant self. He had been briefed by the embassy not to favor any of the Asian members of his audience (for fear of upsetting the racial applecart) and as usual he did exactly as he was told. He led an all-African daisy chain of small boys on a hop-skip-jump tour of the grounds. He let the bandmaster of the Dar police band conduct the All Americans and then presented him with a souvenir baton. He danced with an African lady who, in her delight and enthusiasm, came close to hurling him to the ground.

"I can sure pick 'em," he said as he stumbled back to the podium for his final, farewell rendition of the "Dar es Salaam Blues."

The little pocket of friendship and bonhomie which enveloped

Taubman during his stay in Dar vanished with him and the plot rushed in to fill the void. For the Americans, things went from bad to worse. First the plot and then, far off in the Congo, Stanleyville. *The Nationalist* whipped itself into a frenzy over the Belgian paratroop drop to rescue the rebels' hostages. The fact that American planes were used in the operation was, for the newspaper, simply a further manifestation of the giant anti-African conspiracy. As for Dr. Paul Carlson, the rebels were not to blame for his death. On the contrary, his life surely would have been spared if the Americans had bargained in good faith with the reasonable and patriotic leaders of the Congolese struggle for true independence.

I am afraid that I took the intemperate and violent *Nationalist* reaction to the Stanleyville rescue operation too personally. My good friend George Clay, the National Broadcasting System's correspondent for Africa, had been killed by sniper fire as the armed convoy in which he was riding approached Stanleyville from the south, and, when I noticed that the display windows of the USIS library remained devoid of the Stanleyville atrocity photographs which had arrived some days before, I suggested to one embassy official that we were behaving as if we were embarrassed by our role in the Stanleyville operation.

"Things are tense enough here without that kind of stuff," the official said. "Besides, Stanleyville isn't our problem. We've got enough problems without bringing in Stanleyville."

The American policy of restraint may have been making itself felt within the inner councils of the Nyerere regime but it was not doing much, as far as I could judge, in calming the storm in the hinterlands. A Peace Corps teacher who appeared in Dar for a few days of rest and rehabilitation said it had been rough out there. The Regional Commissioner in his area had made the usual speech about the plot but had embroidered the theme, saying among other things that the Peace Corps was not the Peace Corps but the Spy Corps. When the Peace Corps representative remonstrated with the Commissioner and pointed out that he just might have to pull his teachers out of the area for their own safety, the Commissioner had thrown up his hands in what seemed a genuine display of horror.

"You can't do that," the Peace Corps teacher quoted the Regional Commissioner as saying. "Oh my God, no. You can't believe what I said. I only said those things on orders from Dar."

Nevertheless, that night and for several nights thereafter local patriots traveling in groups urinated on the front porches of Peace Corps dwellings.

Among Americans of African descent, skin color was neither camouflage nor protection. I had a long talk about this with an American Negro with a long and apparently unblemished record in the civil rights movement.

"I came over here because I wanted to help," he said, mournfully eying the motionless revolving fan in the ceiling of his office. "But the color of my skin hasn't done me a damn bit of good. More the other way around. They think I'm either a spy sent over by the CIA or that I've come to take their jobs away."

If the plot did not exactly thicken (Kambona had introduced no new evidence since the three letters), it nevertheless succeeded in congealing all efforts then being made to re-establish a useful working relationship with the Tanzanians. It became increasingly clear that the next move was Nyerere's. He had said nothing of any substance since the Kambona announcement and, as the day of his appearance at the Jangwani Playing Grounds dawned, the atmosphere grew electric. I arrived at the appointed spot well ahead of the crowds, with the idea of taking pictures as they arrived, and stationed myself on a bluff which gave me a view of the playing fields and the intersection of United Nations Road and Morogoro Road. I was joined by an American Negro who worked for the Tanzanian government and who was dressed for the occasion in a Nehru-style cloth cap and a striped sleeveless smock of the kind affected by Nkrumah and other Ghanaians. He had with him a South African Negro who was asking him about elections in America. The South African, who had probably never voted in his life, wanted to know all about them.

"I didn't vote in the last elections," the American was saying as he drew close. "I'm over here so I didn't vote, but even if I'd been back in the States I wouldn't have voted. There's no difference, you see, between Johnson and Goldwater." The South African nodded with admiration. I think he felt it must be marvelous to have the vote and not use it.

The organized part of the crowd was now beginning to stream past us down the Morogoro Road. They were in a festive mood and carrying banners and signs reading, "Yankees Go Home," "This is Our Country," "We Warn Those Who Are Plotting for Tanzania —They Never Get Chance," and "To Hell with Your Heinous Plans African United Will Chase You Like Rats."

After a while I joined the sign carriers. Dressed as I was in shorts and sandals, I felt whiter than I usually do in an African crowd, but the marchers were friendly, posed willingly for pictures and asked me where I was from. When I said I was from America they seemed delighted. Together we crossed the ditch that ran parallel to the Morogoro Road and headed across the field toward the speakers' platform which had been erected in the center of a row of flags denoting the new African nations. I tried but there were too many to count.

Draped with cameras, I had no trouble talking my way into the inner enclosure. On the speakers' stand, two cheerleaders (one wearing a leather, fleece-lined snow hat with ear flaps) were not having much luck persuading the crowd to chant, "Nyerere, Sí! Yankee, No!" The crowd seemed unresponsive, perhaps because its knowledge of Spanish was limited. At any rate the slogan was not catching on. I browsed around, taking pictures, and then climbed up on one of the chairs on the platform to get a better shot of the cheerleaders. It was a bad mistake. A policeman and a man in a scraggly beard who turned out to be from the Information Ministry pulled me down and asked me for my credentials. I produced one of my calling cards identifying me as a travel writer. It was not sufficient. What newspaper was I working for? No newspaper. I was writing a book. Yes, but a book for what newspaper? The argument ended with me well out of the inner circle, squatting on my heels among a group of green-uniformed young national servicemen. Forbidden to take pictures, I concentrated on the crowd and noticed not only that I was the only white man but that there were few Indians.

Despite the incident of the closing of the shops in Morogoro and that morning's TANU Central Committee warning "to all those people who stay in their houses or shops and peep at others during processions and demonstrations," it seemed that the Indians would never learn.

There was some but not much applause when Nyerere arrived at the head of a long line of cars, got out and strode to the speakers' stand. He seemed preoccupied and waved to the crowd mechanically, holding whispered conversations with aides in mid-wave. At length he positioned himself in front of a brace of microphones and raised both arms. The crowd was immediately silent. Nyerere wore an open-necked sports shirt loosely hanging over his trousers, and it billowed behind him in the wind like a spinnaker. It was a stiff breeze, Nyerere is small and slightly built, and the thought crossed my mind that the wind would catch his shirt and blow him away.

He spoke for an hour and a half in Swahili. I could not understand a word but there was no doubt in my mind that he was a good speaker. His voice was a veritable organ—not the kind found in churches but the movie theater variety, which comes equipped with boat whistles, bells, klaxons and every variety of musical instrument. He whispered ominously; he shouted threateningly; he raised and then narrowed his voice to a nasty, carping falsetto. I wasn't sure but it sounded to me as if he were imitating somebody for whom he had nothing but scorn. He understood the musical quality of Swahili and used words as notes; sentences came in cadences; paragraphs ended in cadenzas. But Nyerere was a soloist, seldom using the crowd as an orchestra. Perhaps he knew better. Tanzanian crowds, unlike those in Ghana and even in Kenya, make poor orchestras. But it was a well-behaved crowd; it listened intently and seemed to be mulling over what the President had said when it rose at the end of his speech. Walking back, I asked one of the audience what Nyerere had said. Oh, he said, it had been about the plot and America's complicity. The President had told them that they must beware of spies.

I am still not certain precisely what Nyerere told the crowd at the Jangwani Playing Grounds. According to *The Nationalist*

Nyerere said that the American ambassador had protested that the documents presented by Kambona were forgeries.

"I told him that he should know better and that if he knew that it was not true we will sit down and pray," Nyerere declared in *The Nationalist*. "But they should not expect us to be ready to accept that they are forgeries. I say they will agree that they are not forgeries when we present them with the document. According to a Swahili saying, once you have been bitten by a snake you must be alert. It is not a sin to be alert."

This version was at variance with the one carried in the *Tanganyika Standard* and the official translation released several days later by the Information Services Division of the Ministry of Information and Tourism. According to these sources the President had said:

"Now the Americans are denying the plot and the authenticity of the documents discovered. Mwalimu [which means 'teacher' in Swahili and is the title Nyerere bears] said that if it were true that the documents were forgeries and that no plot was planned at all, the people of Tanzania would be the first to thank God and rejoice."

The American embassy chose the official version, viewing it as a comedown and Nyerere's way of preparing the people for a future admission that the plot did not exist. It was, I was told, the African way.

The American way seemed to me equally mysterious. For some weeks, in a vacant lot at the corner of Morogoro Road and Bibi Titi Street, the Americans had been erecting a considerable structure consisting of a geodesic dome and a courtyard surrounded by a white-washed cement block wall. Viewed by daylight it had a light and airy quality; at night it resembled a strategically placed pillbox.

Paul Taubman had given the Tanzanians a "cultural thing." Now, in the battle for men's minds, we were about to raise the curtain on a consumer "thing." "Plastics–USA" was the name given to the exhibit being assembled under the pillbox and Maurice Gusman was the man chosen to give it voice and meaning.

But who was Gusman? Little was known except that he was flying out to Dar as President Johnson's special representative and that he would officiate at the opening of "Plastics–USA." The information that the State Department cabled to the embassy was sparse, describing Gusman in vague terms as an industrialist and philanthropist. A cautionary note had been appended by a State Department physician, pointing out that Gusman was elderly and frail and that every effort should be made to guard his health. This led to worried speculation as to what the Dar climate, which is hot and humid, might do to a man of Gusman's age. One embassy official remembered having taken a course in embalming during a tour of duty in India. But he had never put his knowledge to the test and was not, repeat not, going to start now. It took Maurice Gusman himself to put minds to rest. To everyone's relief he was the picture of health. His eyes were red-rimmed after the overnight flight from Rome but they sparkled with intelligence and curiosity. They sparkled even more brightly in the presence of ladies.

"My dear," he said, taking each and every one by the hand, "you are beautiful. I never seen a girl so beautiful like you."

The ladies, who loved him on sight, were enchanted when he disclosed that he had made his fortune by manufacturing contraceptives in Akron, Ohio, before selling out and retiring to Florida.

"I could have sold it for forty million," he confided. "But, being the kind of business it was, I took ten."

Gusman himself was unclear as to why the White House had tapped him for this assignment. What was clear was that the White House had made the perfect choice.

"It's so beautiful here. Like Florida," he would say, and when they tried to tell him about the plot he brushed them away. "I don't know anything about politics. You just tell me what you want me to say."

"It doesn't matter what you say, Maurice," said an embassy official who, like the rest, had fallen under his spell. He was at that particular moment preparing the visitor for his first session with the American ambassador.

"What should I wear?" Gusman asked him. He was wearing a sports shirt, the standard daytime uniform in Dar.

"What you're wearing now. You're fine."

"I've never met an ambassador before."

"Ambassadors are just people."

"It's a great honor."

"It's a great honor for *him*. Remember, you're President Johnson's personal representative."

"You're right. I'll put on a tie."

I was not present at the meeting between Gusman and the ambassador but I would not be surprised if Gusman had disarmed him with one of his "afroisms," among which his favorite was "Honesty is the best policy because it's good business to be honest." Whatever he said it was enough to convince the ambassador that here was the man he needed to throw into the breach. A meeting between Gusman and Nyerere took on a high priority. Perhaps (hope springing eternal even now) Nyerere himself might be persuaded to join Gusman at the opening of "Plastics—USA" exhibit.

But it did not turn out that way. Nyerere would see Gusman later. But the exhibit was out. On the opening day, while gray-uniformed officers with police dogs kept a pleasant and patient crowd at bay, Gusman and one of the lesser Tanzanian ministers made brief speeches, cut a ribbon and led a group of diplomats and observers (most of them American) into the exhibit proper. Inside, under the dome, there were stalls containing plastic objects—dolls, dishes, beach mattresses and the like. I had seen many of the same products for sale in the Indian shops of Dar, and the exhibit reminded me of those displays in factory outlet stores on the edges of American superhighways.

Gusman led the invited guests into the courtyard, where a semicircle of chairs had been ranged in front of a covered platform. An attractive girl with orange hair grasped a microphone and announced in Swahili that this was to be a fashion show. The models, she said, were all Tanzanians. Indeed they were—the American embassy, to make sure that there would be no racial "misunderstandings," having fired the Indian and European girls who were originally included in the show. This decision had nothing to do with the dilemma faced by the producers on the afternoon of the opening. Of the dozen or so African girls picked to model the synthetic-fiber dresses, more than half had walked off the job. I never did learn exactly why they had gone on strike although I was given a variety of reasons by several sources. The embassy claimed that Tanzanian politicians had forced the girls to walk off the job in protest against the American plot. Another informant said that it was a matter of money—that the girls had only just learned how much American models were getting for similar work in the United States and were demanding the same. Still another said it was all the fault of the exhibit sponsors (the U.S. Commerce Department), which had reneged on a promise to give the girls the dresses at the end of the exhibit. Whatever the reason, there were only a handful of models on hand at the opening, and, because they had trouble changing dresses fast enough, the show dragged. But not for Gusman. While the rest of the guests stole to the tables piled high with canapés and gorged themselves, Gusman sat entranced, and when the entertainment finally came to an end it was he who led the applause. He gave the Tanzanian minister, who had every appearance of wishing he were elsewhere, a warm handshake and a newly minted Kennedy fifty-cent piece and invited him to visit him in Florida.

"I invited him to Florida," Gusman later told me.

"I know, Mr. Gusman," I said.

"Such a nice man. We talked about his family. . . ."

Not until several days after his arrival did I learn that an American "documents expert" flown over from Washington had been working on photostatic copies of the plot documents. Perhaps because they did not have them, the Tanzanian government had not seen fit to turn over the originals. But this apparently had not deterred the examiner, and his findings, duly transmitted to Nyerere, were said to be devastating. Nyerere's reported reaction ("This is *exactly* what I wanted to see") ran like wildfire through the American community. The tide seemed to be turning. With almost miraculous speed word came to the embassy that Mwalimu would see Mr.

Gusman—now! This time there was no question about what Mr. Gusman would wear.

"Give him hell, Maurice," somebody advised as Gusman and the ambassador, both dressed in dark blue suits, prepared to step into the embassy car which was to drive them to the presidential palace. The ambassador winced.

"It's a social call," Gusman replied. "No politics."

Apparently Gusman's supply of charm had been anything but depleted by his days in Dar. I wish I had been there to see the look on Nyerere's face (it was, I gather, one of total delight) on hearing Gusman's opening gambit.

"Mr. President," he said, "where is your throne? I expected to see a President on a throne." The rest of the conversation concerned itself with Kennedy fifty-cent pieces, invitations to Florida, family life—in short *everything* but the plot. The meeting could not have gone better and Gusman emerged the hero of the hour.

"You were great, Maurice," they told him all the way to the airport. Gusman basked in the glow.

"It was nothing," he said.

"But it was," they said. "You did it. We're back on the tracks and it's all your doing." Gusman's eyes twinkled with pleasure.

"So I had a nice time with a nice man," said Gusman. "For this I should get a medal?"

As in the case of Taubman, the situation deteriorated after Gusman's departure. An anti-American demonstration, led by two cameramen from Communist China, was staged by students outside the building housing the American embassy. But the innate reserve of the students, coupled with the fact that the embassy was out of reach on the fourth floor, made it a forgone conclusion that nothing would happen.

On Tanzania's own Independence Day, Nyerere again appeared at the Jangwani Playing Grounds and said that he had received a long letter from the Americans about the plot. As far as he was concerned, the matter was now closed. The American embassy construed this to mean that Nyerere had accepted the American denial. The United States (in an African way) had been exonerated. I asked several Tanzanians whether they felt the same way about it. They said they weren't sure. The President, they said, had not made himself entirely clear, had he?

The day after Nyerere's remarks, I caught sight of a familiar face in the pages of the *Tanganyika Standard*. It was Paul Taubman in Uganda. According to the caption he was presenting Prime Minister Milton Obote with a pen. A brass-banded pen.

CHAPTER 4

BLUES FOR MISTER JULIUS

At any rate before we begin to hope for the improvement of races so long benighted let us endeavor to discover some of the virtues they possess as men.

–H. M. STANLEY

DAR es Salaam teems with European and American scholars who have spent months and sometimes years in the dank and algal archives of old German colonial buildings or living with and recording the peculiarities of tribes in the interior. I talked with one of these and told him that I just plain did not understand the Tanzanians. I understood them as long as they confined their suspicions to us (every nation, it seemed to me, needs a villain at some time or another in its history) but it puzzled me when they extended their suspicions to include all outsiders. Almost from the start, I had found Tanzanians given neither to quick friendships nor lasting hostility. Not that they were superficial. They were anything but superficial; behind their vague and erasable smiles they seemed introspective, deeply troubled and profoundly reserved. Whatever was on their minds had been there a long time.

The scholar listened until I had finished and then told me to get out of Dar. Dar is too new, he said—too unsettled, too exposed to political crosscurrents, too confused. Did I have transport? I told him I had rented a car. Then go to Bagamoyo, he said.

Bagamoyo lies about forty miles up the coast from Dar. It is an easy drive, a good deal of it on asphalt and the rest on a white sandy road which winds through coconut palms and huge, beer-bottle-shaped baobab trees. Occasionally, on the way north, the road bends toward the Indian Ocean and there are fleeting glimpses of deep blue sea through the tall palms. Having started late, I arrived in Bagamoyo at high noon, and found I had intruded on a scene out of a Grimm fairy tale. It was as if the town, together with its inhabitants, had been turned to stone.

I had driven into Bagamoyo at that precise moment in time when the sun reaches its apex. In Africa there is something sinister about the sun at midday. Time and motion hang suspended in a vise of heat. Where there was movement, now there is none. Where there was sound, now there is only silence. It is not a benevolent sun. It does not make green things grow as does the sun of the North. Instead, it robs trees of their shadows, leaves of their moisture, and man of his ability to think, to feel or to act. In Africa, the weak, the wounded, the newly born and the very old die at midday. Even the lion and the leopard wait until dusk or dawn to make their kill. They too are afraid of the African sun.

High noon and empty streets gave Bagamoyo a spectral quality as I walked past the massive, delicately carved Arab doorways and the old German administration buildings close to the beach, their heavy coral-stone walls cracked and crumbling and scabrous with decay. But then the sun passed its zenith; a faint breeze stirred the branches of the palms. The dogs began to bark and the inhabitants, awakened from their trance, looked on the stranger with suspicion.

It was in Bagamoyo that my thoughts about Tanzania and the Tanzanians began to come together for me. I suppose this was because Bagamoyo, like so many ancient landmarks, turned the mind to history. One by one, the incidents, events and conversations of the past few weeks began to arrange themselves in a historical context—whether they belonged there or not.

Less than a century ago, at a time when Dar was still an obscure fishing village called Mzizima, Bagamoyo had dealt in slaves and ivory and was rich. For the Arabs who built Bagamoyo, headquarters was on the island of Zanzibar, an easy day's sail to the east. Bagamoyo served as the assembly point and jumping-off place for the interior. From Bagamoyo foot caravans marched inland, bargained and battled with the local chiefs for slaves and elephant tusks, placed the tusks on the heads of the slaves, and marched them back to the coast. A great many slaves died en route but the Arabs always made sure that they started the return journey with more slaves than tusks. This way there were always enough porters to carry the ivory back to Bagamoyo. From Bagamoyo, the goods and chattel were shipped by dhow to Zanzibar, where the middlemen took over, sawed the ivory into manageable chunks, castrated those slaves who required castrating, then held their wares on the island until the trade winds were right for the sea voyage to the Arab kingdoms of the Red Sea, to India and beyond.

Demand always exceeded supply and the hunt for slaves and ivory carried the Arabs deeper and deeper into the heart of Africa. They cut through the majority of Tanganyika's tribes like knives through pats of soft butter. Given time I suppose the Arabs would have depopulated Tanganyika. As it was, they only decimated it. The survivors (in most cases those considered by the Arabs to be too weak to make the march to the coast or not salable once they got there) became the forebears of the Tanganyikans of today. And their heritage? It does not take much imagination to conjure up a vision of the old chief, fever-racked, emaciated and dying on his pallet, calling his elders together for the last time and saying to them: "If I have any advice to pass on to you it is this: *Beware of the foreigners*."

This legacy of suspicion and fear was reinforced when the Germans occupied the country and introduced Prussian discipline, a long working day and corporal punishment for those who believed in neither. Then (immediately following the First World War) came the British, who confused the Tanganyikans by doing just about nothing (either for or against the inhabitants) until a few years before independence, at which time there was a brief spurt of school building, road paving and the introduction of a crash course in parliamentary democracy for the indigenous politicians. Independence came in 1961, startling even Julius Nyerere, who not long before had agreed with the United Nations Trusteeship Council that his country would be ready for independence in another twenty or twenty-five years. The British just couldn't wait to get out. It had never been their colony anyway.

Enslaved, then overworked and finally abandoned, the Tanzanians, not surprisingly, were suspicious of foreigners. Perhaps this suspicion helped spark the desire for independence among the Tanzanians. Once lighted, however, the flame burned dimly indeed and, instead of casting a rosy glow, thrust dark and spectral shadows over the landscape. Poverty, illiteracy, disease and death—these were the vulturine chickens which came home to roost on independence day.

The Tanzanian of today can count himself lucky if he survives his first year on earth. Perhaps lucky is not the word. If he is a typical Tanzanian he will never learn to read or write. He will not feel the pangs of hunger often but his diet will consist in large measure of tuberous white roots which his wives will beat into a pulpy substance resembling and possessing little more nutritional value than wet Kleenex. During his days on earth he will be plagued by at least one and probably several debilitating diseases which, in the end, will kill him off in his late thirties or early forties (when the rest of us are in mid-stride). Should he be one of the very few who acquires an education, cures himself of the diseases which sap his strength, his energy and his ambition, he is followed into the city (where he has found a salaried job) by still another problem, known to the sociologists as the "extended family." Custom and tradition dictate that he aid and support as many members of his family, his village and his tribe as he is able. His "family" expands or contracts in direct proportion to fluctuations in his earning power. Thus, the more he earns, the larger his "family" and the less he seems to have for himself and his own children.

Disease, malnutrition, the parasitic extended family and a deep-seated suspicion of foreigners—all these combine in the Tanzanian to produce a man who, to put it bluntly, does not much enjoy working. Feeling sick most of the time, how could he? And with that leechlike family, why should he? The answer, of course, was that his newly independent nation would never get off the ground unless he did. Julius Nyerere knew this and, during my stay in Dar es Salaam, related in one of his "nation-building" speeches how he himself had toured several government ministries after hours and had found only Indians and Europeans working overtime. Nyerere's ministers knew about this too. They were always making speeches –the Minister for Information and Tourism telling a meeting of hotel and bar workers that the tourist industry depended on their being "charming, good looking and . . . at the same time hard working" and the Minister for Communications and Works exhorting the telephone operators at Telephone House to "pull their socks up." The trouble was that the ministers themselves, with some notable exceptions, did not enjoy working either.

It is all too easy for the dilettante historian, sociologist and psychologist to lapse into jargon and generalization. I am no exception and in Tanzania I began to use the phrase "energy quotient," or E.Q. It was not I.Q. that was lacking in Tanzania; it was E.Q. In casting about for historical parallels, America came most naturally to mind. There were obvious differences as well as similarities between the United States and Tanzania (too obvious to belabor here) but what came most forcefully to mind was the sheer and sustained physical and mental energy that was expended by the Americans in building their nation. And every bit of it was necessary. If it took a high E.Q. to make America what it is today, how much of an E.Q. would it take to turn Tanzania into what it might be tomorrow? Plain, common decency requires that the question be withdrawn.

Until the very day of independence, everything that plagued the Tanzanians could be ascribed to the fact that the country was not free. *Uhuru* would change everything. That is what the leaders told the people. Naturally, the people believed them. But, when the day finally came, the Tanzanians awoke to find that nothing had changed. And, worse still, nothing *would* change. *Uhuru* was a door in a false-fronted building. When opened it led not into a gilded palace but out into the bush again. Profits, such as they were, still went to the white farmers. Commerce, such as it was, remained in the hands of the Asian storekeepers. All the Tanzanians were asked to contribute was cheap labor. And it had better stay cheap too, because the coming of *Uhuru* coincided (was it a coincidence?)

with the outside world's decision that it was paying too much for such things as sisal, copra, tea and coffee and would, henceforth, start paying less. For the outside investor—even those whose pockets bulged with venture capital—Tanzania had become a conspicuously uninteresting place. And so, having celebrated the defeat of colonialism, the Tanzanians set out on a desperate and increasingly frantic search for the fruits of freedom.

There was a brief period, in the month of January, 1964, when it seemed as if those fruits were within their grasp. The moment occurred during the short-lived and abortive army mutiny, which was snuffed out, at Julius Nyerere's request, by a humiliatingly small number of British Marines. But before the British stepped in the mutinous soldiers ran unhindered through the streets of Dar. According to a friend of mine who was there when it happened, there was some looting and there were several incidents of savagery. But what was important, he said, was the way the people responded. For the first time since independence, the people in the streets (especially the poor ones) felt that something was changing, that something had happened which would, at long last, alter the pattern of their lives. What happened, my friend said, was typified by an incident which took place one night. A band of mutineers, drunk but not too disorderly, caught sight of an old *mzee*, or grandfather, huddled on a sidewalk in his tattered British Army greatcoat. Like so many men of his age, his days of physical labor were over and he was performing night watchman duty for the building behind him. The soldiers asked the old man whom he was working for. When the *mzee* replied by pointing to a lighted window above, the soldiers raised their rifles and fired a volley of shots through the window. They kept on firing until the Indian occupant, trembling with fear, appeared on the street below. The soldiers told the Indian that it was a shame to keep an old *mzee* in the streets at night, away from his home and family.

"Give him ten shillings," the soldiers told the Indian. The Indian merchant complied with speed. The soldiers then asked the *mzee* where he lived and, after he had answered, asked the Indian whether he knew who in the neighborhood had a car. Another window was pointed out. Again there were shots and still another Indian descended to the street.

"Drive the mzee to his home," the soldiers told the second Indian.

Apparently this sort of incident repeated itself frequently in the streets of Dar es Salaam and the word spread rapidly. My friend told me that he himself was convinced that if the mutiny had continued for another two days the Nyerere government would have collapsed. Popular as Nyerere was and is with the Tanzanians, there was a great hunger for change. Anything would be better than the status quo.

The mutiny also served to remind the Tanzanians that they were still not the masters of their destiny. It was after all the British, not the Tanzanians themselves, who had brought the mutineers to book. Could they do nothing right? Was the old German planter speaking the truth when he told them happily and with obvious affection that they were "just children?" Was the Nigerian judge whom they had imported from the other side of Africa to preside in one of their courts to be taken seriously when he was overheard saying that the Tanzanians were inferior? And what of the Ghanaian technician (a black man like themselves) who amused his white friends at parties by telling them that the Tanzanians were "not quite bright"? Why were all the cars in Dar still being driven by white men? Why were the shops still run by Asians, and why was the patriarchal *mzee* still doing guard duty in his threadbare overcoat at night?

Everywhere they looked, everything they saw seemed to tell them that they *were* inferior.

If ever there was a time for critical self-appraisal it was now. There were some (among them Julius Nyerere) who thought the Tanzanians should be made to face the facts of life. But there were those who thought otherwise and chief among these were the Chinese Communists—and the Americans. The Chinese approached the Tanzanians with cynicism, the Americans with idealism, but both joined in the insidious work of taking the Tanzanians' minds off the problems at hand. The Chinese did this by telling the Tanzanians that nothing that went wrong was ever *their* fault but always the fault of the white imperialists and their lackeys. The Americans countered by insisting that all problems were soluble and that everything would turn out just fine in the end. The Chinese preached the cant of Communism and taught the vocabulary of political invective. The Americans, on the other hand, invented euphemisms for the harsher realities, telling the Tanzanians that theirs was no longer an undeveloped country, or even an *under-*developed one, but would be known henceforth as a *developing* nation. Congratulations! Tanzania became Othello with Iago at one ear and Pollyanna at the other. The old chief was right: "*Beware of the foreigners.*"

It is, I think, to Nyerere's credit that he paid so little attention to either side. He continued to preach tolerance for the foreigner and hard work for the Tanzanians. He drew up a development plan which envisaged an increase in the annual per-capita income from £19/6 to £45 by 1980. He organized some of the nation's youth into work parties and told them to go off and clear land and build houses. Teachers would be trained and facilities expanded so that education would be available to everyone. But the gulf between what Nyerere preached and what was practiced widened. His own people kept missing the point. When he noted that the farms of expatriates occupy "a tiny 1 percent of the total land but at present account for 40 percent of our exports," I am sure he meant only to show the Tanzanians what *could* be done. Instead, his followers thought they heard the opening gun in a race to expropriate European and Asian land and began to do just that—even though it meant an almost immediate drop in production. The fruits of freedom withered.

Even the lowly nuts of the forest turned to dust in their hands—i.e., cashew nuts. In its raw state the cashew, one of Tanzania's major export crops, is encased in a hard shell. It is difficult to open without shattering the soft kernel within. Over the years, it had been the practice to ship the nuts to India, where they were shelled and processed by Indian women. After independence, according to a German economist with whom I talked in Dar, an effort was made to cut India out of the picture and the raw nuts were turned over to

African women for shelling. The experiment failed, however, because it was soon discovered that the Indian women could shell the cashews ten times faster and thus more cheaply than their African counterparts. Today the cashews still go to India and the greater share of the profits still slips through the less dextrous fingers of the Tanzanians.

So it went, and when it finally dawned on the Tanzanians that what Nyerere had been saying (about hard work and the long and rocky road ahead) really *was* true, they could not face it. It was more than they could bear. Abandoning their search for the fruits of *Uhuru*, they set out on a hunt for scapegoats (the Chinese loved this)—for anything which would take their minds off the real and pressing problems at hand. Prestige must be enhanced, and so there were frequent and belligerent speeches at the United Nations. Dar es Salaam must be made a headquarters for the Pan-African movement and super-secret training camps carved out of the bush for superhuman African freedom fighters. All these helped inflate the ego, and if the ego faltered that, too, could be blamed on the spies and saboteurs from without.

It was this atmosphere—this search for distraction—which gave rise to the "Western plot." I think the Americans in the embassy made a mistake when they ascribed it to a power struggle within the Nyerere cabinet. Given time and luck (or so the Americans thought) Nyerere would defeat the extremists, purge his government of Communists and once again resume his walk down the Western-oriented road to democracy and the better life. Certainly there was a power struggle under way, but there was never much question in my mind that it was one in which Nyerere always had the upper hand. Plainly and simply (like most astute, pragmatic and sensitive political leaders), he had found the consensus and was riding with it. Perhaps the consensus was not to Nyerere's liking but there was little else he could do. The "plot" and the President's unwillingness to admit its patent fraudulence reminded me of a story Nyerere is supposed to have told a friend of his some years ago in Ghana. The friend repeated it to me in Dar es Salaam and it went like this:

"Long ago, in Tanganyika, a prosperous tribe fell on evil days. The rains failed, the crops dried up and there were starvation and death. The chief of the tribe called in his witch doctor and asked him what to do.

"The witch doctor, after due deliberation, said that he could save the day and that he would be able to provide food. It would be good food and provided in abundance. But, he warned the chief, the food would make his people mad. Therefore the chief himself would be unable to partake of the food.

"The chief agreed to the witch doctor's conditions and in due course the food was produced in abundance. Just as the witch doctor had prophesied, the people of the tribe went mad.

"The chief himself abstained. After a certain time, however, the situation became intolerable for him and he called in his witch doctor.

" 'I can no longer lead my people because I do not understand them,' he said. 'Give me the food too, and I will eat it and become mad.

" 'Only as a madman can I lead my people.' "

I think a great many foreigners in Tanzania really did believe that the Tanzanians had gone mad, or if they had not gone exactly mad at least they were behaving irrationally. But it was a temporary madness. They were sure of that, and hopefully—in time—they would recover. I felt the same way during my first few weeks in the country because I could make little sense out of their behavior, but after a while it occurred to me that we were all dead wrong. We were wrong because we had based our thinking on false premises. We had assumed from the start that the Tanzanian wanted either to be like us or (heaven forbid) to be like the Chinese or the Russians. Or, if he did not wish to be exactly *like* the foreigners, he certainly wanted the things the foreigners had. But did he want those things the foreigners possessed at the expense of giving up what he was himself? Was he willing to become a white man, or an Indian or a Chinese, in order to acquire what they had? Would he turn his back on the old tribal customs, cut short those long and informative conversations at the side of the road or forgo the deeply satisfying pleasure of doing nothing whenever there was too much rain—or too little?

The answers seemed to lie written in the crumbling stones of Bagamoyo. Once there had been nothing here but jungle. Then the foreigners had come and built a town with roads leading to it to give it life and walls around it to make it safe. Later the foreigners had gone on to build other towns in other places. But the natives who had been left behind by the departing foreigners did not take Bagamoyo and make it their own, or add to it, or even keep it as it was. They had no use for Bagamoyo. It belonged to the foreigners. It reminded them of the foreigners, and so they turned their backs on Bagamoyo and the jungle returned. In time there will be nothing left of Bagamoyo to remind the Tanzanians of the foreigners who took them as slaves, made them work, and gave them nothing in return—nothing, that is, except a town which they did not want or need.

Bagamoyo—the great trading post of the past and the decaying ruin of the present—had been the Dar es Salaam of the nineteenth century. Would Dar become the Bagamoyo of the twenty-first? For a Westerner, it is an almost unthinkable thought. We can imagine the clock of progress slowing down, or even stopping for a while. But turning the hands back! No!

And yet the door *is* swinging shut on the foreigner in Tanzania. I do not know whether this is good or bad—only that it is happening. Perhaps what goes on behind that door after it is shut tight will not be to our liking, but for those who would rush in now to batter it down—to save the Tanzanians from themselves—let me recall an observation made by an expatriate white South African who found he preferred living in a country where he had little voice to living in a country where the majority had no voice at all.

"I tell you this," he said, and he was speaking of the Tanzanians. "If you're going to be buggered about, it's far better to be buggered about by your own kind."

CHAPTER 5

THE MORE WE ARE TOGETHER

It is a most sobering employment, the organising of an African expedition.

—H. M. STANLEY

THE days slipped by. Each morning now, with the clouds that heralded the approach of the rainy season gathered on the horizon, I appeared at the offices of the shipping company to ask about the whereabouts of the freighter carrying my Land-Rover to Dar es Salaam. The shutters on the office windows were shut to lock out the heat, and the Englishman behind the desk, a young man in white shorts and an open-neck white shirt, was always polite. The visits became a ritual. Would I care for a spot of tea? Ah, the Land-Rover. Yes, they had just had a report on that, but the news was not encouraging. There had been a delay getting through the Suez Canal and now, further south, the ports were crowded, the facilities overtaxed. No, there was not more shipping on the coast. It was just that everything was slower now. We all knew the way it was in Africa, didn't we? Not like the old days.

More tea?

In the office next door I asked about insurance. Yes, vehicle insurance could be provided for Tanzania, Kenya and Uganda, but not for Rwanda and Burundi. They were "disturbed areas." As for the Congo—absolutely not. Could I imagine any insurance company sending an adjustor into the Congo? Funny thing about insurance, he continued (there was always time for talk). During the Mau Mau emergency in Kenya, the cost of burglary insurance dropped precipitously because almost every householder carried a weapon, slept with a pistol under his pillow. The burglars just didn't care to try anything. Now, of course, the premiums were higher than ever.

Spot of tea?

In Africa, the dividing line between impatience and resignation is thin indeed and I crossed it frequently. I was, according to my London-conceived timetable, three weeks behind schedule. I had neither Land-Rover nor traveling companion and the rains were coming. The rains, they told me, would wash out bridges and turn dry-season roads into quagmires, and if they were heavy enough my proposed route could become impenetrable. There was nothing I could do about any of this and I found it best not to think about it. Thinking about it, I discovered, led only to frustration and despair. So I killed time, trying as hard as I could to kill it constructively.

On most mornings I went shopping for the things I would need on the expedition which lay ahead. My requirements, when compared with those of Stanley, were minute. Stanley did most of his shopping in Zanzibar, purchasing colored cloths for chiefs and their wives, a large and varied assortment of colored beads and a vast quantity of brass wire. In *Through the Dark Continent*, Stanley's two-volume chronicle of his trip, he wrote:

> The total weight of goods, cloth, beads, wire, stores, medicine, bedding, clothes, tents, ammunition, boat (the Lady Alice in eight sections), oars, rudder and thwarts, instruments and stationery, photographic apparatus, dry plates, and miscellaneous articles too numerous to mention, weighed a little over 18,000 lbs., or rather more than eight tons, divided as nearly as possible into loads weighing 6 lbs. each, and requiring therefore the carrying capacity of 300 men. . . . The entire amount disbursed in cash for advances of pay and rations at Zanzibar and Bagamoyo was 6260 dollars or nearly £1300.

My own shopping list was supplied by a TEA (Teachers for East Africa) teacher who had spent several months in the bush, and consisted, among other things, of a length of sisal rope (for towing the Land-Rover out of mud holes); a snake- and scorpion-proof tent; a snakebite kit consisting of a vial of serum, a syringe and a needle of great length; pots for cooking; a pick and shovel; a *panga*, or machete, which I was told should always be carried in the front seat for protection; two collapsible British army surplus canvas cots and sleeping bags; a table for eating and for the portable typewriter; two large metal trunks, which would be bolted to the floor of the Land-Rover and used to store food, camera equipment and writing material; a Coleman lamp for reading and a portable gas stove for cooking; plastic four- and five-gallon jerrycans for water and kerosene; and then food. My taste in food on my first expedition to the Indian grocer proved erratic and I had to return a second time to fill the gap between the tinned artichoke hearts and the pork and beans. I carried all these things back to my bedroom. There was, of course, too much, but knowing nothing of life on safari I didn't dare cut back. Happily, the tins of food fitted into the larger of the two trunks and my two bottles of Scotch whisky nestled safely among rolls of shock-absorbing toilet paper. One can stretch preparations of this nature over a period of several days and I did just that.

One day (four weeks late) my Land-Rover was dumped onto the docks of Dar es Salaam. Unlike the Lady Alice, it arrived in one piece, and I drove it to a repair shop, where a German with an acetylene torch constructed a wire mesh cage inside the vehicle just behind the driver's seat to make the baggage as theft-proof as possible. I was told that everything detachable and portable would be stolen; so I bought six padlocks for the two jerrycans mounted on the front mudguards, the cap on the gasoline tank, the spare tire on the hood, the hood itself and the tool kit under the passenger seat.

I had almost forgotten the brief talk I had had with the newspaperman in Nairobi, and when the letters started coming in from Rhodesia and the Union of South Africa I was both startled and pleased. The reporter worked for a string of papers in these countries and had written a short piece about me, saying that I was looking for "an adventurous South African or Rhodesian" to accompany me while I retraced Stanley's "epic journey" to the mouth of the Congo. Apparently he (or I) had touched a universal nerve because the letters of application came in by the dozen. I liked one in particular.

"Dear Sir," it began. "I am not a man. . . ." She described herself as "snub-nosed and shapely," this girl from South Africa, but she spoke no Swahili and confessed she could not drive. Besides she carried a South African passport which, as far as I could make out, was about as effective in independent Africa these days as a Nazi party card in a synagogue.

But there were other letters, most of them from young men who claimed they were willing to abandon home, family and job on the spot if given work. One letter caught my eye because the writer had enclosed a photograph of himself riding a rhinoceros. The rhinoceros seemed worried but the rider was obviously at ease. He lived now in a place called Louis Trichardt in South Africa but hailed from Kenya and, as luck would have it, carried a British passport. In addition, he claimed he spoke a fluent Swahili and knew more about the insides of a Land-Rover than was decent. I cabled him immediately and in due course (due course in Africa being a week longer than anywhere else) J. J. Kruger—blond, tall and bristling with an assurance that belied his twenty-one years—arrived at the Dar es Salaam airport.

"I'm a Keen-yan," he announced with a thick, instantly recognizable South African accent. I pointed out to him that times had changed since he had left the country of his birth the year before. Kenya was now independent and was pronounced "Ken-ya" with the "Ken" rhyming with "pen" or "den,"—the theory being, I suppose, that if you couldn't change the name of your country on independence (as in Northern Rhodesia to Zambia and Nyasaland to Malawi) the least you could do was change the pronunciation.

"Ach, man, it will always be Keen-ya to me," Jay said.

It took us a week to get going—a week which Jay spent going over the equipment I had bought and doing his best to be polite about it. He liked the Land-Rover, especially its short wheel base and its reconditioned engine, but wondered why I had spent so much money on a new tent when an army surplus one would have done as well. Also the fragile mantles on the Coleman lamp would shatter en route so we could send that back. Instead, he would fix up an electric light leading from the battery. The snakebite kit with its awesome needle was all right but he himself would much prefer to cut deeply into me with a knife and suck out the venom with his mouth. Penicillin and antibiotics? I told him I hadn't thought about that.

"Never mind," he said reassuringly. "We'll never be more than four hundred miles from a doctor."

He packed and repacked the Land-Rover, each time taking it for a short drive with its full load. He did not like rattles and found a new one every time out.

"Have you ever driven for miles and miles of bloody Africa with the same bloody rattle?" he asked. "Man, it will drive you out of your bloody mind." And so he packed and repacked while I, feeling useless and extraneous, painted a map of Africa on one side of the Land-Rover. At length, after achieving five minutes of comparative silence at thirty miles an hour. Jay pronounced us ready for the great trek and, on the following morning, with Jay at the wheel, we pointed the Land-Rover due east and roared down the Morogoro Road into the interior.

It was December 11 and the six weeks I had spent in Dar had been too long. It was a good feeling now to be leaving the claustrophobic atmosphere of the city for the great unknown. Mentally I transferred all of my worries about the mechanical side of the trip to Jay's shoulders and began to realize that, for the first time in my life, I could go where I pleased and do what I pleased. There were practically no limitations. I would try to stick as closely as possible to Stanley's route (allowing myself the privilege of cheating here and there) and eventually the money would run out. But aside from these restrictions the world was my oyster. It was a heady notion and it carried me all the way down the paved road to Morogoro. The Indians there must have apologized to the Regional Commissioner for their lack of patriotism because their shops were open again. In one of these we bought cold beer and then continued along the road (dirt now and with a washboard surface) toward Dodoma. The sky was dark with clouds; lightning flashed on the horizon, and since it was already late afternoon we agreed to pull over and set up the tent before the rains came.

Our campsite was well off the road and in a grove of scrub trees. Fire had burned the grass underfoot and the ground was hard, black and bone dry. The rains were late and the new grass, just beginning to push its way up through the ashes in scattered clumps, was green at the base but yellow at the tip. There was an air of desolation about the place. Obviously the creator had spent a minimum of effort here, but when I mentioned this to Jay he seemed surprised. Most of Africa is like this, he said. Bush country. All the way from the plains of the Serengeti down to South Africa. Maybe it wasn't much to look at but it supported game. He pointed to a circular indentation in the ground at his feet, a shallow hole filled with dry leaves. Elephant. A man could ranch in this kind of country, he continued. Of course, since it was the kind of country it was, you'd have to keep your cattle moving. Maybe you'd have to think in terms of thirty, forty acres a head. Maybe more. But it could be done. His family had just bought a farm in South Africa but it was too small. This was better. He liked the wild, wide-open spaces.

We held opposing theories as to how a tent should be put up and consequently spent a considerable time doing it. Jay made a lamp from a jam jar, a small bulb and some wires, and then we collected dry wood and built a fire. We drank the beer and then some Scotch, heated up two cans of spaghetti and meatballs (Jay rejected the artichoke hearts) and waited until the sky changed from gray to deep purple to black before turning in. The canvas cots were hard but the beer, the whisky and the silence put us to sleep and we did not awaken until well after dawn the following morning. We arose to the sound of raucous shrieks and found the treetops twitching with birdlife. Tanganyika parrots, Jay said. I had grown up watching parrots hook and claw their way around brass cages in pet shop windows, and to watch them now, flying singly and in great flocks through the branches, was to me enormously exciting. It was also reassuring to know that there was something alive in this barren land. The sky was still overcast but it had not rained. Jay said it could go on like this, without rain, for weeks. Sometimes the rains failed entirely.

According to my calculations we had now joined Stanley's trail.

He had started from Bagamoyo and we from Dar es Salaam to the south but our route had been bending north and the two tracks converged on the road to Dodoma, about thirty miles out of Morogoro. At this early stage in his voyage Stanley was already in a certain amount of trouble. Several porters had deserted and his two mastiffs, gifts from admirers in England, had died of heat prostration.

Soon after lunch the terrain turned into rolling cattle country sprinkled with clumps of gnarled gray trees and outcroppings of gray granite. At dusk we went off the main road again and down a dirt track, and made camp on the brow of a hill overlooking a small valley. About two hundred yards to the west was a small hill of solid granite, bare of foliage and, as far as I could see on our arrival, completely lifeless. But, as the sun sank behind the horizon, a silhouette appeared on the crest of the hillock. A baboon sentinel, Jay said, and threw a rock in his general direction. The rock fell short and the sentinel did not move. Gradually, one and two at a time, more figures appeared on the rocks—mothers and their young. Although we were not close enough to see their eyes, we could tell from the way they were sitting that they were looking at us. At length most of the baboons grew bored and melted into the darkness of the granite hill, but the sentinel stayed where he was, sitting on his hunkers, until he wearied of his upright position and lay down on his side. I do not think he closed his eyes. Later, when the flames of our fire had turned to red embers, Jay told me to shut up and listen. He had heard a leopard cough. Sure enough, the sound was repeated—a rasping, staccato explosion. The baboons answered with a volley of angry barks. Eventually the leopard must have wandered away because the barking stopped and silence returned to the baboon fortress.

Taking a standing bath the following morning in a small plastic tub under the surveillance of sixteen pairs of unblinking baboon eyes was not my idea of privacy. I had also never associated cattle with stealth before and the realization suddenly that I was surrounded by a herd of them was even more disconcerting.

"Jambo, bwana." I wheeled, soap in one hand, washrag in the

other, to find myself eye level with a smiling individual wearing an ochre sheet and carrying a spear. The tops of his ears were crenelated like a medieval tower and his lobes, perforated and heavy with rings of copper wire, drooped to his shoulders like limp elastic bands. His face was deeply lined by age and the elements.

"That's a Wagogo herdsman," Jay said. Walking over to him, Jay began the ritual of greeting. It is an elaborate affair and, according to Jay, must be completed before the conversation can be turned to anything substantive.

"Jambo, mzee," Jay said.

"Jambo, bwana."

Then followed in slow Swahili, interspersed by grunts and sighs and "a-a-ah's" and long, drawn-out "eh's" of understanding and agreement, the stately and traditional inquiries after health. The old man was well. Jay was well. The old man's family was well, and so was Jay's. Finally, Jay managed to pose the breakthrough question.

"Habari gani?" he asked. What was new? The old herdsman thought about that for a while. Still covered with lather, I wrapped a towel around my middle and waited. A fly explored the old man's furrowed forehead and settled in the corner of his right eye. In the distance a male baboon, with a rocking motion like a hobbyhorse in a child's nursery, loped across a clearing.

"Eh-heh," said the old man. Times had been bad. The leopards were stealing the goats around his shamba and the Europeans had increased his taxes. Jay translated. Europeans? I was puzzled. How could Europeans impose taxes now that Tanzania was independent? I asked Jay to put the question to the herdsman. The old man did not seem to understand. Had he heard of TANU?

"TANU . . ." The herdsman reflected deeply. "Eh-heh." Yes, he said at length, smiling, he had heard of TANU, but he did not know what it was. We gave the old man two cigarettes, which he placed like cannons behind each of his crenelated ears, and he departed with his cattle. They left, as they had come, without a sound.

We drove on. The land turned flat and the dust from our Land-Rover hung in the air behind us, white and unmoving. We changed to shorts and sandals, swung off the road to chase a herd of ostriches, and sampled the nut-like fruit of a baobab tree. The kernel inside was white, fibrous and bitter. Jay said it was good for the thirst and we chewed and spat until Kongwa, where we turned off at a sign reading "Kongwa Club—Members Only." Inside it was cool and dark. There was a dart board on the far wall and we ordered two Allsop Pilsners at the bar. The customers, Englishmen most of them, seemed pleased to make room for the strangers and told us that this was headquarters for a large-scale cattle-raising scheme. They were working, they said, under two-year contracts with the Tanzanian government as technical advisers, looking after 13,000 head of Bohran beef on 75,000 acres. Jay was surprised at the ratio of six acres per head and one of the men admitted that it was not sufficient and that the cattle were thin. But they had been drilling wells and if the rains did not hold off too much longer most of the cattle would pull through all right. One of the drinkers was a young Ohioan attached to the Peace Corps not as a teacher but as an agricultural expert. I asked the American about his reaction to the atmosphere of suspicion I had encountered in Dar. He said there was little of it in his field but that it was otherwise with those of his colleagues who were teachers. He said that he had been in the Kongwa area for only two months and counted himself lucky to be spending most of his time off in the bush. Kongwa, he reminded me, was also a training camp for "freedom fighters" from Mozambique, and just a week before the authorities had arrested four American missionaries and a young student on suspicion of spying.

The Peace Corps man said the arrest of the missionaries had not surprised him in the least because here every foreigner was considered a spy. But his teaching friends had grown disillusioned and bitter because their students had been instructed not to believe anything the American teachers said. I told the young Ohioan of the Englishman I had met a few weeks before who had remarked with some heat that the Peace Corps in Tanzania had made a bad name for itself because, in his words, "they won't talk or associate with any of the whites; they only talk to Africans."

"Well," the Ohioan replied, surveying the all-white customers of the Kongwa Club. "I started off that way too. But I guess times have changed."

While we were talking, eight Africans, neatly dressed in white shirts and trousers, entered the bar and there was some talk with the proprietor in Swahili. Then, shy and smiling, they left and the proprietor opened eight bottles of beer, placed them on a tray and handed them to a black waiter. The Peace Corps man said that it was always this way. Beer, he said, could be obtained by anyone who asked for it, but it was a shilling a bottle cheaper if consumed outside. You couldn't call it discrimination but the practice did serve to draw a line between the races.

The towns in this part of the country reminded me strongly of the sets built for Hollywood Westerns. Singida, a small town almost in the dead center of Tanzania, was no exception. The same main street, wide and dusty; the same ramshackle two-story buildings, and the same look of idle curiosity on the faces of the inhabitants as the travelers rode into town. We ate a tough and bony chicken curry in an Indian hotel while the waiter, a boy of about twelve, solicitously sprayed us and our food with insect repellent. We had tied a covered plastic pail to the front mudguard of our Land-Rover and filled it with our dirty shirts and soap and water. It had jiggled and sloshed over the bumpy roads since morning, and after lunch I took the bucket to a faucet in back of the restaurant and rinsed its contents under running water. They emerged surprisingly clean.

We spent the following two days and nights north of Singida at a leprosarium operated by a group of American Lutherans on a high plateau called Iambi. Our stay there convinced me that it was food as much as faith that sustained the missionaries in Africa. We ate prodigiously: tea before breakfast; breakfast of hot cereal, eggs, jam and toast, fruit and coffee; coffee and cakes at 11 in the morning; lunch, including wildebeest steak, potatoes, vegetables, dessert and coffee; tea and cake at 4 in the afternoon, and then an enormous dinner at 7 P.M. We left with a hamper of sugared buns freshly baked by the wife of the colony's director and felt our way through a maze of rocky roads which, we were told, would lead us eventually to the Rift Valley and the village of Mklama. I wanted to see Mklama because it had been the site of a German *boma*, or fort, and the setting for a story which, if apocryphal, at least fitted my conception of the manner in which the Germans ruled their old colony. According to the tale I had heard, a Tanganyikan *askari* had been caught asleep at his post on the ramparts of the *boma* by his German captain. As punishment, the Germans had dug a hole in the walls, placed the sleepy sentinel inside and buried him in concrete. As a permanent warning to the other *askaris* under their command, they had left the tip of his bayonet protruding from his grave. The bayonet (or so I was informed) was still visible in the ruins of the *boma*.

Because there were so many roads and no sign of any kind to point the way, we stopped often to ask directions. At one crossroads Jay pulled up in front of a shamba.

"Jambo," said Jay, and the owner rose slowly from the chair he had placed next to his front door. As usual, Jay remained seated in the Land-Rover. I had asked him about this, wondering whether it was not more polite to get out and approach those we wanted to speak to on foot. No, he had said, he could never do that. He would lose face that way. The Africans would simply not understand a white man who got out of his vehicle to ask a question. We argued about this for a while and then compromised. When it came time to ask questions, Jay remained in the driver's seat and I got out.

"Jambo," the man replied. He walked toward us slowly and went through the ritual of greeting in reluctant monosylables. When in Jay's opinion the time had come to ask more specific questions, the man confounded him by countering each of Jay's with one of his own. The way to Mklama? Yes, but where had we come from? Dar es Salaam? That was a great distance. Why had we come so far? And who were we? Travelers? The answers did not satisfy him. Travelers, yes, but from what region, of what race. By this time Jay too had climbed out of the Land-Rover and we were standing on the roadside, but the man remained on his side of the ditch, on his property. What race? Well, said Jay, speaking for himself he was a Kenyan. For this reason he too was an African. The bwana farmer and the bwana traveler were brothers.

For a moment the man said nothing. Then, stooping down, he picked up a tree branch which had fallen into the ditch at his feet. He propped the branch up. The tip of it reached to his shoulder.

"This," he said, speaking in Swahili and pointing to the trunk, "is Africa. And this," touching one of the lower branches, "is the Wagogo tribe. This is the Masai." He stopped and looked at Jay to see if he was being followed. Jay nodded and the man continued.

"This," he said, indicating still another branch, "is the Mu Ingareza (English) and this the Mu Amerika. We are all African, but the Wagogo and the Masai are more African than you."

The old German *boma* at Mklama had been placed strategically on the floor of the Rift Valley, that great fracture that splits Africa from North to South. From its weathered walls we could see both escarpments, east and west, and closer still small herds of bony cattle kicking up thin clouds of dust in their search for forage. There were several workmen in the *boma* and one of them explained to Jay that they were converting the old officers' quarters into a hostel for tourists. Jay told them the story about the unfortunate *askari* and asked where we might find the protruding bayonet. The workmen looked blank and then began to remember. Yes, said one of them, he remembered now having heard the story, but the bayonet had been removed and the grave obliterated. I was disappointed and wondered how many tourists would bother to make use of the new facilities once the word got around that the famous bayonet had been taken away. I suppose it had been too painful a reminder of the past. Besides, even the wildest chauvinist in the Ministry of Information and Tourism would have difficulty in making a national hero out of a soldier who had gone to sleep at his post.

North from Mklama, it was a story of dust and heat and dried-up river beds. The sky remained an ominous blue. We passed a dead calf on the side of the road. It must have died just an hour or so before because the vultures, heaving themselves into the sky reluctantly as we approached the corpse, had only consumed its eyes. The calf's body was incredibly thin and we guessed that it was no more than a day old. Its mother had simply failed to produce enough milk and the calf had died of starvation. Jay said it was often this way during times of drought. The vultures and the hyenas, themselves starving, watched the herds closely, often tearing a calf to pieces as it is being born and while its mother is defenseless.

The heat made us sleepy, the track through the plains was monotonous, and we were both surprised to find ourselves suddenly confronted by a cluster of buildings and a white man standing in the middle of the road. He was dressed in a pair of faded, striped cotton trousers, dusty black shoes with pointed toes, a torn white shirt and two felt hats, one worn on top of the other as double protection against the sun. He looked like an emaciated scarecrow.

Would we have a cup of coffee? The voice was unmistakably Irish, an undiluted brogue, and he introduced himself as Father Ryan from Tipperary as he led us into a ramshackle building and made us sit on a stained and threadbare sofa. The room was sparsely furnished but Father Ryan, angular and awkward of movement, seemed about to bump into every article in it. The refrigerator door was held in place by a black rubber band cut from an inner tube. Father Ryan took off his hat and then his glasses, revealing a white band across the bridge of his nose where the glasses had been. He made some coffee on a small stove in a corner of the room. We offered to help.

"No, no," he said, bringing the coffee over to us. "You stay just where you are." There was so little to do now that the children were all on holiday. It wasn't often he had visitors. Yes, we were quite correct in inferring that he was a missionary and that he taught school. Those other buildings we had seen were the classrooms. I started to say something about how neat and kept up they looked but Father Ryan interrupted. It wasn't necessary for me to say things like that. He knew they weren't much. And he was sorry about the condition of the furniture. Were we quite comfortable? An ashtray? He leaped to his feet, apologizing for not being a smoker himself, returned with a saucer and apologized for the fact that it was not an ashtray. Seated on the edge of his chair, he leaned forward. Could he tell us about anything? Education?

Well, times were changing, hopefully for the better, but as he understood the situation only some 40 percent of Tanzanian children got any education at all. Of the 40 percent who were eligible in his area . . . ah, it was a sad business. He himself had to turn down half because there wasn't room for them in his school. Those who were chosen were not selected on the basis of their intelligence but according to their size.

"If they're too little we say come back next year," he said. Then, pausing as if ashamed, he added: "We also turn them down if they're too big."

Since there are three tribes in the area Father Ryan continued, the student body was tailored to reflect this. He kept his students in school throughout Standard VI and their average age was thirteen when they left. Of those who completed Standard VI, only 25 percent went on to further education. Did they work hard? Father Ryan smiled and searched our faces in an effort, it seemed, to determine whether we could be told what he really thought. Evidently he was satisfied because he went on to say that he was afraid they did not work very hard. For some reason they did not see the connection between education and the better life. I asked him why this was so and Father Ryan began by saying he did not know. But then, as he talked, it became apparent that even if he did not know precisely, at least he had some ideas on the subject. Maybe it was different in the cities, he said, but out here on the plains there was no reason for people to work harder than they did. Not only had the better life not penetrated this far but even the *idea* of the better life was so remote as to be unreal. Oh, they had seen the better life go by once in a while in the form of a car or an airplane, but they had never seen the pilot of the airplane, and the owner of the automobile, if he was known to them at all, was either a white man or a politician from some other part of the world. He was certainly not a member of *their* family or *their* village. Out here there was no friction between the haves and the have-nots. Out here *nobody* had anything.

Uhuru? Yes, there had been changes after freedom but as far as Father Ryan could tell they had not been for the better. As far as he himself was concerned, it had simply made his job more difficult.

The people in these parts had interpreted freedom as meaning freedom from all the things which had irritated them or had made life difficult or had demanded a certain amount of discipline. Consequently, after *Uhuru*, church attendance had dropped and those who did come back attended irregularly. Father Ryan supposed it was true that if he and the other missionaries left tomorrow the vast majority of the people would go back to the old ways. He did not appear to be crushed by the thought.

"Oh, we always hope," he said. "Especially the older fathers. We all hope that there will be some who will stay with the Church."

Perhaps it was because the Catholic Church demanded certain things of its members which the African religions did not. Pagan religions gave satisfaction more readily since they were concerned with the problems of today—rainfall, a wedding, an illness and things of that nature. Immediate problems for which the witch doctors provided immediate answers. The Church had tried to teach them that there was more to life than a series of todays, and that there was a life after death. But it was a difficult concept, Father Ryan admitted, and one which was seldom grasped by minds concerned only with today. Yesterday and tomorrow, foresight and memory were alien words in these parts and perhaps (Father Ryan was extremely thoughtful now), perhaps it was just as well.

After seven years on these windswept plains Father Ryan doubted that he knew the African.

He had stopped talking now and seemed lost in thought. I interrupted and asked him whether he had noticed any other changes since independence. Father Ryan leaned forward again and lowered his voice. Isolated as we were, Father Ryan considered it necessary to lower his voice.

"There is great unrest," he said. His voice was close to a whisper. "The people are not happy. They are not satisfied. Partly it is the lateness of the rains, but it isn't only that. It is more than that."

Just that morning, he said, some of his workers were building an addition to the school when several TANU officials came up and said there was to be a meeting. He had learned by now not to argue, Father Ryan continued, so he had let them go. But the workers did not go joyfully. One of them had come over to Father Ryan and told him that he had thought that when *Uhuru* came it would mean that he would not have to do anything he did not want to do—and that included going to meetings.

"Before Uhuru," Father Ryan added, "there were taxes on cattle and hut taxes and the like, but the white man never really made them pay. Now they are made to pay, and all they get in return is a drought which kills their cattle and politicians who make them go to meetings. Not so long ago the police rounded up a group of tax delinquents and put them in jail for a day or so. That had never happened before. They're beginning to learn that the white man wasn't so cruel after all."

I stood up. It was time for us to go, but Father Ryan would not hear of it. It was so seldom he had visitors, people with whom he could talk. It had been so interesting for him. Was there nothing more he could do for us? What news could we bring him from the outside world? More specifically, had we heard anything more about the Congo? That was all he and the other fathers seemed to talk about at night after the day's work was done. I told Father Ryan that he probably knew more than we did since he had a radio and we did not, but I added (as long as we were on the subject) that it had occurred to me that too many missionaries, priests and nuns had held on in the Congo for too long, long after they had been warned to get out.

"That's odd," said Father Ryan. He was quite excited now. "That's exactly what we were talking about the other day with our bishop. You know it is not impossible, not at all impossible, that we could have another Congo right here in Tanzania. We asked ourselves whether, under similar circumstances we would leave or stay on . . . and become martyrs."

"And do you know what?" Father Ryan's expression was almost sheepish. "We couldn't decide."

He followed us out to the Land-Rover. Were we sure we could not spend the night? There was so much still to be said. The Congo . . . With the wind whipping the dust around us in the center of that vast and empty landscape, Father Ryan bent even closer. The

Congo. He had heard on the radio that Foreign Minister Spaak of Belgium had told the United Nations that the basic conflict which must be faced in Africa was the racial one. Did we agree? This really *was* the case, wasn't it? And what made it all so sad, so terribly sad, was that there seemed to be so little anyone could do about it. Perhaps it would just have to happen . . . as in the Congo.

We left him standing in the middle of the road as we had found him, a thin and angular scarecrow waving his two felt hats at sharp-clawed birds of prey he could not see but knew were there.

We drove northwest for another day across parched and eroded plains and arrived at Shinyanga in darkness. The manager of the Pamba (Cotton) Hotel found us an airless room next to the generator, but there was cold beer at the bar and we listened to a civil servant recently transplanted from the coast tell us how much he hated his new assignment. It was refreshing to hear a Tanzanian gripe about his own government for a change.

Next morning we studied our maps and found we were about half a day's drive from Mwanza on the southern shores of Lake Victoria. As we started north, I opened my copy of *Through the Dark Continent* and discovered that our reactions to the countryside and Stanley's were not far different.

> Usiha [he wrote] is the commencement of a most beautiful pastoral country, which terminates only in the Victoria Nyanza. From the summit of one of the weird grey rock piles which characterize it, one may enjoy that unspeakable fascination of an apparently boundless horizon. On all sides there stretches toward it the face of a vast circle replete with peculiar features, of detached hills, great crag-masses of riven and sharply angled rock, and outcropping mounds, between which heaves and rolls in low, broad waves a green grassy plain whereon feed thousands of cattle scattered about in small herds. . . . Fresh from the tawny plains of Monangah, with its thirsty and sere aspect, I was as gratified as though I possessed the wand of an enchanter, and had raised around me the verdant downs of Sussex.

Stanley arrived at Usiha on February 17, 1875—a month to the day after watching the first of his ill-fated white traveling companions, Edward Pockock, die of typhoid fever. Since his departure from Bagamoyo, he had covered 720 miles in 103 days or, as he described it, in "70 marching and 33 halting days." For Jay and myself, it was

December 17, 1964. We had covered approximately the same ground in exactly seven days.

Our destination was Mwanza. I asked Jay to keep a sharp eye out for the lake and to remember to shout: "I have seen the Lake, Sir, and it is grand!" (as Frank Pockock had shouted when *he* first sighted Victoria). But then the rain came suddenly and with such force that we had trouble seeing through the windshield and neither of us said much of anything when we saw light gray water through an opening in the hills to our left. It was Mwanza Gulf, a stalactite-shaped appendage to Africa's largest lake.

Looking back on my stay in Mwanza, I am still reminded of a shipboard bon-voyage party in which the passengers, knowing they are about to depart, say things they would not say if they were staying. Almost everyone I met in Mwanza was either on the verge of leaving or hoping to leave in the not-too-distant future. Despite its beauty and the view it commanded of the great lake (and it *was* grand!), Mwanza was a disturbing and unhappy place.

At the local tennis and golf club, to which Jay and I had been given temporary memberships, the British civil servants seconded to the Tanzanian government gossiped venomously about the Tanzanians. Africans had been asked to join the club after independence but none of them had, so the white members continued to speak freely. Of the many stories I was told at the club bar, these two are typical:

In the town of Ngudu, two magistrates have been held in detention without charges since March. The guess is that the first of the two was jailed because he had ruled against a TANU official in a civil case. The second magistrate had also incurred the ire of TANU. When several members of the party invaded his courtroom to tell everyone to clear out and join a big demonstration, the magistrate replied firmly that court was in session and that it would stay in session until he was ready to adjourn it. He was seized on the spot by the TANU members and taken away. Neither magistrate has been heard from for nine months. Their families do not know where they are.

A new magistrate moved into the Singida area and, in pursuit of extra-judicial activity, found what he thought he was looking for in the wife of a man who traveled frequently. The magistrate engaged the services of a boy who lived next door to the couple and promised to pay the boy a shilling if he came to his court and told him the moment the woman's husband left town. After a few weeks, the boy appeared in court and told the magistrate that the husband had departed on one of his periodic voyages. The magistrate, adjourning court, raced over to his potential paramour's house and was beginning to enjoy himself when the husband unexpectedly returned. I was not told the husband's reaction, but the magistrate was incensed and brought charges against the boy on two counts: (1) for taking money under false pretenses, and (2) for giving "false information to a public servant."

It was with difficulty that his fellow magistrates persuaded their colleague to drop the charges as well as abandon his insistent determination to try the case in his own court.

Nothing as stimulating as this took place during the hours I sat in the Mwanza magistrate's court. For the Tanzanian magistrate as well as myself, it was a slow and unproductive day. Case after case, most of them involving driving without a license, was adjourned either because warrants had not been issued or because they had not been served. I left with the magistrate upbraiding two glum policemen for failing to produce witnesses in a case which had been adjourned twice before for similar reasons. The lost and found notices on the bulletin board outside revived my spirits. Item No. 50/60 in particular:

> Eight long trousers in different colours. One basket six pair Khangas, 3 bed sheets, one Bugi-Bugi, one gown, one hand bag, one elastic basket, one standard stover, one water-bottle, one torch, two small porches, one blous, one blush, two knives, one hair comb, one shewing machine, one handkerchief, and seven dried timbers.

Perhaps the stories I was told at the golf and tennis club were not entirely true, or were exaggerated. The point is that the members believed them. One of the drinkers, an Englishman who was "not bloody likely" going to renew his two-year contract with the government when it ran out said it was too bad, really.

"We're the only ones who really understand them," he said. When I asked whether he and others like him would be replaced, he said he doubted it. The Tanzanians might hire "a few Swedes or Russians or people like that," he said, but nothing like the number of British they had working for them now. Already, he added, there were fewer doctors in the country than there had been before independence.

I met the regional Peace Corps representative and his wife surrounded by packing cases in their living room. They had come to the end of their tour of duty and were leaving in a few days. They had not, the Peace Corps man acknowledged ruefully, been to any farewell parties given by any Tanzanians, but perhaps that was to be expected now because of the plot. His wife was less philosophic.

"We've worked hard here," she said. "I don't expect them to kiss us or even be grateful. I just wish they weren't so damn snotty—like they thought they were doing us a big fat favor by letting us stay here."

The Peace Corps man shrugged his shoulders. As far as he was concerned, it hadn't all been a great waste of time. Had I, for instance, seen the report on the Peace Corps's first year of activity in Tanzania, the one which showed that classes taught by Peace Corps teachers had done far better in their examinations than those taught by Tanzanians? I shook my head.

"No," he said, "I guessed the report wouldn't get much publicity."

Unlike most members of the white community in Mwanza, Barbara Johansson did not go often to the golf and tennis club. Gaunt and stooped now, she had come to Tanzania from Sweden twenty years before as a missionary teacher, had supported the nationalist movement almost from its inception and had been appointed (not elected) member of parliament from Mwanza by her old and good friend Julius Nyerere.

I found Miss Johansson in her home on a hill above Mwanza waiting impatiently for a telephone call to come through from Bukoba just across the lake. The telephone call, she explained as she paced the floor, had to be routed through Dar, then up through Nairobi to Kampala in Uganda, and then down the western shore of the lake to Bukoba. The call had been in since yesterday but each time Bukoba came on the line it was only the operator to inform Miss Johansson that the number she was calling did not answer. Since the number she was trying to call was that of a business establishment which she was certain was not closed, Miss Johansson took a dim view of the operator's explanation.

"Oh," said Miss Johansson, "if I can only get through I can stop something terrible from happening." Miss Johansson said she could not tell me what it was she was trying to prevent but I heard that she was something of a crusader and unofficial public defender and I rather imagined that one of her friends in Bukoba had got himself into trouble with TANU. Tanzanians who were on good terms with TANU never seemed to be in trouble. I had also been told that Nyerere had appointed Miss Johansson to her present post over the objections of TANU and I asked her what her relations were with the party. She answered by saying that she had not joined the party at the beginning, because it was then solely African, but only after the writing of the constitution which stated that the party was to be multi-racial. The telephone rang and Miss Johansson seized the receiver and spoke several sentences in rapid Swahili. She sighed in exasperation, repeating the word "Bukoba" several times, and then hung up sharply.

"Now they tell me the line is down," she said. "Something is wrong. Something is very wrong."

While Miss Johansson was on the telephone, I had risen to study the books in her library. The bookcase was less than half filled, the stock obviously depleted.

"Yes," she said, answering my question before I had asked it. "They are not all there. Most have been borrowed by Tanzanian friends. There is such a hunger, such a thirst for knowledge."

We talked for a while about her recent trip to America, where she had gone to lecture. She was angry with the Americans. In Mexico, she said, American Secret Service agents had detained her at the airport, and asked her a good many questions about her just-completed visit to Cuba. As a consequence she had missed her plane. Was she absolutely certain that her interrogators were American and members of the Secret Service? Yes, she said, she had been sure they were Americans because they had spoken the language and their questions had been offensive. What right had they to ask her, a member of the Tanzanian Parliament, about her trip to Cuba? I suppose it was Miss Johansson's assumption that anyone who questioned her rudely must have been American that prompted me to say that I had not been made to feel exactly comfortable in Tanzania myself. I said it struck me that the government-endorsed anti-American atmosphere was both short-sighted and foolish, in that it would not conceivably profit the Tanzanian people themselves. I did not know what Miss Johansson thought, but it had been proved to my satisfaction that the American "plot" was a hoax.

"You may be right," said Miss Johansson. "But the fact that somebody gave those documents to us proves that somebody was plotting. Maybe it was to get America into trouble with Tanzania but to this extent there was a plot. We have done everything to keep the Cold War out of Tanzania, but the Western and the Eastern powers are forcing the issue on our country. You have your agents everywhere—asking questions, asking questions, trying to find out which minister is strong and which one is in favor or out of favor. Asking questions, spying . . ."

I said it was my impression that the gathering of political information was a fairly common and accepted function of embassies on foreign soil. Miss Johansson looked at me impatiently.

"If that is so," she said pointedly, "then we must teach our people to be suspicious of foreigners who ask questions." We were arguing now and I was under the impression that both of us were enjoying it. There was a rumor, I went on, which I had been unable to track down, to the effect that cinema cameras were banned in Mwanza. I did not know the basis for this rumor; I had checked with the police and they professed to know nothing, and yet I had been told again and again that even tourists were forbidden to take motion pictures without special permission. What, I asked, would this do to the tourist industry? And what was there in Mwanza that was of any possible military or strategic interest? Miss Johansson glared at me and then began to talk rapidly and indignantly.

"A few weeks ago we had a trade delegation here from the People's Republic of China," she said. "I have forgotten how many of them there were. We were told that they were important and we were prepared to do our best for them. But I do not think they came in the spirit of friendly cooperation. Each of them had a camera and they took pictures of everything—the facilities at the port, the airport, the railroad terminus. Everywhere they went they took pictures. This was not right. I did not care who they were. They were spying. So you see *I* am the one responsible for the restriction on the use of cinema cameras. . . ."

Suddenly, Miss Johansson broke off. Her expression was that of a trapped animal.

"You have tricked me!" she cried. "You have no business to know these things but you have made me talk. Questions. Questions. Always asking. You are no better than the others." She rose, rubbing her hands together in a close approximation of anguish. I had not wanted to alarm Miss Johansson and I did my best now to pacify her, telling her that I had not meant to pry and that my concern was solely with the betterment of relations between America and the Tanzanians. At length Miss Johansson subsided, but during the remaining few minutes of our conversation she remained on guard.

"There is one thing you Americans must understand," she said. "You have always pictured Julius Nyerere in your own minds as being pro-West. I must tell you this. Julius Nyerere is not pro-West, but neither is he pro-East. He is genuinely nonaligned. Until you understand this you will never have good relations with Tanzania."

Miss Johansson had many friends in Mwanza and most of them felt that her days as a member of parliament were numbered. Despite her friendship with Nyerere and her undoubted love for her adopted country, she was not in the inner circles of TANU. I could understand TANU on this. Would Miss Johansson have applauded wholeheartedly had she been in the audience when the former Regional Commissioner at Mwanza told the predominantly Indian Rotary Club during a speech about aid from America: "Let us make sure we get the last egg before we kill the Golden Goose"? I doubt it.

Some months afterward, I was not surprised to learn that Miss Johansson had been relieved of her parliamentary duties and appointed headmistress of the Tabora Girls School.

On my last afternoon in Mwanza, a friend took me to a graduation ceremony for a group of Tanzanian teacher trainees. On the way he told me that he himself had done some teaching and that he had found his students bright and inquisitive. At times, however, he had run into situations which had baffled both him and them. There was, for instance, the case of Long John Silver. His students had enjoyed *Treasure Island* and no problems had arisen until the final chapters. How was it possible, his students had asked, that Long John Silver could now be bad? He had been good in the beginning and now he was bad. My friend had tried to explain that such things happened often, not only in literature but also in life, but his students would not believe him. They had been deceived. A man was either good or he was bad. It was not possible to be both.

The young teachers were gathered in the auditorium of a school on the outskirts of town. Chairs had been arranged in rows facing a small stage but the rear of the room was filled with tables on which the teachers had placed drawings done by the students they had been teaching during the past semester. The teachers, dressed in white shirts and ties, were eager to show us what they had accomplished and pleased when we asked questions. The drawings were, I thought, like drawings done almost everywhere by children, but there seemed to be a uniformity about them. I examined one pile and asked the teacher what they represented.

"Going to school," he said. There were about fifteen drawings, done, he said, by ten-year-olds. In each case the sun had been placed in the left-hand corner, the school building in the center, the tree to the right and the schoolward-bound student to the left.

At a signal the students and guests seated themselves in the chairs facing the stage. There were several speeches, some in Swahili and some in English, about the importance of teaching and the need for education. Each speech was followed by enthusiastic applause. Then it was announced that a special treat had been prepared for the honored guests. With that, a beautiful, statuesque Negro girl (my friend told me she was with the Peace Corps) walked over to the piano on one side of the stage and hit a key. There was a tuneful humming among the teacher trainees in the seats behind us and we turned to look at them. They were smiling broadly. To the tune of "Ach du lieber Augustine" they began to sing.

"The more we are together, together, together,
The more we are together, the happier we'll be."

Gaining confidence, the basses and the high tenors joined the baritones, until finally the little auditorium pulsed with harmony and song.

"Together, together, together, together
The more we are together, the happier we'll be!"

I noticed that the Peace Corps representative and his wife seated close by were singing along with the students. They were leaving the next day.

CHAPTER 6

A YOUNG AND FRAGILE PLACE

> *. . . they roved in countless numbers over the plain—giraffe, zebra, gnu, buffalo, springbok, water-buck, kudu, hartebeest, wild-boar, and several varieties of smaller antelope; wild birds abounded, ibis, field-larks, fish hawks, kingfishers, spurwinged geese, ducks, vultures, flamingoes, spoonbills, and cranes.*
>
> —H. M. STANLEY

WE left the Stanley trail at Mwanza. While he circumnavigated Lake Victoria (1,970 conscientious, island-and-inlet-charting miles by boat) Jay and I headed east to find the giant herds that once lined his route of march. It was a frivolous mission having nothing to do with Stanley and little to do with anything else. I simply wanted to see the animals. This being the case, Serengeti was the obvious place to see them.

For a while we followed the eastern shores of the lake northward. It had rained heavily during the past several days and we passed a large group of men, women and children (an entire village it turned out) gathered at the mouth of a culvert which ran under the road. They had built weirs of reeds and were trapping fish as they poured out of the culvert. The villagers told us it happened this way only once a year, when the rains caught the water which had been pushed inland by the flooded lake and turned it back toward the lake again. The villagers caught the smaller fish in wicker baskets as they hurtled—shimmering coins in a piscatorial jackpot—through the culvert. The larger fish (catfish, most of them) they speared or picked up in their bare hands and tossed onto the bank, where others waited to club them to death. I had never seen a happier group of people.

We entered the Serengeti National Park at the Ndabaka gate which lies almost in sight of Speke Gulf, named after John Hanning Speke, a predecessor of Stanley's who first developed the theory and later proved that the Nile originated in Victoria. The green-uniformed guard at the entrance to the park took our money and then told us we might have to wait a day or two before proceeding into the park itself. It had been raining "too hard," he said, and much of the track leading to the main camp at Seronera was under water. Jay talked to the guard in Swahili and managed finally to convince him that we stood a chance with our four-wheel drive. It was something else again for ordinary cars, two of which were now parked at the entrance, their disconsolate passengers alternately staring at the skies and looking at their wrist watches. Tourists. I did nothing to suppress a feeling of misanthropic glee as Jay and I left them behind and drove into the park. The ground was grassy and glistening with water and the idea was to keep moving at a steady pace. If we stopped, the heavy Land-Rover would sink gently, and perhaps irrevocably, into the soft mud. We had gone perhaps five hundred yards when Jay said, "Damn," and swung the Land-Rover around in a wide arc. One of the passenger cars (a Volkswagen containing an American couple) had been following us and was mired now in the mud. Jay attached our rope to the front bumper of the Volkswagen and, with much spinning of wheels, managed to pull it out.

"Go back," Jay told the driver. "You'll never get through." The American smiled and when we started off he followed us. Predictably, he foundered after a few yards and again Jay had to pull him out. He told me this was one of the unwritten laws of the bush, that one must always stop to aid a traveler in distress. The third time the persistent Volkswagen bogged down, I told Jay I did not care what the code of the bush said. The Americans had been warned and whatever happened to them now was clearly their fault. We left them, looking puzzled and vaguely alarmed, a mile from the park entrance, and drove on.

The ground sloped upward gradually and after a few more miles of slipping and slithering through the water-logged savanna we found firmer footing and Jay shifted back into two-wheel drive. And almost at the same moment, as if a curtain had parted, we were among them—more animals than I had ever seen before, more than my eyes could absorb. Involuntarily I held my breath as we rounded each corner because in every glade, in every opening among the thorn acacias, there were more of them. Wildebeest, zebra, kongoni, Grant's gazelle, Thomson's gazelle, waterbuck, rhinoceros . . . Jay spotted the rhinoceros first. He always saw things minutes before I did, knowing from experience what the silhouette of a wart hog or a buffalo should look like at three hundred, six hundred or a thousand yards. The rhinoceros, a large male, was in a patch of brush and Jay drove him out onto the plain. He ran like some sort of mechanical toy—tail straight up and body suspended over two sets of churning legs. We followed him while he figure-eighted through the short grass.

"Charge, old rhino," Jay shouted—the maniac matador at the wheel, using *me* as the red rag. The bull rhino would charge. He would reduce the Land-Rover to pulp. It wasn't funny. I tried to tell Jay to cut it out . . . and found I could not speak. It was only after Jay decided that enough was enough and veered away that I started to breath again.

And then into a mixed herd of zebra and wildebeest, the animals swirling away from the Land-Rover as if stirred by a huge, invisible spoon. We were allowed just so close, but no closer, and when we crossed the line the members of the herd simply made way for us, moving off but without panic. This was not the case with a rippling pack of banded mongooses, lunging across the savanna like frantic inchworms on a hot plate. It was clear that they were not running away from us, and, as we drew closer, a hawk interrupted its dive and peeled off at another angle.

"Do you want one?" Jay shouted. When I said I did, he slammed on the brakes and jumped out just as the group (in this case it was men and women first, children last) reached their multi-entranced burrow. Jay grabbed one of the babies by the tail and turned it over to me. It hung there, upside down, squirming, defecating and screeching profanities until I let it go.

We drove slowly, pausing to take pictures, and, finally, just to look. Toward the end of the afternoon I discovered that I had had enough. My eyes, my mind could encompass no more, and we increased our speed and pitched our tent just before nightfall about a mile from the main camp at Seronera. After supper, which we cooked over an open fire, Jay turned on his flashlight and told me to follow him. Not more than a hundred yards from our tent he began to pick out twin embers of light in the darkness.

"Tommies," he said, and as we drew closer the embers blinked out and several Thomson's gazelles turned and were swallowed up in the undergrowth. Jay stood for a while casting the beam of his flashlight about. Then more embers, closer together now and nearer the ground, and Jay motioned me forward. We advanced on tiptoe, gradually insinuating ourselves into a baffled but inquisitive group of dik-diks, the smallest antelope in the Serengeti, no larger than a hare. Holding his flashlight away from his own body and pointing it directly into the eyes of an unblinking dik-dik, Jay reached around with his free hand and gently touched the antelope on its backside. That was enough. The dik-dik wheeled and scampered away. If we had had a net, said Jay, or an overcoat, we could have caught one easily.

Early the next morning, accompanied by an African guide, we set out to explore the park systematically, looking for the animals we had not yet seen. Lion and leopard headed the list. It was Jay who spotted the leopard first—delighted when he saw the tail, dangling like a baroque bell cord from the limb of an acacia, before the guide. When we drove in under the tree for a closer look, the leopard pretended to sleep. I do not know whether he was feigning lack of interest or was genuinely and supremely bored by our presence. He had slung his kill (a little male Thomson's gazelle) over a nearby branch the way some women will toss their minks nonchalantly over the backs of chairs.

Jay said he would eat his kill tonight and perhaps again the next night and the night after—leopards being anything but wasteful and preferring their meat somewhat gamy.

The Serengeti lions, black-maned and massive, posed for their pictures and then lumbered off, lips curled back in mirthless grins, their fawn-furred genitals like suède coconuts. In the Seregenti, you are caught up quickly in the more basic facts of life. You become, for instance, a student of stools.

"Elephant droppings," the neophyte cries.

"Two days old," the expert adds, sending the neophyte back to the bottom of the class. It was this way with Jay and me and the African guide. As we drove along, they exchanged animal stories in Swahili, talking like upperclassmen who have embarrassingly been forced to share a railway compartment with a first-termer. Occasionally, they referred to some distant speck on the horizon and told me what it was. Once, coming on a newborn gazelle, its coat still dark and moist, Jay told me it would be up on its feet in a matter of minutes and would then be able to run as fast as its mother. It was the same way with zebra foals and wildebeest calves. Camouflage also protected the herds from the wild dogs, the hyenas and the larger predators, but Jay could not tell me why there were so many different kinds of camouflage and why, despite the differences, each worked so well. I thought I understood the principle of the leopard's spots and the anonymous dun of the antelope, but what made the zebra, so garishly visible in closeup, vanish under the trees at two hundred yards and melt into the plains at five hundred?

In the Serengeti, nature and not man had the upper hand (a welcome if regressive phase in evolution), and certain men, it seemed to me, began to take on the characteristics of certain animals. At least they revealed something of themselves in talking about the animals they most preferred to hunt. A white hunter in the bar at the Seronera lodge spoke knowingly and lovingly of the elephants he had killed. This was not unusual. Most hunters preferred the elephant, because of his intelligence, the value of his tusks, his loyalty to his friends and family, his sheer size. . . . There were many reasons. Jay himself enjoyed the buffalo because, he said, they were dangerous and unpredictable and one of the very few animals which actually enjoyed the job of stalking and then killing a man. My own favorite was the zebra. He was for me the perfect combination of the exotic and the familiar. I knew a horse when I saw one. I had ridden horses, and this was a horse—but a horse to be envied, a horse out of harness, a horse in fancy dress out on a spree. Would they take his costume away and force him back under saddle the morning after, repentant and hungover? I hoped not.

There was much I liked about the Serengeti. I liked the sign at the airstrip which read:

HERE THE WORLD IS STILL YOUNG AND FRAGILE
HELD IN TRUST FOR YOUR SONS AND OURS

I liked the little museum with its cases and cupboards crammed with bottled snakes and stuffed birds, and the unnamed genius who christened one of them "The Bare Faced Go Away Bird."

And at first I liked the silence. Silences would be more accurate. There were so many kinds—the instant, shattering silence that came just after I turned off the car motor; the awesome silence that came at midday, and the sudden silence like a pause between movements in a symphony, that interrupted the chirruping of the frogs and crickets at sundown. The sounds on the plains came gift-wrapped in silence —the distant cowlike grunt of the wildebeest communicating man's presence to the others . . . and then silence; the explosive whoof of the startled zebra . . . and again silence. The deeper the silence, the more precious the sounds in between.

But the silences of the Serengeti were too fragile to be entrusted to the thick-skinned visitor from the cities. I listened until my nerve ends, long callused by noise, were raw with the strain, and then I gave up and sought my own peace in the sound of clattering dishes and human voices.

Someone had once told me that game wardens looked like parsons. I saw what he meant when I met Myles Turner, the game warden at Serengeti. His khaki shirt was open at the neck, his short trousers were frayed, but he wore his uniform almost primly. Yet he was no simple country parson. There was something fanatic burning behind those pale blue eyes. If the rules of the game permitted, he would gladly bomb our cities and lay waste our farmlands—anything to stem the lava-like flow of civilization into the wilderness.

Turner's office, at one end of the complex of buildings and tents that make up Seronera, was littered with the ugly paraphernalia of poaching—wire snares and nooses, arrows tipped with poison, and traps made of thorns. On his desk there was a human skull. I do not think Turner was particularly fond of the skull but he kept it there as a warning. The skull belonged to a poacher.

For Turner and the forty African rangers who patrolled Serengeti's 5,600 square miles and guarded the park's million or more animals, poaching remained *the* problem. During the past eight years, they had picked up 1,200 wire snares and their arrest record had gone up—89 in 1958, 115 in 1959 and so on up to 160 in 1964. Turner gave me these figures without much comment as if he himself was not sure whether they meant that he and his men were getting better or that there were simply more poachers to contend with. Perhaps it was a combination of the two.

"It's a tribal pastime," said Turner. "We catch them, they get locked up for six months or a year, and then go right back to it again. Not so long ago we found twenty wildebeest caught in snares, dead of course, but with only their tails cut off. They're used for fly whisks."

Turner had seen so much of this sort of carnage that he had lost whatever revulsion or hatred he must once have felt. He was like a professional soldier who has no personal feelings about the enemy he has been told to destroy.

"They have a new technique now," he continued. "Mechanized poaching. They take orders for meat in a village. You know. One wildebeest? Right. Two zebra? Right. Cash in advance please and thank you very much. Then off they go in an old Land-Rover or lorry and shoot what's required. They're in and out of the park before we know it."

I asked Turner how he went about catching poachers and he said it was not terribly difficult predicting their movements because they usually turned up where the wildebeest were. He pulled out an aerial photograph of a section of the park. It was dotted with tiny specks, each of which had been pierced with a pin. This was the way he and the others spent their evenings, he said—counting wildebeest and zebra and piercing each with a pin so that, bleary-eyed and tired, they wouldn't count them again by mistake.

We had arrived in the park too early to witness the height of the annual *Drang nach osten*, the spectacular, massive seasonal migration to the plains after the rains have turned them green with soft new grass. The migration had already started but the animals hadn't really moved out onto the plains yet and were still in the glades and bush country on the western side of the park. This was not a time to be particularly worried about poachers, Turner went on, because the trails leading out onto the plains lay well within the boundaries of the park. It was later, during the swing back during the dry season that he would have to be on guard because some of the dry season trails led north and west, out of the park—so to speak through enemy territory.

"What we're trying to do now," he said, "is to clear the settlers from a strip of land seven miles wide around the Serengeti. They've drifted in over the past few years. They haven't crossed the borders of the park but we think there's only one reason they're here and that's to do some poaching."

Turner and the park people had taken the matter up with the Regional Commissioner and had been pleasantly surprised by his reaction. Was seven miles wide enough, he had asked?

I told Turner that it was my impression that the parks seemed to have suffered little, if at all, since independence and that the alarm bells being rung in London by the wildlife preservation people seemed, in retrospect, exaggerated. I had been told, for instance, that elephants had grown so resistant to the blight of civilization that as many as three thousand had to be shot annually in Tanzania simply to keep the population down to manageable proportions. It was known as "elephant cropping." I had also been told that elephants lived almost cheek by jowl (or trunk to tail) in certain parts of East Africa and that if you disturbed a group of them, let us say, on the coast in Malindi, there would be an outpouring of elephants hundreds of miles inland a few weeks later. It was like squeezing a tube of toothpaste.

Turner agreed that, all things considered, the parks were doing well. What troubled him, however, was that they were not making money. This surprised me. The entry fee Jay and I had paid for four days in Serengeti (170 East African shillings or a little over $24) had seemed high, and the prices being charged at the Seronera Lodge for drinks, meals and accommodations were, in comparison, even higher. A trip to the parks was not a poor man's vacation.

Turner said I was dead wrong. The Serengeti, he said, spent five times as much on itself every year as it took in from tourists. He gave me a 1963 East African Tourist and Travel Association brochure in which it said that overseas visitors had spent £4,017,000 ($11,247,000) on hotels, restaurants and bars in that year and (skipping down to the bottom of the list) £68,000 ($190,000) on laundry—£1,000 ($2,800) more than they had spent in the national parks. The implication was clear. Unless the parks started showing a profit some budget-cutting bureaucrat would notice the gap between income and outflow and move to cut down.

Many of Turner's colleagues had already been replaced by Africans. He himself expected to be Africanized one of these days, and the idea appalled him, not because he did not think his replacement would do as well ("The ones I've seen are really fine chaps") but because it would mean he might have to become a white hunter again. He had been one before and had reached the point where he could no longer bear the slaughter. Now it seemed likely that he would have to desert the animal side of the war and rejoin the butchers. It was not butchery exactly. It was simply that hunting had become too easy. He knew too much about the animals now. They had taken him into their confidence, shown him their hiding places and taught him their secret codes. To turn on them now would be an act of treason. But what else could he do? Wild animals was all he knew anything about—how to save them and how to kill them.

It was dusk when Turner and I finished talking and I asked him if he would join me for a drink at the lodge. He declined, saying something about children and the way it was with them at this time of the year. It wasn't until I arrived at the lodge that I realized what he had meant. In one corner a group of TEA teachers were singing carols, and in the patio, which two nights before had been paved with the pug marks of lions, somebody had scattered tinsel over the thorn acacia.

It was Christmas Eve.

CHAPTER 7

THEM WOT GETS SPAT ON

. . . to lead men astray by taking a too bright view of things.

—H. M. STANLEY

OUR first reaction on crossing the border into Kenya was one of relief. Only then did we realize that the tension had been building up in both of us during our trip through Tanzania. It was a tension made up, I think, of many things, but most of it was born of a growing awareness that we were not wanted. Even if it had not been stamped into our passports, the status of *undesirable alien* had made us furtive. It became *them* versus *us*, and it was both silly and sad—silly in the sense that we all became children playing a childish game and sad because I could see no end to it. The Tanzanians *wanted* us to be spies and saboteurs, to be the enemy, to pigeonhole us in with the other foreigners. In the end, because it was easier to capitulate than resist, we did become spies, taking our pictures quickly and surreptitiously and, when stopped and questioned, lying and saying we were tourists on vacation.

The Tanzanians may have known I was a spy. What they did not know (and it would have confused them if they had) was that I was a double agent. Any latent impulse to cast my lot with my own kind was exorcised on our final night in Tanzania at the bar of our hotel in Arusha, a prosperous town on the coffee-growing slopes of Mount Meru.

The speaker had been drinking for some time and his voice carried into every corner of the room. His monologue went like this:

"My houseboy lost the keys to my flat. I told him: 'You stupid black bastard, I'll give you the sack.' I don't take anything off them and they know it. Respect me for it, they do. I've known exactly three good niggers in my life. One of them, good chap, invited me to a bar for a drink the other night. Shenzi place. He went in first and shouted at them: 'Is this the way to treat a white bwana when he drinks with me? Clean off that table. I want a tablecloth and clean glasses.' By God, they gave that nigger a clean tablecloth. The lot. You should have seen them hop. Bloody good nigger, that. . . ."

I wondered whether the two African bartenders, who had listened impassively to all of this, went home after closing to dream of the Night of the Long Knives. The monologist whistled at one of the bartenders, ordered another beer, and then came over to where Jay and I were standing. The walls of the bar were covered with photographs of motion-picture actors who had used the hotel as headquarters for the location shooting of several safari pictures. John Wayne predominated, and the monologist wanted to tell us all about it.

"Duke Wayne," he said. "We all called him Duke. A real man. Oh, the times we've had in this place. The parties. Those Hollywood people really know how to spend money. One night—I'll never forget it—we were drinking up a storm and the wife of one of the chaps in the company came down those stairs there and into the bar—starkers! Naked as the day she was born. You can imagine what happened. Just as quick as we could several of us wrapped her in tablecloths and whatever we could find and ran her upstairs again."

I asked whether it wouldn't have caused less of a scene if she had been left alone, ignored.

"Oh, I'm sure that's what we would have done anywhere else. Had a good giggle. No damage." The laughter went out of his eyes. "But here, you know, there were niggers. You don't want those black bastards looking at a white woman, now do you?"

What was it in this man (and so many others like him) that permitted him to believe that it did not matter what an African bartender *heard* as long as he did not *see* it? The incident reminded me of Salisbury, Rhodesia, where I had listened some years before to a long harangue on the virtues of *apartheid* from a white couple while they were being served at their dining table by two impassive African servants. And later that evening I joined the same couple at a night club where the African staff was banished to the kitchen during the strip-tease performance.

Nairobi, on the day of our arrival, was bedecked with flags and festooned with banners proclaiming the spirit of *Harambee*. The way President Jomo Kenyatta used the word (and he let it roll out like a thunderclap at the beginning of each of his public speeches) it meant "working together"—not only the African tribes but the Asians and the Europeans as well. *Harambee!* It had a splendid ring to it, especially for the visitor so recently arrived from Tanzania. There were other indications that we had come to a land where tolerance for the idiosyncrasies of others prevailed—at least until sundown. A printed notice in the lobby of our hotel stated:

GENTLEMEN ARE REQUESTED TO WEAR JACKET, TIE AND TROUSERS AFTER 7 P. M.

I had decided to come back to Nairobi, thus veering far to the east of Stanley's trail, for a number of reasons. I felt the need for some research, facilities for which were not to be found in the bush. Then there was the question of Jay. His family needed his help on the new farm in South Africa and his father, now in Nairobi, wanted to talk with him about it. Should Jay decide finally that it was best for him to return to South Africa, I would have to find a replacement. My chances were better in Nairobi than elsewhere.

And so, with the familiar feel of pavement underfoot, I visited government buildings, newspaper offices, libraries and the homes of friends. For a day or so, I was caught up in the atmosphere of optimism which seems to pervade most cities when they are shiny and new. But then it began to dawn on me (and it dawned slowly because I had no wish to know about it) that my first impressions were superficial ones. *Harambee* may have been the official slogan but it was also a cry in the wilderness.

My journey into pessimism began in the files of the *East African*

Standard, where I read that not many weeks before, one of the Senators from Nairobi, C. K. Lubembe, had presented a motion in the Senate urging the government to study and recommend ways and means of controlling the "Indian population problem in Kenya."

"This motion," the *Standard* reported, "was warmly received by cheers from other members of the Senate. [Mr. Lubembe] said that in view of the rapid increase of Indian population in Kenya, due to their high birth rate, and in view of the fact that there was a danger of having a non-African government in Kenya in the future, the Senate should urge the Government to seek ways and means of fighting this problem."

Further perusal of the files did not disclose what, if anything, happened to the Senator's motion (although I strongly suspect that it was defeated) but it seemed to have worried the Indian community. I talked about the motion with a young Indian who met me in a curry joint dominated by a large soft-drink sign bearing (appropriately I thought for an Indian establishment in Nairobi) the following inscription in bold red letters: SAY PLEASE.

For the Indians, saying please to the Africans had become the password to survival. What bothered my Indian friend was just how long the password would remain valid. He said that the problem these days was whether or not to take out Kenya citizenship. He and most of his friends felt it would be the decent and patriotic thing to do but what would happen if, after becoming bona-fide Kenyans, they were "Africanized" out of their jobs? As Kenya nationals, they would have enormous difficulties emigrating elsewhere. So perhaps it was better to hold on to the old United Kingdom passports. Then, should life become intolerable in Kenya, he and his friends could always try their luck elsewhere—in England or even India (although he knew the last thing India wanted was more Indians). It was all pretty much of a bad joke, wasn't it?

"The trouble is we can't get even Jomo Kenyatta to tell us what will happen to us if we *do* take out Kenya citizenship," the Indian continued. "No guarantees at all. Any promise made today can easily be broken tomorrow. No single politician speaks for all of

Kenya. It is difficult enough to find one who speaks for his tribe."

As we went on talking, my eye caught the SAY PLEASE sign again and it occurred to me that the Indians had been saying please gracelessly, almost insultingly, the way an army private will use the word "sir" when addressing an officer he loathes. The young Indian was talking about currency restrictions designed to halt the outflow of capital from Kenya. The Indian community, he said, had never been particularly concerned by restrictions of this nature and a way had yet to be found to stop businessmen from banking their profits abroad. The secret, he said, was never to allow your profits to flow into Kenya in the first place. In essence, the system worked like this: The Indian merchant buys goods (can openers, tractors or what have you) abroad, paying for these goods out of his foreign bank account. The goods, shipped to Kenya, are sold there and the money from their sale is used to buy such exportable products as sisal, tea or coffee. These in turn are shipped out of Kenya and sold to importers, who pay for them in sterling or dollars and deposit the money in the Indian merchant's overseas bank account.

"You see," said my Indian friend. "We never ship money out of the country. It is always goods."

The Indians gave lip service only to the spirit of *Harambee* because they were suspicious of it. Having never been allowed to practice it under the British, they questioned the motives of those who were preaching it now. Discrimination was more their cup of tea. They knew all about discrimination. They had had centuries of it under their own caste system and in Kenya they had grown accustomed to the idea of being discriminated against by the whites —in the same way that they had grown used to discriminating against the blacks. It all reminded me of the wonderful line from a Cambridge undergraduate production: "There's them wot spits and them wot gets spat on!"

Except now the pecking order had been rearranged and they, the Indians, were being spat on by all sides. It was not a comfortable sensation, knowing as they did—*knowing*—that the black Africans were inferior.

I was told that the East African Institute of Social and Cultural

Affairs was doing useful work in the field of race relations but I did not get the warm gush of optimism I expected when I walked into the office of its director, a bearded young American named Richard Garver. The institute, he said, had just conducted a five-day seminar on race relations, attended by sixty delegates representing trade unions and educational organizations in Kenya, Tanzania and Uganda. Their findings made for gloomy reading. For one, the delegates rejected multi-racialism and non-racialism as solutions to racial tensions. Non-Africans, they said, would have to learn to live within an explicitly African society.

"Minority groups," read their concluding statement, "will live within this developing culture; respect it; learn from it; and where possible contribute to it. This will be in fact a great advantage to such groups which have in the past and would in the future lose a great deal of intellectual vitality by trying to nourish themselves entirely from within their limited resources. Asians, Europeans and other groups in East Africa can only benefit by opening themselves to the developing African life of that area."

The document, if read quickly, sounded innocuous enough but I thought some of the wording ominous. There was, for instance, the clear implication that the minority groups (the Asians and Europeans) might eventually find their proffered contributions to Africa's developing culture rejected. After all, hadn't the delegates applied the adjective "limited" to Europe's and Asia's spiritual and intellectual resources? The seminar's conclusions were so obviously part of a pattern of thought, a line of reasoning which seemed to be gaining credence, that I could not dismiss them as a one-shot aberration. What disturbed me most was that the entire approach to racial harmony appeared to be based on the premise that whatever was African was right and whatever was imported from elsewhere (or might be imported in the future) was wrong. The theme ran through any number of speeches made by politicians and any number of periodicals sold on the street corners. In *Pan Africa*, a magazine which pictured on its cover a bust of the defunct Congolese leader Patrice Lumumba, I read an article titled "White Man's Crisis," which was written by someone identified only as a "special correspondent." I think it is worth quoting at some length.

> It will not longer be very profitable to remain [wrote the special correspondent of the white man still resident in Africa], and those who stay behind will do so either because they lack the initiative to make the move, or because their bonds with Africa are strong enough to survive the loss of privilege. Since resented and resentful minority groups are too dangerous to be tolerated for long, in particular by young states, considerable pressure will be brought on those who fail to gain acceptance into African society, and the remnants of the white communities will be forced to disintegrate. Acceptance into African society presupposes the shedding of all patronage—the white man's burden—down to the last shadow of paternalism. Whether they came to rule or to save souls, to extract wealth or to instill knowledge, the white men were imbued with an all but unshakable conviction in their own white superiority. Since Hitler, it has been admitted that the superiority is "innate"; instead the modern type of paternalism has at its back what it considers to be a "superior" culture and civilization. In fact, the only superiority the white man can really claim to is the superiority of the gun over the spear, the machine over the simple tool.

The writer concluded by saying: "Idealism by foreigners on behalf of Africa is always patronizing, suspect, and resented."

If the idealist was suspect, so too was the down-to-earth, dollars and-cents businessman. In *Africa and the World*, a magazine published in London and retailing in Nairobi for two shillings, an unsigned article warned against colonialist businessmen—especially the friendly ones:

> They invite the African business men and managers to dinner and cocktail parties. They make friends with them. They give them the sense that they are now all together, serving a common interest.
>
> Superficially this appears progressive. Africans are now accepted as equals with Europeans. Colonialism is ended! For the present even the impoverished African masses are glad to see some of their number, they think, rising in the social scale, living and cohabiting on equal terms with the former colonialists.
>
> Opportunities to "get on" are created. It becomes the great African dream to live in a splendid house, to have servants, to own a motor car, a refrigerator, expensive radiograms and television sets, to wear a dinner jacket at cocktail parties, to be in positions of authority. . . .
>
> Africans rising in positions of public authority are also given the

opportunity to acquire extra luxuries by being given gifts either in kind or money, sometimes euphemistically described as "commission."...

The African bourgeoisie rises on twin horns of corruption—the physical corruption of bribes of money or gifts and the psychological corruption of flattery and social snobbery. It is an easy situation to slip into. It is a situation which has developed to larger or lesser degree throughout independent Africa.

The writer wound up at the top of his voice:

IT IS THE SITUATION IN WHICH NEO-COLONIALISM HAS BEEN PERMITTED TO INVADE AFRICA. FOR THE NEW AFRICAN BOURGEOISIE IS, IN FACT, THE FIFTH COLUMN OF THE NEW CAPITALIST INVASION OF AFRICA.

Much of the Communist literature circulating in Africa is heavy-handed stuff and I doubt whether words like "bourgeoisie" or "fifth column" mean much more to the city dweller than they do to his spear-carrying relative in the bush. But just so long as the Communists had something to say against the whites or the Asians; as long as they railed against the status quo, their message fell on receptive ears.

Garver's point, after we had talked about these things for a while, was that you could not really blame the Africans. Almost everything the Europeans did or said these days rubbed them the wrong way. He himself employed a house boy who lived in a basement room in his apartment building. After some months of service, the house boy sent for his wife and she moved in with him.

Soon afterward the white building agent came to Garver and said: "Do you realize that your boy has a woman in his room?"

Garver replied that he did but pointed out that the woman in question was the man's wife.

"Makes no difference," the agent told Garver. "It's against our rules."

After further argument from Garver failed to persuade the agent to change his mind, Garver said he guessed that he would have to take the matter up with the Attorney General. Being an African, the Attorney General might not agree with the position taken by the landlord. A few days later the agent returned and said there had been a meeting of the board at which it had been decided to make an exception in the case of Garver's house boy.

It struck Garver and me as incredible that the British-owned holding company which owned not only the apartment house in question but also much other real estate in Nairobi would jeopardize its investment by ruffling the feelings of an already sensitive citizenry. Not so incredible perhaps as just plain stupid.

The same company, Garver went on, was totally indiscriminate in its exercise of discrimination. It also owned the building in which Garver had his offices. On her first day at work, his new Indian secretary had been told ever so politely by a white woman in the ladies' room: "You will find that Asian ladies use the ladies' room at the other end of the hall."

Without complaint the secretary did as she was told. I would not blame the Indian secretary for dreaming of her own Night of Long Knives. But what would she and her Indian friends be fighting for—to get into the white washroom or to keep the Africans out of theirs?

As in Tanzania, independence had meant change but not enough change to satisfy the black inhabitants. The Africans now had the political power but the basic pecking order remained where it had always been—with the Africans still at the bottom, the Asians in the middle, and the whites on top. There were many whites, Africans and Asians in Kenya who believed passionately in the spirit of *Harambee*, who rushed in with soothing ointments whenever the harness chafed. There were others who thought it was all a great waste of time, and unworkable, and sought to circumvent or wreck it. And then there were a very few who had spent their lives trying to put it into practice. One of these was a Dane who drank to forget and, in so doing, remembered everything. When I told him I was writing a book about Africa he looked at me as if I had at that very moment gone out of my mind.

"If you ever do understand them, you will have become African yourself—and then your readers will not understand you," he said.

The Dane was now in his fifties. He had been in Africa since his seventeenth birthday and he liked the Africans more than he did white people. But he could never become one of them because there was a gulf, you see, a difference. He could not explain it. He just knew it was there.

"The Danes," he said, "think the Masai are just little Danes with black skins. They are not little Danes with black skins. They are Masai."

I asked him what a Masai was.

"I know them. I speak their language. I have lived with them for months on end. They know me and they like me," he replied. "But I am certain of only one thing and that is that they do not think of me as a little Masai with a white skin."

And then he told me a story which I set down now as I wrote it out on the typewriter in my hotel room immediately after he had told it to me.

"I was eighteen at the time," he said, "and was managing a plantation on the coast in Tanganyika. There were no white girls available and we all—all of us white lads—had African women. Mine? Well, she was lovely, you know, a coastal girl with perhaps a little bit of Arab blood in her. She knew how to make love and we used to love each other. God, how I loved that girl.

"At the beginning I couldn't even talk to her. I didn't know her language. We made love often. After we had made love, she would kiss me right here, you know, at the corner of my eye. . . ."

He paused, remembering, and then continued: "Sometimes I would come home and she would be sitting outside the shamba making pombe in a pot, holding the pot between her knees and singing softly. Always the same song, the same tune, gently, softly, and looking up into the air. Never at me. Always up in the air. And she had lovely legs, long legs, and she held the pot between her knees so that I could see the inside of her calf. And she would sing and look up in the sky and not at me and stir her pot and she knew exactly what she was doing with that song because pretty soon I could resist no longer and I would carry her inside and we would make love. God, how I loved that girl.

"Then I was made a big manager, the youngest manager in Africa. I was twenty-one and I had more than thirty whites under me and hundreds, maybe it was thousands, of blacks, and I had to entertain. And it didn't work any more, with my position and the entertaining and the big directors from Europe with their wives. . . . So I had to let her go. I set her up with her own duka, her own little shop, and she became an important lady in her village.

"Many years later I took my wife to that village. I didn't tell her about the girl and we went together to her duka. She had gray hair but her figure I could see was just as lovely as ever, her breasts, those lovely little breasts, firm under her dress. Well, she saw me and she flung herself across the counter of her little store and held on to my arm. And she was sobbing, 'Bwana, bwana. . . .' I took her hands away from my arm and I told my wife, who had seen all of this, that this was a crazy woman. And we left."

The Dane's eyes were now wet with tears. Then he shook his head angrily.

"They do not think as we do. They do not feel as we do. She had probably become a prostitute. They all do. It means nothing to them," he said, and then, looking at me, his eyes still glistening with tears, he added, "Now do you understand why I love them and despise them at the same time?"

I was more disheartened by what the Dane had told me than by anything else I heard in Nairobi. Thirty years in Africa and he and the Africans were still poles apart. He had tried but, in his effort to build bridges, he had only succeeded in burning his own, so that now, by his own admission, he was totally unfitted for the white man's world.

Despite its injustices, the old, pre-independence system did work. With the whites on top, the Asians in the middle, and the Africans at the bottom, the division of profits was obviously inequitable. But there *were* tangible assets. There *was* something to divide. If the trickle-down system left little for the Africans, at least it left them something.

Under the new system, the old equations were rejected and suddenly there seemed to be nothing at all to divide.

Assuming that the colonialists stole the Africans blind, undermined their tribal civilization, thwarted their natural ambitions for a place in the twentieth century, denied them an education and then, staggering under the load of their ill-gotten gains, withdrew from the Dark Continent at the stroke of independence—assuming all this to be true, there is a tendency on the part of African leaders, and the foreign technical assistants they have brought in to help to size up the situation, to rub their hands together with pioneer enthusiasm and say: "Well, now we know the worst. We've hit rock bottom. There is nowhere to go but up!"

My own assessment, arrived at without enthusiasm, is that there is nowhere to go but down.

What started me off on this doleful line of inquiry was a thoughtful and devastating piece by a journalist called Aaron Segal in the *Kenya Weekly News*, a publication written primarily for Kenya's farming community. What Segal seemed to be saying was that no matter how hard everybody tried, and even with the best will in the world, things were going from bad to worse in Kenya.

Segal began with an analysis of the government's six-year development plan, which, as one of its first orders of business, envisaged the creation of 144,000 new jobs between 1964 and 1970. In view of the fact that there were at Segal's time of writing 205,000 registered as unemployed with the Ministry of Labor, this was a conservative target indeed. The planners, however, seemed to have ignored Kenya's population explosion. I tend to believe that the omission was deliberate since its inclusion would have made a mockery of the entire plan. Come to think of it, its absence has the same effect.

Kenya's population, now at something over 9,000,000, is growing by 3 percent, or about 300,000, annually. This is one of the highest rates in the world. A little over half the present population is under sixteen. During the next six years about 720,000 young men will reach the age of seventeen. According to Segal, even if the six-year plan is achieved there will be no available paid employment for any of these young men unless they are given preference over those who now hold jobs.

For the job holders of Kenya, the future is anything but bright. Of a population of more than 9,000,000 Africans, only 540,000 are established in wage-paying industries (March, 1965, report of the Kenya government National Wages and Policy Advisory Committee.) But instead of increasing, the number of those gainfully employed is decreasing. According to an American embassy economic survey dated October 18, 1964, the wage-earning figure dropped 126,000 between 1960 and the end of 1964. The jobless congregated in Nairobi and other population centers—and their friends and relatives joined them.

"The problem," said one economist with whom I talked, "is that unemployment is moving from the bush, where it was hidden and unnoticed, to the cities where of course it raises hideous problems of health, sanitation and overcrowding which never existed in the bush."

The Kenya six-year plan further proposes that the economy grow at a rate of 5.7 percent annually. Allowing for the 3 percent population increase, that would leave 2.7 percent available for increased consumption and investment. What investment? The Kenya government is almost wholly dependent on the outside world for development finance. As an example, the foreign aid component of the various development budgets within the plan is 91 percent. The job-creating part of the plan counts on an investment of about $90,000,000 a year from the private sector. Nothing like this sum is being invested in Kenya these days. As a matter of fact (again according to the American survey) there was a substantial flight of capital from East Africa following the Zanzibar revolution and the various army mutinies on the mainland. (Kenya had one too.) If any of it is coming back today it is doing so timorously and tentatively.

At first glance, the planners' estimate of an annual 5.7 percent increase in the Gross Domestic Product does not seem unrealistic. According to the government, the GDP actually did grow by 6.5 percent in 1963 and by 7.2 percent in 1964. But what the planners did not mention was that past increases in the GDP (and one must assume any hopes for continued increases in the future) were based largely on a 50 percent rise in the price obtained for sisal, Kenya's second-largest export crop. After 1964, however, sisal prices came down again and threaten to continue in that direction. Together with sisal, coffee and tea account for the bulk of Kenya's exports (55 percent in the years 1960-1962). Sadly enough, there is no reason to believe that prices for these products will go up or even maintain their present levels. The opposite seems more likely. Between 1954 and 1962, export prices fell by an alarming 24 percent. One local economist goes so far as to think that an average decrease in export prices of 1 percent in the coming years is an *optimistic* assumption.

I have been searching my own mind and others far better equipped than mine for solutions. There seem to be few that do anything more than rearrange the problem, like shuffling a deck of cards, so that its several aspects come at you in different sequence. The government itself has tried various schemes, including the introduction of the so-called Tripartite Agreement, under which, for a period, labor unions promised not to strike or press for wage increases; employers in the private sector agreed to take on an extra 10 percent of staff, and the government an additional 15 percent. The Tripartite Agreement was signed on February 10, 1964, but by the time I had arrived in January of the following year not many more than thirty thousand had been accommodated under the measure. The agreement was due to expire the following April and the government still had employed only half the number it had agreed to add to its rolls. Needless to say there had also been a good many strikes although most of these were of short duration.

Africanization (the replacement of Asians and Europeans by Africans) has also taken up some of the slack. But almost invariably Africanization has been accompanied by a loss of efficiency and a drop in standards. Perhaps because of this it is difficult to get fresh figures. The most recent ones I have from the East African Railways and Harbors Administration refer to the year 1963 and record, among other things, an 8 percent drop in railway turnaround times at the port of Mombasa. Mombasa could count itself lucky. During my stay in Kenya I heard much talk about what, in retrospect, became known as "Black January" in the annals of Tanzanian railway history. During that month, something between £50,000 and £60,000 was lost as a result of accidents involving freight trains. On

January 14, seven freight cars were derailed in a crash on the Mwanza line. The following day fourteen were derailed and turned over between Pugu and Mpiji, and on January 30 six more cars suffered the same fate on a downgrade near Dodoma. In commenting on "Black January" several months later, the *Reporter*, an excellent fortnightly resembling *Time* Magazine and published in Nairobi, noted that Tanzania's annual average figure of forty to fifty derailments over thirteen hundred miles of track was not high in comparison to railway standards elsewhere.

"In the past three years," the magazine declared, "there has not been a single passenger fatality–apart from passengers who jump from moving trains when the ticket inspector appears–and this is a record comparable to none."

The problem of unemployment is not Kenya's alone. In Tanzania the authorities have met the problem head on by banishing beggars from the streets of Dar es Salaam. Out of sight, out of mind. What is happening in Uganda is, if anything, more depressing because Uganda (unlike Kenya and Tanzania) possesses much rich and fertile soil. In Uganda, a study made by the Minimum Wage Advisory Board shows that, since wages began rising in 1960, employment has dropped by nearly 10 percent–and this while the population has risen by half a million. Of a population of 7 million, only 208,000 (1964 figures) were in paid employment. Incidentally, 27 percent of these were immigrants from neighboring countries.

In all three countries, the one possible panacea–birth control–is still talked of in whispers, since it runs counter to tribal tradition and the fundamental, almost sacred, conviction that it is right and proper to have as many children as is humanly possible. Fecundity is the ultimate virtue; barrenness is grounds for divorce. For most East Africans such a thing as birth control would be unthinkable. No politician in his right mind would make birth control a plank in his platform. On the contrary, there are many politicians who tell their constituents that birth control is a diabolical plot cooked up by the colonialists to stifle Africa's growth and, eventually, snuff her out entirely. I think the politicians believe this and I think their listeners do too.

What I have just written is based on statistics. Some may be accurate and others may have been manufactured to fit some economist's version of what he thinks must be true. Cooked or uncooked, they are part of the public record. I will not apologize for them or, if attacked, defend them. They are not mine and anyone is welcome to juggle them to suit himself. I could have used others, the optimistic ones, which show that school attendance is up, that the African farmer is yearly getting a larger slice of the agricultural pie, that disease and hunger are down, human life prolonged—all these and many more I could and perhaps should have mentioned. But they strike me as irrelevant, and in the end all are reduced to rubble by the population explosion.

TANZANIA: The Land-Rover fords a stream near Singida.

TANZANIA: Drought, and a dead calf. The vultures take the eyes first.

NAIROBI: Curry joint. The Indians say "Please."

NAIROBI: Population explosion. Children at play in automobile junk yard.

Campsite at Serengeti National Park.

y Kruger holding a young
nded mongoose in the Seren-
ti.

Ol Kalou: Takeover day at the Sparrow farm. Who will look after the Kipsigis?

Ol Kalou: Chase after cat
thieves. "The old man's fa
was red with rage."

UGANDA: Elephant at Queen Elizabeth National Park.

KIGALI, RWANDA: The author at work. Natives mark area into which they advance by spitting into it. Spit, step, spit, step.

GITARAMA, RWANDA: Dancer at Day of Democracy celebration.

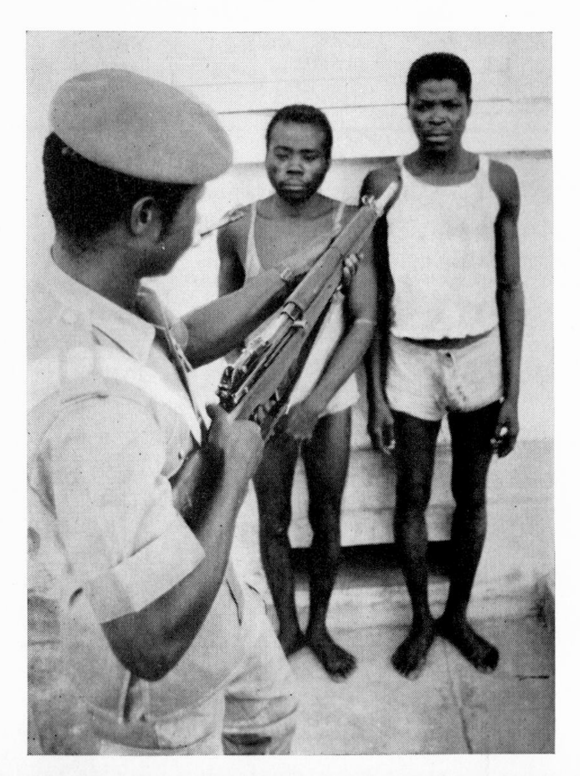

ALBERTVILLE, THE CONGO: Mulelis prisoners. The guard raised and aim his rifle for the picture.

Freddy

Yves Corroy

"Cactus"

Christian

Mr. Nathu

NEAR KAMPENE, THE CONGO: After seven months under the rebels, the cry goes up "Wazungu! Wazungu!"

NEAR KAMPENE, THE CONGO: Author witnesses the burning of rebel leader Stanislaus village.

CHAPTER 8

THE MOST HAPPY FELLA IN THE WHOLE HAPPY VALLEY

. . . each tribe, with rage and hate in its heart, remains aloof from the other.

—H. M. STANLEY

IN the evenings we would sit around the fire in David Frazer-Allen's cabin and talk—David, the old man, Jack and I. Jack was my new traveling companion, foisted on me in Nairobi by a friend of mine after Jay had decided, with considerable reluctance, that his primary responsibility lay with his family and not with me. Jack should be grateful to me for not using his real name. Even now, months later, nothing would give me more pleasure than to beat him within an inch of his life. And yet I remember Jack with something close to affection. Like all true rogues, he had great charm and I have no wish to reduce his chances for rehabilitation and reform. They are marginal enough as it is. Hence the pseudonym.

It was David Frazer-Allen's cabin, with its wonderful view of the valley of Ol Kalou; it was his food we ate as his guests; and it was his liquor we drank so copiously. But, always, it was the old man who dominated the conversation. Invariably, as the evening wore on, the old man would drop the guard he had been holding during the daytime and then what he truly felt for the black man would pour out of him and fill the cabin with hate. There were times when I had to excuse myself, open the front door and stand on the lawn under the starlit skies until the knot in my stomach went away again. David was luckier than the old man and felt sorry for him. Being by nature a man of peace, he would wait until the old man and I were on collision course and then intervene, usually on the old man's side. David was reasonably sure that I would cool my temper out on the lawn. No one was ever sure what the old man would do.

"Quite right," David said late one night, disagreeing with me. "It took the Nignogs three thousand years to get nowhere and the United States and Britain expect them to be like us in fifty."

The old man shifted his attention from me to David and nodded vigorously.

"Niggers are naturally inferior, boy," he said. "You've got to admit that."

"Give them time," David said.

"Time, hell. We had to bring them down from the trees. With us gone they'll climb up again. It's only natural."

"Poor Nignogs."

"Black apes is more like it. Hanging by their tails from the trees."

"Apes don't have tails."

"Niggers do." The old man laughed. It was a mirthless laugh, the same laugh he used when he told me that the white settlers' name for Ol Kalou was the Happy Valley. In the days Jack and I spent as Frazer-Allen's guests in Ol Kalou, I saw the old man happy only once. That was early one morning when three Kikuyu night watchmen came up to the front door of David's cabin with their ankle-length army coats buttoned to their chins and told the old man that some cattle had been stolen. The thieves, they said, had driven them out of the valley and were headed uphill now, making for the crest of the ridge above us.

"Come on, boys," the old man shouted. "We might catch them." There were no arms, no weapons of any kind—just seven African herdsmen, Jack and me, and the old man. David was away at the time. Later, when he heard what had happened, he said it was a stupid thing for the old man to have done. He could have driven into Ol Kalou and contacted the local police, who maintained radio communication with roving police patrols on the ridgetops surrounding the valley. But then, that would not have been in character. The old man liked to take direct action. Besides, the police superintendent in Ol Kalou was black and the old man had never asked a black man for anything.

So we went tearing off through the grove of wattles which clung to the sides of the ridge above Frazer-Allen's place, the old man increasing his lead until he was lost from sight. But we always knew where he was by the sound of him thumping and crashing through the thickets ahead and cursing the one African herdsman who managed to keep up with him. Then the cursing and the thumping stopped. When we caught up with him, he was sitting down under a clump of brush and his face was red with rage and the effort of the climb.

"Must have been the rear guard," he said, speaking in short gasps. "In this bush here. Almost had him. Black bastard jumped out of the bush and went ahead. Looked like a Masai. If I'd had a weapon I'd have filled his ass full of lead."

We sat for a while on the hillside, looking down at the floor of the valley with its triangles and rectangles of barley and wheat and the stands of trees that served as windbreaks. In the language of the Masai, whose territory this once had been, Ol Kalou meant the place of a certain kind of grass. The Masai had long since gone and now the white men who had plowed under this 130,000-acre valley in the Kenya highlands for their wheat and barley and their sheep and cattle were going too. Already there were signs that the valley was reverting to its original state, but the old man wasn't thinking of that right now. Instead, he was smiling. Chasing cattle thieves had reminded him, he said, of the old days, the good old days during the Mau Mau emergency when he and his friends had hunted the wily terrorists through the forests of the Aberdares.

The Mau Mau were Kikuyu, members of the same tribe that once worked for him on his farms. A sly and treacherous tribe, the Kikuyu. You were never sure when your most trusted foreman would put a knife in your back. The old man's eyes narrowed. Come to think of it now, he wasn't so certain that the cattle thief he had just flushed out of the bush was a Masai after all. This one had looked like a Masai all right, covered as he was with ochre mud and stinking to high heaven of urine. But he might just as easily have been a Kikuyu. That was an old Kikuyu trick, disguising themselves as Masai so that the blame would fall on their oldest and bitterest enemies. Besides, the old man continued, a Masai had courage. A real Masai would have stood his ground and fought. No, the thief must have been a Kikuyu. Trouble in the Happy Valley had always been traceable to the Kikuyu.

"You can't trust them," he said with finality. The old man was always delivering final judgments, most of which seemed to contradict each other. You could not trust the Kikuyu and, in the next breath, the Kikuyu were loyal and industrious servants. As Mau Mau they made a formidable and worthy enemy and, on the other hand, they were born cowards. The Kikuyu on his farms loved him and prayed for the white man's return. Yet they and their leaders had plotted the white man's downfall. When I confronted the old man with some of these seeming inconsistencies, he brushed me aside with the statement that I had never "lived among them" and would, therefore, never understand. That morning on the hillside I went after him again—this time because of what he had said about the Masai.

Cattle theft had become one of Kenya's chief problems. Some European farmers had reported it to be running as high as 15 to 20 percent of their herds. At the opening of the Mount Kenya Show just a few days before, the Minister of Finance, James Gichuru, had said that some 29,000 head of stock valued at £395,000 had been reported stolen between January of 1963 and May of 1964. Many of these stolen cattle, it was known, had found their way into the Masai herds, where the demand apparently was insatiable. In view of this, could not the smelly savage the old man had almost caught have been a Masai after all?

That was doubtful, the old man replied. The Masai almost never stole from the white man. They respected the white man. If the cattle stolen that morning did eventually find their way into the Masai herds . . . well, that would be because the Masai had in turn stolen them from the original thieves. The thought that the Masai would triumph over the Kikuyu in this manner pleased the old man no end.

"Damned old Masai," he said fondly. "Tell you one thing, boy. Just give me one old Masai with a spear and we'll stop all the cattle thieving in Ol Kalou in no time. That's all it would take—just one old Masai."

That evening, in David's cabin, the old man waxed prophetic.

"Mark my words, boy," he said to me, "we whites are the only ones standing between the Masai and the Kikuyu right now. When we clear out, the old Masai are going to come back in here and take their land back. Talk about a blood bath, man . . ."

There was no question that the old man's return a few weeks before after an absence of a year had made the residents of Ol Kalou—white, Indian and African—extremely nervous. He had abandoned his farms on Kenya's independence and, in the interval between his sudden departure and his return, they had been left idle and the acres that were once in wheat had gone back to grass. It had been his version of the scorched-earth policy. Of course the price the Kenya government was offering him now was far less than it would have been if he had not left his land to the ravages of time, nature and his Kikuyu workers, who had already started chopping down his windbreaks for firewood and timber for their *shambas*. Everyone agreed that the old man had been stupid to leave his land that way. Frazer-Allen (and others like him) had held on and, as a result, would be quitting the highlands shortly with something like $800,000 in his pocket, which was not bad for a young man of twenty-eight. Ostensibly the old man had come back to sell his land at the highest price possible—to seek justice—and in this the remaining white settlers wished him well.

But it soon became apparent that the old man was not seeking justice so much as revenge. Every day, in an old Land-Rover he had borrowed from Frazer-Allen, the old man prowled the valley like a malevolent ghost, reopening old wounds and disinterring the bones of long-forgotten feuds. And at night, when he spoke of blood baths, his voice throbbed with excitement. He viewed the gradual disintegration of his own farms not with resignation or alarm but with impatience. It was happening too slowly. Perhaps, under the next full moon, the tribes would assemble in full war regalia; the spears would flash in the moonlight; drums would sound and, in the morning, the Happy Valley would be a smoldering charnel house. For the old man, that would have been the proper ending. But, instead of ending with a bang, it was ending with a whimper, and this too contributed to the old man's fury. He loathed his friends for the equanimity with which they accepted their downfall. "Shoot the next nigger you see cutting down one of your trees," he told them, hoping to goad them into an act of sufficient violence to provoke more violence. And he could not abide Frazer-Allen's proclivity for ridicule.

"We were like children with a sandcastle," David once said in speaking about the white highlanders before independence. "We were having a lovely time and now they've kicked it apart and ruined our day." I don't think the old man ever forgave David for saying that. Humor had no place at Armageddon.

As the old man's anger mounted, so too did the fear among his friends. They worried that he would do something or say something that would get him and them into trouble. For some reason, he hadn't been able to get it through his head that times had changed, that the balance of power had shifted drastically, and that the black men were now running Kenya. There was something pitiful about his arrogance, or at least so it seemed to his friends. But for the Africans and for Mr. Unia, the Indian proprietor of the main store in Ol Kalou, the old man's arrogance only served to reawaken bitter memories.

"He is not so popular here, you see," Mr. Unia told me over a vegetarian curry dinner in a room off the compound in back of his store. Before independence, the old man had served a term or two as town manager. During this period, according to Mr. Unia, he had torn down the African shantytown which had grown up over the years. In so doing he had also demolished several shacks the Unia family had built to shelter their merchandise.

While Mr. Unia's toothless father, in his chair in the corner of the room, chortled and nodded like the Aged Parent in *Great Expecta-*

tions, Mr. Unia produced a sheaf of photographs of the Unias and Jomo Kenyatta. Mr. Unia and his brothers had gone in a body to visit the old leader while he was still under restriction and, with uncommon prescience, had presented him with a gift-wrapped pull-over they had bought in Nairobi. The photographs, taken by a fellow Indian, had been kept out of sight until the time of independence. After independence they were shown to every KANU politician who ever visited Ol Kalou. The Unias wished to survive. But now, with the old man charging in and out of their store every day, the Africans might start thinking that the Unias were his friends and not Jomo Kenyatta's. The Unias hoped the old man would go away.

I had come to Ol Kalou (a five-hour drive northwest of Nairobi) because I had reached the conclusion that the future of Kenya, if any, lay not in her cities but in her land. Two-thirds of the country is arid and impoverished bush, sand or rock. If there was an answer, it would be found in the one-third which is considered arable, which receives more than thirty inches of rainfall a year. Most of this kind of land lay in the highlands (the *white* highlands before independence) above Nairobi. Before independence, some 3,500 Europeans (most of them British and South African stock) had 3 million of the highlands' 8½ million acres under the plow. With the hunger for decent land what it was among the Africans, it was obvious that independence would bring changes. With the help of the British government, which cooperated in the form of grants, low-interest loans and salaries for those needed to carry out the program, the Kenya government created what came to be known as the "million-acre scheme." The idea was to buy out European farmers in designated areas of the highlands and replace them with African families who would either run the farms as cooperatives or carve them up into 7- and 15-acre smallholdings. Ol Kalou was not part of the original scheme and the white settlers in the valley were told they could continue farming if they so desired. But the scheme surrounded the valley and all but a handful of Ol Kalou's white farmers chose to sell out and move on. Willy-nilly, the scheme absorbed the Happy Valley.

On my arrival at Ol Kalou, the old man told me ("Don't take my word for it, boy; see for yourself") that the scheme had already failed ruinously; that Africans were not cut out to be farmers and that, even if they were, the complexities of distribution and organization would be too much for them. I would have given almost anything to have proved the old man wrong. Alas, what a bigot says is true is not necessarily false.

The scheme called for the settlement of 55,000 African families by 1967. At the beginning of 1965, when I was in Ol Kalou, there were only 18,000 on the ground and the settlement officers were doubtful that the scheme would ever be able to take care of more than 30,000. On the newly created smallholder farms which bordered the Ol Kalou salient, children were picking the daisylike pyrethrum blossoms. It was a pleasant sight. But the African settlers who had been put there and who had borrowed money from the government to pay for their land said the land was not right; that they were having trouble meeting the payments; that they had been discriminated against because of tribe. Where was the machinery the government had promised to give them? And the cattle? And where was the money they should have been paid for their last crop of pyrethrum? In a farmhouse abandoned the year before by a European family, the white settlement officers for Ol Kalou said there was always hope but that they didn't really see how they were going to manage without more money. Taking Ol Kalou as an example, they had arrived at a rock-bottom figure of 3 million pounds ($8,400,000). It would take that amount to recondition the land abandoned by the European farmers (an estimated £7 an acre for the old man's property), purchase the necessary machinery and then settle the Africans. But all the settlement officers had to work with was £1.2 million. In addition, the scheme was desperately short of trained technicians.

"An increasing number are Africans, and this puts a greater load on us," one of the officers said.

Their work, they agreed, was an interminable, uphill struggle—against the politicians in Nairobi, against African apathy in general, against nature itself. And nothing would succeed without constant and emphatic white supervision. The Africans would not take this sort of pressure from their own kind and it was only a matter of time before they refused to take it from the whites.

"I wish I could say I felt this was all a great leap forward, but it's more a rear-guard action," the settlement officer said. He sighed wearily and turned to one of his white assistants.

"Don't forget," he added. "We've got fourteen new assistants coming in tomorrow and they're all black as charcoal."

I spent my last morning in Ol Kalou watching part of "takeover day" at J. W. Sparrow's pig and dairy farm. Three white men from the settlement office, armed with checklists, were on hand to make certain that the machinery and livestock they had contracted to buy from Sparrow were still there. It was an informal and entirely amicable procedure, Sparrow having even agreed to stay on a few extra months to help during the transitional period. The sale of his farm coincided with Sparrow's decision to retire and there were no regrets. After they had counted the dairy cows and the heifers as they passed through the gate joining one pasture to another, and had satisfied themselves that the number of boars, sows and piglets tallied with their lists, the takeover men asked Sparrow to call his work force together. In a few moments about forty Africans, ranging from small boys to old men, had gathered in a semicircle in one of the fields. Speaking in Swahili, one of the men from the settlement scheme addressed them at some length. He explained that they were no longer working for Bwana Sparrow but for the government. In a sense, therefore, they had become the owners of the land, but with this ownership came responsibility. They should remember the wise words of their leader, Jomo Kenyatta, who had told them repeatedly that *Uhuru* would mean nothing unless all Kenyans worked hard and in the spirit of *Harambee*.

The farm workers listened impassively. When the settlement officer had finished his speech, Sparrow walked over to him. The expression on his face was one of concern. What, he asked in English, what about his Kipsigis? His labor force was divided about equally between Kikuyus and Kipsigis. Under his protection they had been working side by side and, with minor exceptions, there had been no trouble. But what would happen to the Kipsigis now? The settlement officer paused and thought it over for a while and then, speaking again in Swahili to the entire group, said that it would probably be a good idea if the Kipsigis made preparations to return to their own tribal areas. If the Kipsigis were astonished or alarmed by this information, they did not show it. Perhaps they had known this would happen all along.

The takeover formalities were now concluded and the group of white men started walking back to Sparrow's house for the coffee Mrs. Sparrow had been preparing in her kitchen. At this moment a large chauffeur-driven car pulled into the driveway and stopped. An African dressed in a sports jacket climbed out of the back seat and introduced himself. He was from the ministry, he said, and had come to witness the takeover and make a report.

"You're a little late," said one of the settlement officers curtly. "We're all finished here."

"I see," said the African. He looked abashed, and when it became plain that he was not invited for the coffee being served by Mrs. Sparrow, he climbed back into his car and instructed his chauffeur to drive away.

Later, I told the old man that everything had gone very well at the Sparrow farm that day and that I would be leaving Ol Kalou with high hopes for the land scheme. The old man gave me one of his mirthless laughs.

"You haven't learned a thing, have you, boy? Not a thing." I said nothing. Let him think what he pleased. I was damned if I would give him the satisfaction of knowing he had changed my mind.

CHAPTER 9

RUNT OF THE LITTER

. . . that land of bananas and free entertainment.

—H. M. STANLEY

TRY as I would (and in the end I did not try at all) I could not take Uganda seriously. Even before we drove down from the Kenya highlands and crossed the border into the lush, green countryside that crowns the northern rim of Lake Victoria, my growing collection of newspaper stories about Uganda leaned toward farce. One in particular seemed to catch the flavor of the place. Datelined Jinja (a town on the banks of the Victoria Nile) it reported that the Jinja branch of the Uganda People's Congress Youth League had taken strenuous exception to the behavior of an Italian in a Jinja bar on Christmas Eve. It seemed that the Italian had "insulted the citizens of this country" by giving his dog a glass of beer. Calling for "stern" action by the Minister for Internal Affairs, the Youth League's publicity secretary declared: "To give a dog liquor from the same glass human beings use in any bar in this independent country is but to undermine the African integrity as well as insulting the images of Uganda." Obviously times (or dogs) had changed since the days when Stanley's bulldog had "amazed the wondering savage with his bold eyes and bearing, and by his courageous form caused them to retreat before him. . . ." But much else remained the same—especially the bananas. The bananas of Uganda fascinated Stanley and he wrote about them at some length in *Through the Dark Continent*, noting that there were several varieties ranging from three-inch green ones through lighter green sixinchers, "considered the best," to a dark-tipped species unfit for food and reserved for the manufacture of a wine called *maramba*. Stanley found a small draught of *maramba* taken at dawn "beneficial to the system." He also noted that the banana fronds served as thatch for houses and as bedding, that the stems could be used for fences and their hearts made into sponges which "may be seen in almost all Kiganda lavatories." The stalks, he discovered, could be turned into cord, battle shields or sun hats and the leaves into tablecloths or parcel wrappers.

"With the banana plant," wrote Stanley of the Uganda native, "he is happy, fat and thriving; without it, he is a famished, discontented, woe-begone wretch, hourly expecting death."

In the course of circumnavigating Lake Victoria, Stanley spent several months in Uganda and never managed to generate much enthusiasm for the people. "They are," he wrote, "crafty, fraudful, deceiving, lying thievish knaves taken as a whole, and seem to be born with an uncontrollable love of gaining wealth by robbery, violence and murder, in which they resemble—except that they have the lawless instinct to a greater degree than most—nearly all African tribes."

I must admit that I was much more interested in the Uganda of Stanley's time than I was in the Uganda of today. It paled in comparison. I did my best to steep myself in local lore and learned (although it had no meaning for me) that the country was divided into four regions; that there were, in addition, four kingdoms, and that there was a Kabaka of Buganda, an Omukama of Bunyoro, and a Omugabe of Ankole. Ankole also had an Enganzi, but all I knew about him was what I read in the papers.

"There will be no more elections in Uganda in 1967," the Enganzi was quoted as saying, "because there is no more opposition."

Since Stanley's day, the opulence had disappeared from the Kabaka's court (where, for instance, was the guardian of the Imperial Lavatory?) and the steam seemed to have gone out of the "crafty, fraudful" natives. Those I met in Kampala struck me as not particularly good copies of their brothers in Kenya and Tanzania. As a matter of fact, everything about Uganda—her politics, her attitude toward white men, the speeches made by her leaders—seemed to have been borrowed from her neighbors to the south. She was, in comparison with Kenya and Tanzania, the runt of the litter. Uganda did not originate. She imitated and, in an almost frantic effort to make herself more important than she really was, she exaggerated. The leader of the parliamentary opposition, in explaining why he had joined the government party, said his old party was "dangerous" and that anyone who voted for it in the future was a "criminal." Dr. Milton Obote, the Prime Minister, complained that America's policy in the Congo might well result in the extinction of "all the black men in the heart of Africa." At the Makerere University College campus, a TEA teacher said the anti-white atmosphere had reached ludicrous extremes. The day before he had taken his female tennis partner directly from the court to tea in one of the university's halls. Now he showed me a typewritten notice which he had torn from the hall bulletin board: "The Hall [it read] is not a museum in which particular cultural differences are displayed. This applies particularly to a certain young man who brought a certain young woman to tea, making it difficult for the Hall to decide whether she was dressed or naked."

I spent most of my days in Kampala feeling bored and wondering why it was that I *was* bored. Occasionally, something was said which did not sound derivative. One morning I joined a group of about thirty students in one of the smaller lecture halls to hear "christianity in East Africa" discussed by a theologian called Dr. Mbiti. The group was attentive and seemed in complete agreement as Dr. Mbiti criticized the missionaries for having adopted what he called a "superior" approach to their potential converts. What the missionaries had failed to comprehend, said Dr. Mbiti, was that the Africans had always been steeped in a religion of their own, a religion which enveloped them even before birth and stayed with them long after death. The Africans' religion, he continued, permeated every nook and cranny of life; it was in the food they ate, the beer they drank, the songs they sang, the dances they danced, the wars they waged and the very stones they fashioned into tools or weapons. Before the time of the missionaries, there were no such things as atheists or agnostics. No one was heard to say: "I believe." One simply knew. Then came the missionaries, who quickly made it plain to the Africans that everything they had been doing was heretical.

"They gave us a fantastic list of dos and don'ts," said Dr. Mbiti. "But their most serious mistake was that they set boundaries to the Christian religion. They put it in a building and locked it up except for a few hours on Sunday or Holy Days. They told us that this new religion could not solve our marital problems. It forbade ancestor worship. We could no longer enjoy dancing as a religious experience. The tunes they taught us were utterly devoid of rhythm and we were told to sing without moving our bodies or clapping our hands. Except for those few hours on Sunday, religion left our lives untouched."

Christianity, Dr. Mbiti added, was still at a distance today. Now the time had come to rescue Christianity from being a religion, from "being asleep six days a week."

"It must be stretched to every moment of space and time," he said.

I was impressed by the lecture and was even more impressed by the questions which followed. All reflected Dr. Mbiti's feelings about the missionaries themselves but nowhere was there a suggestion that the Christian religion itself was wrong. It had simply been introduced to the Africans by a band of short-sighted and inflexible bunglers.

At one point, after Dr. Mbiti had suggested that it was important to allow Christ to permeate everything, a student rose and said he didn't see exactly how "I can put Jesus in my father's beer." There were several questions referring to Christianity as "the white man's religion," one of the students asking whether "we should make Christ think like an African or make the Africans think like Christ." Dr. Mbiti said he guessed the student would just have to figure that one out for himself.

In a sense, Uganda served as a kind of watershed in my trip through Africa. Not that Uganda could be called the high point of the voyage. Nadir would have been more like it. Up until Uganda, it seemed to me that I had been learning something new every day. Now, suddenly, I was learning nothing—and two-thirds of the mid-section of Africa (the most difficult part) still lay ahead. In addition, the three months I had allocated in London for the entire voyage were almost up. Clearly, the time had come to go. What prompted me to decide on immediate departure, however, was Jack's discovery that his passport did not contain a visa to the Kingdom of Burundi. Taken by itself, this might appear to have been a minor and easily rectified omission but he chose to bring it to my attention the day that the newspapers reported the assassination of Burundi's Prime Minister, M. Pierre Ngendandumwe. According to the reports he had been gunned down on leaving a maternity clinic in the capital of Bujumbura where his wife had just produced a baby. Burundi's relations with Rwanda, through which we planned to pass before entering Burundi, had always been tense. Now it seemed likely that the borders would be closed or, worse still, that war would break out between these two tiny but bitter enemies. This was not a time to try to sweet-talk our way across frontiers without visas. I sent Jack down to the Burundi embassy in Kampala immediately. Naturally it was closed. When it opened two days later, Jack presented himself before the ambassador and, in an effort to ingratiate himself, expressed his sincere condolences for his nation's recent and tragic loss.

"Oh, well," the ambassador replied while stamping Jack's passport with an entry permit, "it happens in every country, doesn't it?"

There was nothing on the horizon (literally or figuratively) to lighten our spirits as we drove out of Kampala and headed due west down the road toward Fort Portal on the Uganda side of the Congo frontier. Dark thunderclouds loomed ahead. The radio reported that Ngendandumwe's assassin was employed in the American embassy in Bujumbura. A few days before, the Obote government had deported two journalists for paying an "unauthorized" visit to the West Nile and Madi districts through which passed arms en route from the Sudan to the Congolese rebels. Both Uganda and the Tshombe government were accusing each other of border violations, and war between the two seemed imminent. All in all, it did not seem to be the best of times to be traveling (Stanley himself furnishing the historical precedent when he observed that "it was not customary in Uganda to permit strangers to proceed on their journeys while the Kabaka was engaged in war"). At Mubende, about halfway between Kampala and Fort Portal, the clouds suddenly dropped to the ground and we were enveloped by a tropical downpour ferocious enough to drive water through the metal roof of our Land-Rover and tear to shreds the spastic leaves of the banana plants on either side of the road. The storm lifted as we approached Fort Portal (our spirits with it) and beyond, almost black against the gray sky, lay the Ruwenzoris, the Mountains of the Moon.

A sign at the edge of town warned travelers to be sure to obtain the necessary passes for disturbed areas. Not knowing the whereabouts of any disturbed areas nor whether we would be traveling through them, I thought it best to check with the police. It was an unfortunate decision. At the central police station we were told that such passes could only be obtained at the District Commissioner's office and that was closed for the day. We thanked the police officer, climbed back into the Land-Rover and then backed into the station's porch, neatly and quickly breaking one of its wooden supports in two. Our whole strategy, we had agreed on our way to Fort Portal, would be based on behaving unobtrusively. And now this. We climbed out of the Land-Rover and presented ourselves at the desk.

"Please wait," said the sergeant in charge. We did and, when nothing happened for several minutes, I asked the desk sergeant who we were waiting for.

"He is coming. You wait."

"Who is coming?"

"He is coming right away."

We waited. We examined the splintered beam. We discussed the splintered beam with the desk sergeant. The desk sergeant discussed the splintered beam with a friend. We shook our heads. We frowned. We laughed. We shrugged our shoulders. We read all the notices on the bulletin board. Then, because dusk was descending rapidly and I wanted to find a campsite and set up our tent before dark, I blew up. Were we being held? If we *were* being held what were the charges? If there were *no* charges against us, and if we were *not* being held, would the sergeant please let us go so that we could find a place to spend the night? My raised voice did not alarm so much as embarrass the sergeant and, after we had established that we would be spending the night at the campsite operated by the Mountains of the Moon Hotel, he let us go. The campsite, only a few hundred yards from the police station, commanded a splendid view of the Ruwenzori Range. From here it was less than twenty miles to the Congo border. Several army tents had been erected at one end of the campsite and, as we parked and began to open up the back of the Land-Rover, a corporal detached himself from a group of soldiers and walked over. Could he be of any assistance, he asked. Jack replied that we could manage perfectly well ourselves and we started to unpack our tent. The corporal motioned to a sergeant, who walked over and informed us that we would not be allowed to camp here since this was now army property. I asked what the Uganda army was doing here.

"We know what we are doing," the corporal replied. Neither he nor the servant volunteered any further information.

The proprietor of the hotel apologized to us, saying that the army really had no right to camp on his property but that there hadn't seemed much point in making an issue of the thing. I asked him whether the presence of the army had anything to do with the disturbed areas referred to in an announcement on the police bulletin board and he said he doubted it. It seemed more likely that these army movements had something to do with the Congo. The frontier, he said, had just been closed. As for the disturbed areas, they were nothing new. "Just the usual tribal nonsense," he said. "They hate each other, that's all. It's been going on for the past thirty years and it will go on for another thirty."

We had just finished setting up our tent in the hotel garden when two men in a police jeep drove up and asked us to accompany them to the police station. There, one of the patrolmen told us that the O.C. wished to see us. The desk sergeant turned on the patrolman.

"Don't say O.C.," he said. "Don't you know better than that? Say

Officer in Charge." Then, turning back to me, the sergeant said: "The Officer in Charge would like to see you."

In a small office next door, the Officer in Charge, his shirt glistening with starch, went through my papers and asked me what I intended to do about the porch. Did I realize that I was charged with a traffic offense? I said I most certainly did and that I would be most grateful if he would let me plead guilty and make the necessary restitution for the splintered support beam. This struck the O.C. as fair enough and together we drove in the O.C.'s car to a lumber yard, where a turbaned Indian agreed to come back to the police station. He measured the beam, penciled a few figures on a sheet of paper, and announced that he could hew a replacement for five shillings.

While the O.C. drove the Indian back to his lumberyard I talked to a Catholic father who had appeared at the police station to validate the passport of a newly arrived Peace Corps teacher. He said he and the other fathers had gotten into the habit of listening to the radio that past fall, tuning in to the short-wave broadcasts of every Notre Dame football game. Because of the time difference they listened each Saturday from 11 P.M. until 2 A.M. and he was glad the season was over. They had all turned into insufferable bores rooting for their old alma mater. They still listened to the radio a great deal but now most of the news was about the Congo. That morning, he went on, they had heard that the Prime Minister's assassin in Burundi had said that the Americans had paid him to do it; that Tanzania had sealed its borders to all Americans, and that Uganda was about to declare war on the Congo. As for the Congo, the radio had informed the fathers that the rebels were gaining ground and that the strength of white mercenaries fighting under the command of Colonel Mike Hoare was now down to one hundred which hardly seemed enough. They had heard all of this on Radio Brazzaville, which probably accounted for that fact that none of the items was true.

There were still a surprising number of missionaries in the Congo, the father said, but in recent weeks they had been bringing their cars across the border into Uganda for safekeeping. His own mission, he said, was full of them.

"You can't keep a big car in the Congo any more," he said. "Just little cars like Volkswagens." I asked how he would rate chances for my Land-Rover. He gave my vehicle an appraising glance.

"That would go in no time," he said.

Before leaving Fort Portal, I stopped by the large office occupied by the police commander of the Toro District. He grew increasingly suspicious as I told him about following Stanley's second trip through Africa, and when I added that I would be interested in joining any of his officers who might be planning an inspection tour of the border, he called in his white assistant and together they began to ask me what sort of credentials I was carrying. At that I began to ooze toward the door.

"It's a little dicey right now," said the white assistant. "I wouldn't be trying anything if I were you."

"I won't," I said. The white officer began to smile. He knew a prying journalist when he saw one.

"Just stick to the main roads and you'll be all right," he added.

With the Congolese border on our right, we drove south. Our destination now was Kisoro, a town which lies at the juncture of the Ugandan, Rwandese and Congolese borders. We spent the first night after Fort Portal in the Queen Elizabeth Park at the Mweya Lodge on a bluff overlooking Lake Edward. Stanley had planned to circumnavigate Edward but had been unable to lower his boat, the *Lady Alice*, down from the cliffs to the east of the lake and, after viewing its shores, had been forced to turn back. The approaches to Lake Edward—the "peaks, cones, mountain humps and dome-like hills"—had enchanted Stanley and he had called this "singularly wild and beautifully picturesque" country "the Switzerland of Africa." We watched the sun go down behind the hills on the other side of the lake (the Congolese side) and, drinks in hand, listened to the radio in Swahili. The announcer said nothing which would have altered our plans. Winston Churchill was dying in London. Overhead, marabou storks, the tips of their wings like extended fingers, circled in the twilight.

At dawn next morning, a ferry carried our Land-Rover from the spit of land on which we had spent the night across the Kazinga Channel to the mainland. The countryside as we drove south was indecisive—partly bush and partly open savanna—but it seemed made for buffalo and elephant. The elephants tended to move off when we drove close, gliding like ships under sail among the islands of bush. The buffaloes, shoulder deep in pools of muddy water, held their ground, their horns parted in the middle like the mustaches of turn-of-the-century bartenders. Signs on our right pointed to Parc Albert in the Congo, but we were determined not to stumble into the Congo by mistake and followed the tracks leading south rather than those heading west. Late in the morning we started to climb into a range of mountains. The road, well cared for by gangs from the Uganda Ministry of Works, led through forests of giant trees and clinging vines and there was in the cool mountain air the rich, sweet smell of rotting vegetation. Patches of gardens, all carefully terraced as if every inch counted, clung to the steep and sometimes almost perpendicular mountainsides. Villagers on either side of the road stepped back as we drove past. The children waved and the men took their hoes off their shoulders and curtsied. Fog shrouded the heights and we began our descent through close-packed bamboo forests in almost total darkness. It was raining heavily when we drove into Kisoro and the police said the border wouldn't be open for another hour or so because the customs officials had gone for tea. This seemed like a good idea for us, too, and we pulled up in front of the Travelers Rest, a small hotel run by an old German called Baumgartel. The walls of the reception-hall-cum-dining-room-cum-bar were lined with lacquered bamboo and Baumgartel served us tea and cookies and said he had plenty of room for us for the night. When he found out that we planned to follow Stanley down the Congo River, he started to laugh.

"No," he said, "you can't go to the Congo now. They will take your car and anything else you have and then they will knock your teeth out and kill you."

Baumgartel seemed to know what he was talking about. He had lived and worked in these parts for forty years. Now he had had enough and he was looking for a way out, for somebody to buy his little hotel.

"I will either sell it and retire or commit suicide," he said. Even though independence had come far too soon in Uganda there had been a chance, but now the Congo had changed everything. The Congo was drawing the rest of Africa in after it, like a terrible whirlpool, and if he stayed on he would be drawn in too. Until recently he had been going in and out of the Congo on business (it was just a few miles down the road) but that was finished now because you could never be certain what would happen. It made absolutely no difference which side you were on. The soldiers were drunk most of the time. It could be safe in one place and a mile away they could be raping and killing nuns.

"It was a good place under the Belgians," he said and then he added: "Well, perhaps not so good. The Belgians . . . I didn't like the Belgians. They were a hard people. No humor. But there was no bloodshed and the people worked and the children went to school and were fed."

Here on the border, in Uganda, the situation was still not dangerous but the atmosphere was unpleasant, and Baumgartel spoke of the climate of fear which had produced a widely shared belief that every stranger was a spy.

"Two nights ago, in my bar here, there was an Israeli technician," Baumgartel said. "I think he was agricultural. He was writing letters at this table. In Hebrew of course. An African standing at the bar—he was of course drunk—came over to the Israeli and said he was a spy, and that he should stop writing. He should have a drink instead. I told the African, although of course I don't think I was correct, that Jews never drink. But the African wasn't satisfied and asked why the Israeli was writing in code, and backward too. I explained that this was the way they wrote and I also told him that his own Bible had been written in that language and by people like that. But it was no good. The African became very angry and abusive. The police were brought in and we talked and they managed to calm the African down. But this was only after the police—and they insisted—had been allowed to read the Israeli's letter—backwards and in Hebrew."

In answer to my question, Baumgartel said he understood that it was still calm in Rwanda. A Baptist missionary had been through a few days before and had said he was going back to Kisenyi, a town in Rwanda on the northern shores of Lake Kivu, for a meeting with an American consular official. There was, I had heard, a sizable contingent of Baptists in Kisenyi. They had fled the Congo several months before and were said to be living more or less as refugees in a lakefront house until the situation in the Congo clarified. When Baumgartel said he thought the meeting with the African consular official was scheduled for the following day, I decided to drive to Kisenyi immediately. The meeting sounded interesting. Baumgartel seemed crushed.

"We do not get many visitors here any more and I could use the business," he said. He overcharged us for the tea, which made me feel less guilty. By the time we reappeared at the customs post, the Uganda officials had returned and we passed through the formalities without trouble.

Instead of continuing straight down the road into the Congo we branched left and followed the road south for a couple of miles to the Rwanda border. In contrast to the Uganda side, the Rwanda post was slovenly, populated by shoeless men in dirty shorts who jostled each other for a look at our passports and the car papers and eyed the Land-Rover with looks that were disconcertingly closer to longing than interest. This was French-speaking territory now and the customs officials and I practiced the language on each other without achieving any breakthrough in the field of communication. I was also reminded that Rwanda had once been in the hands of the Belgians by the hyperbolic signature the customs official in charge affixed to our visas. All over the Congo, officials initial documents with elaborate, spiraling scrollwork, and the official at the Rwanda border post, head down and right eye an inch from the paper, was no exception.

We drove on now, with our headlights on, past groves of eucalyptus trees, and I was relieved to see that the male pedestrians still curtsied as they had on the other side of the border. We reached our first checkpoint outside the town of Ruhengeri. The soldiers who surrounded our Land-Rover were drunk, but they were unarmed. We were asked for our *carte rouge*. We did not have one.

"Carte rouge, carte rouge," the soldier repeated.

"Touriste, touriste," I replied while going through my papers. I found a pink piece of tissue paper which the Rwanda border officials had given us and showed it to the soldiers. They examined it upside down in front of the Land-Rover's headlights and then waved us on. Jack, accustomed to the polish and politeness of the British-trained soldiers in East Africa, was incensed. I told him this was nothing compared to what he would probably encounter later on. On the outskirts of Kisenyi we almost ran through our second checkpoint and had to brake hard to avoid smashing the barrier. By the time we reached a stop the soldiers had their weapons to their shoulders. They seemed drunker than the first batch, and the officer in charge, weaving and gesticulating, was extremely angry. Did we not realize that we had violated regulations by not stopping fifteen meters from the barrier? I explained that we were tourists and that we had meant no wrong. He thought about that for a moment and then demanded the *carte rouge*. I had not eaten much of anything since breakfast. It was now past nine in the evening and perhaps this contributed to my feeling that we would get along better if I displayed some arrogance of my own. I said in French that I didn't have a *carte rouge* but I had a *feuille rouge* and that if he didn't know the difference between a *feuille* and a *carte* it was time he learned. He took this in silence, and when I told him he had better open the barrier quickly or I would see to it that my good friend the Minister of Tourism heard about it, he signaled the guard and waved us on. As we drove by the officer saluted. If my previous visits to the Congo had taught me anything it was that checkpoints must be played by ear. If shouted at loudly enough, some would crumble. Others cost money. Most, however, could be penetrated if the guards were persuaded that you were a huge joke. A laughing man or, more specifically, a man who could be laughed at was seldom an enemy. The difficulty, of course, was to determine which of the several approaches to take. The wrong one led frequently to arrest, and arrest, in most cases, was accompanied by a beating. Beatings in the Congo were seldom administered scientifically but always with enthusiasm.

There seemed to be no center to the town of Kisenyi (no cluster of bars or restaurants) and we drove up and down several dark streets before Jack spotted a policeman wheeling a bicycle. As we pulled abreast of him he flung his bicycle into a ditch, opened the door of the Land-Rover and squeezed inside. He was enormously friendly and enormously drunk and the cab of the Land-Rover was immediately enveloped in brandy fumes. He said he would take us to where the Baptists were staying and directed us to a large house surrounded by a high hedge. The policeman got out, staggered to the front door and began beating on it with his fists. After a long wait an obviously terrified female voice from behind the door asked us who we were and what we wanted. She was speaking in French but with an American accent and I replied in English. At length she opened the door, revealing a gray-haired lady in a faded print dress. The policeman looked at her and beamed.

"Don't let him in," the woman said to me.

"It's all right," I replied. "He's a policeman." But I got rid of him by pressing some francs into his palm and the woman took her hand away from her throat and asked us inside. If we would care to wait she would try to find the Rev. Mr. Peters. When he appeared a few minutes later, dressed in an open-necked shirt, he made it plain that he was not glad to see us. I asked if this was where tomorrow's meeting with the American consular official would be held.

"How did you know that?" Mr. Peters asked. I told him we'd heard about it in Kisoro.

"Well, nobody is supposed to know about it. It's private."

I asked whether we could talk to him anyhow, after the meeting, sometime tomorrow, at his convenience.

"Maybe," he said. "But I warn you, I'm not talking."

Curiosity thoroughly whetted, we said good night to the Rev. Mr. Peters and found rooms and good food at Le Relais next door. On the following morning we discovered to our pleasure that the windows of our room overlooked Lake Kivu, blue and clear in the early-morning sun. Kisenyi (the signs leading into the town had spelled it with a "G") had the look of a substantial summer colony. The houses were large and well built and their lawns, still carefully tended, wandered down to the shoreline. But now a great many of them were unoccupied, their former owners having left the administrative centers of Leopoldville and Stanleyville or their ranches in the Kivu to return to Belgium. It was a summer colony after Labor Day in America or the August Bank Holiday in England.

Jack and I wandered about, trying to pick up as much information as we could about the Congo. Since the Congolese border and the town of Goma lay not more than a few hundred yards along the road which follows the lake, it was not difficult to do so. Goma, we were told, was still a quiet town except when the troops were there. Then it became a worrisome place. The troops were government—either just back from the Stanleyville area and hell bent on having a good time after the fighting, or fresh troops up from Elisabethville in Katanga and equally hell bent on having a good time before going into combat against the rebels. In any case when the troops were in Goma cars were stolen and civilians were beaten up. It was a good idea to spend the night in Kisenyi when the troops were in town. And beyond Goma? The man who answered that question (a planter) moved in and out of the Congo almost every day.

"It is calm up to fifty miles west of Goma," he said. "But further on if it was peaceful we would hear about it. But nobody is going in there and nobody is coming out. So we do not hear."

Two American consular officials (one from Bukavu in the Congo and the other from Kigali) were eating a late breakfast at Le Relais. I asked them about their mysterious meeting with the Baptists. Nothing very mysterious about it, they replied. It was simply that the Baptists represented the largest concentration of Americans in the area and it had seemed like a good idea to see them. One of the officials said he'd received the impression that the Baptists had hoped the United States government would take the decision out of their hands and order the entire group out of the Congo.

"But we can't order them out," he said. "We can only advise."

I had hoped to make friends with the Rev. Mr. Peters. I had heard he made periodic trips into the Congo and it occurred to me that it might be interesting to accompany him on one of them. But when we met again he was if anything more suspicious than before.

"We have decided to say nothing," he told me. "We're not talking." I broached the idea of joining him on one of his trips across the border and he said that it was out of the question. He himself had not had any real trouble so far but that was because the people knew him. If a stranger joined him, the people might become suspicious and then there might be trouble for both of us. He could not afford that risk right now. Besides, newspapermen were always trouble. They were always distorting or exaggerating, or misquoting innocent people. . . . Mr. Peters looked at me expecting, I think, some sort of denial which would, in turn, terminate the interview. Instead, I lapsed into silence, and as the silence became prolonged Mr. Peters, obviously uncomfortable, began to talk. We were standing on the lawn in front of his house, watching the lake, and he began to talk about how things had been before independence. It had been a beautiful place, with flowers planted along the beaches as far as the eye could see. A wonderful place for children. There was a time when he had thought of retiring here, but of course everything had changed. Thirty years in the Congo. You would have thought a man would have learned something in that length of time, something about the people, but they were completely unpredictable. He had never expected it to turn out this way.

"In Goma," he said, "you see civil servants—civil servants, mind you—sitting on the curb with a bottle of beer in each hand. Drunk. In the middle of the day. Now I'm a minister and I don't drink but I don't mind other people drinking. All I say is that you should do your drinking in your own home. This morning, here in Kisenyi, I had some business with the perfecture about my children's passports and I congratulated them after it was over. I said: 'At least you *try* to behave like civil servants.' They were very pleased."

Mr. Peters also seemed terribly pleased with himself for having said it. As I listened to him talk, it occurred to me that Mr. Peters was less disturbed by what the rebels had done in the Congo than by their effect on the people. He had built up his mission carefully, meticulously, expanding gradually over the years, appointing African deacons ("we were the first to Africanize"). It must have looked good on paper, in the reports sent back home to headquarters. But the rebels had done more in a few short weeks than the missionaries had managed to accomplish in a lifetime. Now on his trips into the Congo Mr. Peters did not know whom he could trust. Something deep, something primordial had been released among the members of his flock. Oh, the missions were still functioning under the black deacons (those who were still alive), but now an uncertainty had crept into his relations with even the most trusted of his assistants.

How many more times would he be able to enter and leave the Congo in peace? How many more visits before something happened, before they—perhaps even one of his African deacons—turned on him? How could this be explained to an outsider, to headquarters back in the States? Could Mr. Peters explain it to himself, this failure? Because that was what it was and, although Mr. Peters was not saying so now to me, I thought I understood why it was that he had no wish to speak to anyone. Thirty years of work which end in failure is not something one can easily talk about. Was there any hope? Perhaps, he said, but only if Tshombe stayed in power. Mr. Peters remembered a speech by Tshombe in which the Prime Minister had said: "After me there will be nothing." Tshombe was right about that. The Rev. Mr. Peters only wished that the American embassy would . . . well, the missionaries often knew things that even the State Department did not know.

"They think we're nuts or something," Mr. Peters said bitterly. "So we've given up, a lot of us, telling them about anything. We could have told them what was going to happen, what's going to happen next. . . ."

And what was going to happen next?

"Now you're asking questions." Mr. Peters ended the interview then and there. He had said too much as it was.

That evening, Jack and I speculated on our chances of driving into the Congo with the Land-Rover. They did not seem very good but, in an effort to make certain that we left no stone unturned, I argued for the Land-Rover. After all, we were innocent civilians, obvious noncombatants. With my knowledge of French and his of

Swahili, we could talk our way out of most tight spots. We could feel our way forward, taking risks only when the odds were in our favor. Jack stared moodily into his drink, ordered another, then another. Finally he slapped his hand palm down on the table and said he had heard enough.

"You don't know what you're talking about," he said. What he said after that he said with passion. It must have been building up inside him for some time and it will be some time before I forget it.

"There's no future for the white man in Africa," he said. "You outsiders can go around helping as much as you want but that's because you don't know what the black man knows about you. Not you yourself but the white men like me who have lived here all our lives. The Africans remember all right.

"Make no mistakes about it. We treated them rough. People think we British treated them better than the Belgians. Maybe that's so. The Belgians were really tough, but we weren't exactly saints. Let me tell you something. I remember when I was a kid and I remember this nigger stretched out on the lawn and my father was beating him with a hose. Some of us got together and tied one of them down and tickled his cock with a feather until he had a hard on, and then we threw cold water on it and watched it go down. Or we used to do worse. Like once we tied one to a post and lit sticks around his feet. If it burned his feet, what difference? He was only a nigger. And our daddies used to come out and laugh and say, 'It's just the young fellows having fun.' Once one of them threw a panga at my uncle while his back was turned. My uncle saw it just in time but it caught him on the hand—he must have had it up protecting his face—and *whhooosh*, two fingers off. And my uncle said, 'Right, you bastard,' and they strung him up. Hung him. Now, any African who saw that nigger hanging dead from a tree must remember.

"The same way during the Mau Mau emergency. I was walking to a milk shed and under the door there was this pink liquid—milk and blood, you know. And I walked in and they had killed this woman and cut her up. Part of her arm was there, and her head was there, and her guts all over. And bloody handprints all over the white walls of that milk shed. I was only fifteen at the time and I vomited all over. I'll never forget it for the rest of my life. If I can't forget that, why should they forget all the things we did to them. We had our hotels and we said: 'These are for us and you don't come in.' Now they've got their independence. Why should they let us in? You talk about going into the Congo. Hell, the Belgians were much worse than we were. And you think you can go in and the Congolese won't remember? You think you can just go in there and smile at them and they'll treat you different from other white men? Don't kid yourself. They remember, and they hate you. The only thing that held them back before was fear. Now they have no reason to fear you any more unless you carry a gun and you're just stupid enough not to.

"A white man, some of them anyway, have a feeling of pity. Let the poor bugger go. But not an African. It just never crosses his mind. We had our day. Now it's their turn. Make no mistake about it. We never loved them and you can bet they never loved us. They don't want us around. You still want to go to the Congo? Listen, if you want my advice, if you want to survive in this country, get out. . . ."

Next morning, still shaking his head at the naïveté of certain travelers, Jack drove me to the Congo border and let me out. We arranged to meet at the same place two hours later. If I failed to show up at the appointed time, he would notify the authorities. We did not plan any further than that.

The road to the Congolese border post followed the contours of Lake Kivu and then curved away from the lake toward Goma. The border post, a small shack for the guards and a barrier to stop cars, had been put up at the curve. I produced my passport, and two officials, one in a gray uniform and the other in dark trousers and a white shirt (customary dress for a Congolese clerical worker) studied every last one of the dozens of visas stamped into my passport and then asked me for my vaccination certificate. For this walk into Goma, I had divested myself of everything nonessential—my spare cameras, travelers checks, extra money, and so forth. Of course I had also left my vaccination certificate behind. Despite my argument that I only planned to be in Goma for an hour, I found myself a few moments later walking back down the road to Kisenyi.

The officials at the Rwanda border post looked puzzled when I passed by for the second time in ten minutes and even more puzzled when I reappeared five minutes later. Back at the Congolese post, I received a cardboard disk with the number 17 written on it in exchange for my passport, and walked into Goma. The road now became a dual highway with luxurious mounds of crimson bougainvillaea planted in between. It was a Saturday and, as I walked into the straight main street of Goma, with its neat arcaded buildings, it was apparent that this was a day when the troops were not in town. The streets were almost deserted and the business of those who lounged in the shade of the arcades was to watch the stranger. The atmosphere was that of a western frontier town in the movies just before the big gunfight.

I walked up one side of the street and then down the other. In the windows of the stores there were pictures of Tshombe patting a lion. I think it was one of Emperor Haile Selassie's lions and the photograph must have been taken during one of the many Pan-African conferences at Addis Ababa. The stores were shut but one of the bars was open and I walked in and ordered a large bottle of beer. I was joined almost immediately by two polite and friendly Congolese. After it had been established that I was a tourist and would buy them beer, one of them kicked off his shoes and the other, dropping to his knees, began to polish them. Standing there in his stocking feet, the Congolese apologized for the fact that the tourist bureau had been closed these many months. Goma, he said, had been a lovely place before the trouble. I asked whether he meant before this latest revolution or before independence. He replied that it had not been a happy place for many years but that the period under the rebels had been the worst. They had been bad for the country, he said, because they had killed all the intellectuals. What kind of intellectuals?

"Comme moi, monsieur," he replied. "Like me. Those who know a little how to read and write."

In answer to his question, I told him that I planned to continue on to Stanleyville. My chances of getting through, he said after some thought, were far better than his because I was white. It was virtually impossible for a black man to attempt the trip.

As I prepared to leave, he said he was sad that I was only passing through. If I could stay on in Goma, then perhaps I would be in a position to offer him a job. In the meantime, however (and he began to brighten again at the thought), would I buy him another bottle of beer? I did.

"Merci, patron," he said. "Merci, et bon voyage."

CHAPTER 10

SHORT WEEK IN A SMALL COUNTRY

Wherever we looked, we beheld grassy ridges, grassy slopes, grassy mountain summits, and grassy valleys—an eminently pastoral country.

—H. M. STANLEY

Excerpts from a Rwanda journal:

SUNDAY, January 24. We have set up tent on a ridge above Kigali, the capital of Rwanda; population four thousand; one paved street. Being on the reverse side of the ridge, we can't see Kigali from here. Stretching to the west a wonderful view of range after range of mountains disappearing into the Congo. Have been interrupted and distracted by growing group of small boys and young men wearing rags and leaning on poles. As always seems to be the case with Africans, they have materialized out of nowhere, out of thin air. A few moments ago we were alone and now here they are and more are coming, followed by their long-horned Ankole cattle. It's like the child's game Still-Pond-No-More-Moving. When I look down and type, they inch forward. When I look up they stop. An extremely pleasant bunch. I have been teaching one boy how to say how-do-you-do. It embarasses him and amuses his friends. The semicircle draws closer. Interesting how they delineate the territory into which they are about to advance by spitting into it. Spit. Step. Spit. Step. Do they get echoes back—like SONAR? Jack produces dreadful cigars bought in Kisenyi (three hundred for $1) and hands them out. Mistake, because salivary glands activated. Spitting increases. Joined now by tall girl smoking a pipe. She is probably all or part Tutsi and stands very, very straight. It is getting dark and I can hear conversations a mile away in the valley below. Little cooking fires everywhere.

MONDAY, January 25. *Morning*. It will take Jack a while to pack up the tent. Neither of us slept well and it turns out we both had dreams about the Congo. The pleasant herdsmen, spitting less, are back with us again and this is reassuring although Rwanda has been a bloody place in its time too. Not much more than a year ago the Hutus (something like 85 percent of the population) slaughtered their pre-independence masters, the Tutsis, by the thousand. Most reliable estimates put the figure at between 10,000 and 14,000 Tutsis dead, their bodies tossed into the rivers or left on the sides of roads for vultures and hyenas. Apparently it's all over, at least for the time being–but with an estimated 150,000 Tutsis living as refugees in Burundi, the Congo, Tanzania and Uganda. Have a speech here by the Rwanda President, Gregoire Kayibanda (he's a Hutu but married to a Tutsi) complaining about neo-colonialism (the usual stuff) and about the Inyenzi (translation: "the cockroaches"), the Tutsi terrorists who keep staging raids on Hutus and Belgians from vantage points on the other side of the Rwanda border. The President calls them "those kill-joy Inyenzi," which I like.

Evening. Ed Lollis, the young third secretary at the American embassy, has kindly put us up in the guest room of his house. Tent life is fine when we are on the road but doesn't work when we are in or near a town. Even up on that hilltop the night before we attracted a crowd, part of which followed me as I walked away with my roll of yellow toilet paper. Imagine what life would be like if we pitched tent in the public square of a town, even one as small as Kigali.

The United States ambassador to the Republic of Rwanda, Charles Withers, has a southern accent and is about the most unambassadorial ambassador I have met yet. The only thing ambassadorial about him is that he steers you away from his desk and sits you down on the same low couch facing the same low coffee table that you see in every ambassador's office. Are all ambassadorial desk tops invariably strewn with top-secret papers, or are they working on crossword puzzles? Whatever it is they never let you anywhere near that desk. I dropped in to see Withers this morning simply to pay my respects, and he kept me for over an hour. Affable, unpretentious man. Says the Rwandese come for cocktail parties but don't necessarily appear for dinners when invited. Social life in Kigali limited. No villages in Rwanda. Only a few Belgian-made towns. The rest of the population (2,700,000—the densest of any country south of the Sahara) live in huts scattered over thousands of hillsides. Right now there's a terrible slump in coffee production, the amount having dropped steadily since 1959—22,000 tons in 1961, 12,000 tons in 1962, even less in 1963. The annual per capita "money income" is about $20. President Kayibanda drives around in the front seat of a Volkswagen—unheard of poor-mouth behavior for Africa.

Withers says he himself has it easy in Rwanda. Kayibanda has it written into the constitution that Communism is permanently out and his ambassador makes all the right pro-Western noises at the United Nations. Although Kayibanda makes speeches about neocolonialists, nobody seems to pay much attention and they aren't printed in the papers because there aren't any papers. The Russians moved in a few months ago but have been very quiet. They travel in groups of two or three so you can never have a talk with one of them alone. When the Russian ambassador arrived, Withers gave him a quart of bourbon. The Russian retaliated with a bottle of vodka. The vodka bottle was smaller than the bourbon bottle so the Russian evened things up with a tin of caviar. Withers says he won't give the Russian another bottle of bourbon because he doesn't like vodka, hasn't finished the first bottle yet and doesn't want any more.

The American embassy is housed in what used to be the town butcher shop but I have not yet seen the meat hook that is supposed to protrude from one of the walls.

After talk with Withers, I met the military attaché, a Lieutenant

Colonel Wagoner, and asked about the situation in the Congo. He said the whites in Kivu Province due west of us had banded together as armed volunteers to defend themselves. A recent government decree has allowed them to do this as well as employ private armies to guard the mines, plantations and so forth. Wagoner said I might go to Bukavu just over the Rwanda border on the southern end of Lake Kivu and then tag along with an armed convoy (or a series of them) to Stanleyville. By now I am convinced that it would be no good taking the Land-Rover into the Congo. It will get swiped or commandeered and Wagoner agrees we stand a good chance of getting killed in the process. He says I have a better chance if I travel light and inconspicuously.

Lunch at Le Relais, one of two restaurants in Kigali. Customers mostly white technical assistants and the like. The food, after East Africa's dreary Anglo-Asian cuisine, is good and the chilled red wine is cheerful, but I cannot communicate with the waiters. In French I ask for a fork. Our waiter disappears and fails to return. I ask another waiter and he too disappears. I think I got rid of four waiters this way. The problem of course is not that they have run out of forks but that I have apparently used the wrong word for fork and the waiters, instead of telling me they do not understand, simply vanish. It's the same way on the road. Ask a man whether this is the way to Gitarama and he will say "Yes, yes" rather than say he doesn't understand the question. Saying "No" is practically impossible.

At Withers' suggestion, called at Chinese (Formosan, not Communist) embassy, where first secretary led me next door to the office of Mr. Hung-Fan Wang, Chef de la Mission Agricole Chinoise au Rwanda. Mr. Wang, in charge of the rice scheme here, speaks practically no French and his English is fascinating. Ritelarry evelly "l" is an "r" and vice versa.

"In Lwanda," he said, "there is gleat intellest in lice."

When I asked him how many Chinese were involved in the rice-growing project, Wang said: "There are twelve and me." He works with a local chap called Mafura, director of the Rice Department, who studied a year in Formosa. The Chinese work in the paddies from 8 A.M. to 12 noon and again from 2 to 6 P.M. For the first three months the Africans who worked with them did so according to their traditional schedule—7 A.M. to 3 P.M.—but then asked to go on Chinese hours. Wang very diplomatic about the Rwandese, saying they worked hard and were very interested in the project. The Chinese started with forty-eight varieties of rice but only seven showed good results. Soil and water are no problem but the temperature sinks too low and the humidity is not high enough for really good rice production. Wang says, however, that Rwanda is ideally suited to corn, peanuts and soybean. The problem now is to persuade the Rwandese that it isn't rice they ought to grow after all, but this is an uphill battle because the government officials have got it into their heads that rice is a prestige crop. They want to grow it even if it's uneconomic. Wang has invited me to a soybean party Wednesday afternoon. At dawn tomorrow I am going to join him for a tour of one of his rice-growing operations in what used to be a swamp just outside Kigali.

TUESDAY, January 26. In Land-Rover, Wang and I followed Volkswagen bus filled with Wang's countrymen down winding red dirt road to rice field. Passed a group of tall men carrying something on their shoulders and I waved at them before I realized what it was they were carrying—a dead body on a bamboo stretcher. It must have been a funeral procession. Instead of bowing their heads mournfully, they smiled and waved back. I've been told they have fearful famines here fairly regularly, about once every ten years. If the population increases at its present rate, there will be twice as many Rwandese twenty years hence. Since there are already 265 per square mile at present, it's hideous to contemplate. I suppose when famine strikes again we will drop wheat. Meanwhile, the Catholics (who more or less run the non-governmental parts of this country) will inveigh against birth control. In this way each (the Church and the U.S.) will make absolutely certain that the problem grows large enough to become insoluble.

The Chinese jumped out of the Volkswagen bus wearing conical straw hats. They rolled their denim trousers up to their knees and, barefoot, went to work with hoes in the flooded paddies. Wang led me along the narrow raised portions (dikes?) between the submerged shoots. Being too polite to walk in front of me, he tried to walk alongside and had great trouble keeping his feet out of the water.

"You go on ahead, Mr. Wang."

"Prease, prease," said Mr. Wang. I took several rolls of color pictures of the work going on at the project, most of a group of Africans swinging their hoes in unison.

"It takes a rot of rabol," said Mr. Wang.

Count de Borchgrave lives with his wife and a black Great Dane just outside Kigali in a large house he built in the late thirties. He used to keep lions but had to get rid of one when it tried to get into the bath with Madame. The lion floundered on the slippery tiles on the bathroom floor and never made it. The Count has lived in Rwanda most of his adult life and remembers covering the distance between Kigali and Kisenyi on foot. It used to take him nine days. I imagine he's made a fair amount of money because, at one time or another, (often concurrently), he's been involved in everything—mining, coffee growing, importing, exporting. He likes the Rwandese and has utterly no faith in the future of the country. We couldn't see the Chinese rice project in the valley below his house because of the eucalyptus trees, but we were talking about it and the Count said he wondered just how long it would be before the Rwandese found a way of turning the rice into beer. That's what they were doing with all the bananas. He said there was really no reason for working in Rwanda. All a native had to do was climb a tree and pick his food. If he was too lazy to do that he could wait at the foot of the tree and the fruit would fall down.

The Count's chief concern when I saw him (lunch included delicious cheese soufflé and *vin rosé*) was his dog. His Great Dane hates Africans and the Count is trying to keep the dog from showing his hatred. (Odd, because he's a very black dog too.) If the Africans realize that the dog hates them, they will kill him and the Count doesn't want his dog killed. The Count says it's often the case that white-owned dogs hate black people. Conversely, African-owned dogs hate white people. Seems obvious that the dogs derive this from their masters—but how? Intuition? Is there an undiscovered human gland, activated involuntarily by hate, fear or aversion, that produces an odor which only dogs can smell—like those special dog whistles deliberately pitched too high for the human ear?

If there is such a glandular secretion, is it only the dogs that can smell it? Or can Africans too? There may be something to this, in which case the prospect for harmonious racial relations are dim indeed. Brother Aelvoet, who is in charge of Catholic education in Rwanda, says it is very strange how the Africans will take a dislike to a certain priest or nun despite the fact that the person in question may have been working just as devotedly, teaching just as well or nursing just as diligently as the others. Aelvoet has often had Africans come up to him and say: "This is a good father, and that one is also all right. But this one is bad."

"They can tell instinctively whether you like them or not," he said. "And of course they are right. There are some fathers who don't like Africans. There is nothing we can do about it."

I suspect the Africans could tell that Brother Aelvoet liked them. He is very down on the Americans, who, as their major contribution to Rwanda's future, are planning a waterworks for Kigali. "Why don't they give books?" is the logical question posed by Aelvoet. To be fair to him, he is down on the others too—on the British because all they've done thus far is offer a few scholarships to Cambridge, and on the Germans because their prime (and as far as I can see utterly selfish) mission is the construction of a powerful radio station to allow them to compete in Africa with the Voice of America, the French-supported Radio Brazzaville, Nasser's station in Cairo, and so forth.

During our conversation late this afternoon in Aelvoet's office (walls hung with spears) I brought up what Ed Lollis had told me about America's offer (when Rwanda became independent in July of 1962) of thirty grants to young Rwandese of the government's choosing to come to the States for five or six months to study anything—nursing, police organization, radio engineering, basket weaving—anything. To date, according to Lollis, only seven Rwandese have been sent. Lollis said various people in the government had been reminded of the standing offer from time to time and the answer, always polite, was invariably: "Oh yes, how interesting." Aelvoet said he thought this was probably the President's decision, it having been his (the President's) experience that many of those who went abroad returned unable to fit back into the life of Kigali. Somehow they had been spoiled.

Most of our talk was naturally about education. "On chasse tout le temps," he said, meaning that the savage weeding-out process never ends. He said there are 302,500 children in Catholic primary schools, another 80,000 in schools run by Protestants. In the Catholic schools (he was talking about the 1964-65 school year), there are 108,951 in the first grade. By the second grade, the number has been pared down to 76,589. In the third grade it's 56,119; in the fourth it's 31,274; in the fifth it's 16,659, and it's about the same in the sixth. In the seventh grade (the start of secondary-school education) they really "chasse"—trimming the number of students down to 1,235. Not that education is so good through the first six grades that students don't need any more. Quite the contrary. Primary classes are taught in double shifts. Half (2,036) of the 4,390 primary-school teachers haven't had more than six years of schooling themselves. Of course there aren't nearly enough books. I can't believe it, but Aelvoet insists that the Rwanda budget allocates 13.5 Rwandese francs per child per annum for education—which is about 13 cents.

"All they send us from Europe and America is technicians," says Aelvoet. "Why don't you send us money?" The same point is made again and again. Count de Borchgrave said the same thing, only he would use the money to reopen the tin mines.

Met one of the technicians tonight for dinner at Le Relais and begin to see just what Aelvoet means. His card describes him as "docteur en droit [and] expert économique international ingénieur-conseil en organisation d'entreprises." An indigestible title and an unpalatable man. He kept calling me "un amour," which I found off-putting. Hates and despises the Africans. Says they are always delighted with the reports prepared for them by experts like himself but never read them and never act on them. From his vantage point as advisor to the Ministry of Finance, he is convinced that the situation is utterly hopeless. There is, he says, no work of any kind going on in any of the ministries, and that he will break his two-year contract and go home because "there is no point in staying where it will do no good." At about that point, they turned off all the lights in Le Relais to show the twice-a-week movie. By insisting on a candle, we succeeded in driving every waiter out of the dining room and finished the rest of our meal in total darkness. On the way out the technician introduced me to a junior minister and we made a date to meet in his office tomorrow.

WEDNESDAY, January 27. *Morning.* Two names for the immediate future: (1) Sylvain Gastellier. Jack knew him vaguely in Nairobi and ran into him again last night. Now living in Bujumbura, where he runs a night club. He has asked us to look him up when we get there. (2) John Bennett, the British ambassador to both Rwanda and Burundi, with headquarters in Bujumbura. He has come up here to sniff around and then attend the "Day of Democracy" celebrations at Gitarama (the President's birthplace) tomorrow. He invited me to ride down to Bujumbura with him, but I explained about my Land-Rover and Jack and he said it might be a good idea to make a convoy out of it anyway. Apparently *laisser-passers* had been required to travel from the Rwanda border to Bujumbura but the American embassy here has called the American embassy there and they aren't needed any more.

Evening. Mr. Wang's soybean party. Long table set with dozens of different soybean dishes—soybean cheese, soybean bread, soybean milk, etc. Several tall Tutsi wives (government officials seem to prefer them to their own kind because Tutsi women tend to be better educated and more refined than Hutu women) sampling this and that and making appropriate noises of appreciation. The Minister of Agriculture, a substantial figure in a dark suit and tie, seemed delighted and disappeared to fetch three ministerial colleagues from the adjacent government buildings. Mr. Wang, clutching his English-into-French interpreter firmly by the arm, used him like a battering ram among the groups of Rwandese officials. The Minister of Agriculture drank some soybean milk and made a face.

"Dlink, dlink," said Mr. Wang encouragingly. His interpreter (I guess he was Mr. Mafura from the Rice Department) seemed hideously embarrassed.

Earlier, appeared at the office of the junior minister for scheduled rendezvous but his door was locked. As usual, the adjacent office was filled with Belgian and French technical advisers who grinned knowingly and said they didn't have the foggiest.

The young Englishman who administers the United Nations program was profoundly pessimistic. When I brought up the subject of unread reports, it reminded him of one of his colleagues who, several years before, had spent some time in a West African country doing some sort of comprehensive study. In due course he submitted his lengthy report and returned to Europe. A few years later he was asked by his superiors to do another stint in the same West African country and he said he'd be delighted. But before he went would they send him their file on the country in question so that he could catch up. They did but when he opened the file all it contained was his old report. In other words, nothing had happened since his departure. The UN man declined the proposed assignment.

Something seems to be terribly wrong with what everybody is doing in Africa. The UN chap in Kigali said it was his experience that Africans expected help but were more than willing to let everybody else do all the work. (If you keep doing somebody's homework for him, and never ask him any tough questions in class, is he ever going to learn anything?) He went on to say that it is always "we" (the foreign technicians and the aid people from the outside) who think up the projects; "we" prepare the studies; "we" get the proper minister's signature on the proper documents; "we" raise the necessary funds, and "we" push it through to completion. The local Africans are seldom if ever *involved*. What the UN man says rings true. I cannot quite imagine a delegation of Rwanda government officials beating on the door of the American embassy and pleading for, demanding that water supply system for Kigali.

Eucalyptus trees wonderful to watch when it's windy. When air is still, the leaves are olive drab. With the wind they are suddenly silver, luminescent, like a school of fish turning, bellies up, under your boat.

THURSDAY, January 28 (Urundi Palace Hotel, Bujumbura, Burundi). *Late night.* It seems a triumph that we are here at all.

Rwanda's Day of Democracy dawned early for us and we loaded the Land-Rover and drove down to Gitarama while the shadows from the trees were still long on the ground. Crowd of several thousand assembled in Gitarama's sloping red dirt square. We got through by saying we were tourists which, since we were the only ones, was the magic password for the occasion. The President seated under a long awning and flanked by members of the government and the diplomatic corps (Withers, Bennett, my "amour" of a French technician, etc.) all armed with cameras. The President's small children on a reed mat at his feet—quiet and well behaved like all African children. The crowd surrounding the open space in front of the President's reviewing stand grinning and enthusiastic.

Many school classes, differently uniformed, in the crowd—including charming group of schoolgirls in red tartan dresses. The program begins with these classes pushed up, one at a time, to the microphone to sing or to dance (often with white schoolmarms looking frantic and clapping hands in the background to keep the rhythm from floundering). Then the dancers, the best of them being Tutsi-type (but too short to be real Tutsis) in long jute headdresses, which they snap like whips. They are surrounded by non-dancing assistants whose job it is to dart in and out picking up articles the dancers have dropped—bells strapped to their ankles, arm bands, spears, bows, arrows. . . . The dances seem based on the leader principle. As the mood seizes him, a dancer leaps forward and for a time becomes the leader, leading the others in new steps. There is much chatter back and forth between the leader and the followers. The leader starts off with what sounds like a very fast "bulubulubulu" and the chorus picks it up: "BULUBULUBULU." I liked best the disorganized and totally unaffected group of Twas who straggled out into the arena (old men, boys, nursing mothers, the lot) and proceeded to have themselves a ball. The Twas are pygmoids, probably the earliest inhabitants of Rwanda, and number about 1 percent of the population. (If they were twice as tall, would that make them 2 percent of the population?) It was almost as if this happy, motley group had been let out for this occasion, were determined to make the most of it, and afterward would be locked up again somewhere.

After an interminable speech by the President in the local language, the crowd broke up. Ambassador Bennett said he would have to stay around for the official reception (to which Jack and I were not invited) and suggested that we drive on ahead. Said he'd be an hour or so behind us.

Heavy rain on the way south and we ate greasy pork sausages out of a tin with our fingers and drank Primus beer until the Rwanda border. There we filled out long questionnaires, including the names of our parents and whether they were living or deceased. Jack joked with the customs people in Swahili and we shook hands and parted friends. At the Burundi border it was a different story. First they found out that Jack had lost his health certificates. Then, after the usual study of each of the many visas in our passports, where were our *laisser-passers?* We told them none were needed. Oh yes they were!

A crowd begins to gather. It is a military matter. Where are the military then? A slovenly-looking man in an unbuttoned gray uniform is pointed out and the crowd disgorges him, pushing him up front. I ask if he can take us to his superior officer. He has none. Makes no motion to get one. So there we are. I make some acid comments about what this sort of thing does for tourism. Jack translates into Swahili but of course it does no good. It does, however, make me feel better. I set one of the cameras on a tripod in front of the customs station and the crowd disperses. Nobody wants his picture taken.

After an hour or so, Ambassador Bennett's gray Land-Rover appears and he gets out. He is accompanied by his African chauffeur (but Bennett has been doing the driving) and the diplomatic representative from the Pays Bas. Bennett has changed from the business suit he wore for the "Day of Democracy" into a khaki bush jacket and a wide-brimmed bush hat. Looks resolute. Sends his driver over to talk to the border officials. "Let him handle this one," he says. "He knows this sort of thing." While all this is going on three trucks arrive driven by three Europeans. Their leader walks up from the road shouting greetings to the customs officials and making loud jokes. He picks out the most disreputable of the hangers-on (dressed in tattered shorts), claps him on the back, and calls him "mon chef." This produces laughter among the others. There is much handshaking and backslapping. Bennett (*sotto voce*) to me: "That's the boy who does the paying." Although I haven't seen it happen, money has changed hands and in no time the road barrier is raised, the three Europeans climb back into their trucks and drive north into Rwanda. They haven't said a word to any of us. Bennett's driver has been negotiating with the officials and it is agreed that a soldier accompany Jack and me while we follow the ambassador's Land-Rover south to Kayanza where there is a prefect who can make a decision. It is almost night now but our new companion continues to wear his dark glasses. He wears an American helmet liner and carries a German Mauser between his knees. He is shy and friendly and speaks enough French to be able to tell me that he likes army life but is worried about a war with Rwanda.

On the outskirts of Kayanza we are stopped by soldiers in camouflage uniforms standing outside a large tent with a fire blazing next to it. A small boy with a case of Primus beer stands hopefully by the wayside. We all get out and the ambassador conducts a lengthy conversation with the lieutenant in charge. Bennett asks the lieutenant to let us through. He will be responsible for us. The lieutenant shakes his head. "If you were in the army," he tells Bennett, "you would know that you cannot disobey the orders of a superior officer no matter what." Bennett tells the lieutenant he is perfectly right and gets his permission to drive on into Kayanza to seek out the prefect. If the prefect says it's all right, then it's all right with the lieutenant. In the meantime, I have succeeded in pressing two hundred francs into the hand of the soldier who traveled with us from the border. I ask him now whether he thinks the lieutenant would be interested in a little *cadeau* too and he says he thinks it would do no harm to try. When I offer the officer three hundred francs, he turns me down. I buy some beer from the boy for our fellow travelers (Bennett has gone on alone) and we warm ourselves by the fire.

At length the ambassador returns with the prefect, a tall, very young man exuding intelligence and authority. He listens while the ambassador explains again that it was his understanding that only residents of Burundi needed *laisser-passers* and that we are travelers who have just entered the country. The prefect nods and, using the hood of the Land-Rover as a table while I hold a flashlight, writes something on a piece of paper. He signs it, asks the ambassador to sign, and then I sign too. We thank him profusely, and I remark to Bennett how reassuring it is to find somebody with a constructive and understanding attitude. Bennett smiles somewhat patronizingly. "The prefect cost me 300 francs," he says. "I'll send you the bill in the morning."

I had bought too much beer and, as we were about to leave, offered the remaining bottles to the soldiers. They talked it over among themselves and then allowed that they would prefer some fresh ones. Bennett said there was only one more roadblock now, just outside Bujumbura, and then we'd be home free. We followed his tail lights and had trouble keeping them in sight because he drove fast and well. The road narrow and winding. Large trucks, coming in the opposite direction, pulled over to one side politely and stopped to allow us to pass.

And then, with the lights of Bujumbura twinkling below, the final roadblock. Soldiers drunk and offensive. The ambassador's Land-Rover had stopped before us and I got out of mine in time to see him lean across the passenger in the front seat and shout: "C'est absolument défendu!" What the soldiers wanted to do was search the ambassador's vehicle. Apparently this was the last straw for Bennett. The soldiers started menacing him with their rifles. One of them said something about "Le loi est le loi," and Bennett shouted in English that he knew a bloody bit more about the law than they did.

Would they immediately get him Bujumbura on the telephone before it all became a grave diplomatic incident? It was a splendid performance and I could almost hear the martial strains of Rule Britannia—Bennett sitting there, his nose three inches from the muzzle of a rifle, roaring like a lion. Marvelous. Then, for no reason that I could discern, the soldiers collapsed. Bennett waited until they had checked our passports too (somehow the soldiers didn't seem to want to look at *anything* any more) and we drove bumper to bumper into Bujumbura.

A delicious meal at the St. Michel restaurant—whisky, huge filets mignons, Burgundy, then brandy. Jack's friend Gastellier and his girl Jeannine appeared for coffee and drove us to his night club where (because Jack suddenly remembered it was his birthday) we drank two bottles of champagne. Jack went outside and was hugely sick, returned, and together we finished a third bottle of champagne.

I think it has been a long day.

CHAPTER 11

A KINGDOM OF MANY TENDENCIES

It will depend altogether upon the leader . . . whether their worst or best qualities shall prevail.

—H. M. STANLEY

EVERY night at 9 P.M. curfew descended on Bujumbura with a roar of motors, with squealing tires and vanishing tail lights. As the hour approached the waiters in the restaurants became highly nervous. Dessert appeared with the *tournedos* and table linen was whisked away before the coffee was finished. More often than not the waiters did not linger for their tips but jogged off in packs down the dark streets that lead to the native city. Apparently there was safety in numbers. During my two-week stay in the capital of Burundi, I could never find out why the curfew had been imposed, or, for that matter, who had imposed it. Not that there weren't good and sufficient reasons for a curfew. Only a few days before my arrival, the Prime Minister had been gunned down by an assassin just nine hours after taking the oath of office. Although the assassin, a refugee Tutsi from Rwanda embarrassingly employed as a clerk in the American embassy, had been arrested and had confessed, there were any number of accomplices still at large.

Then, while the Americans were still expecting the worst, the King of Burundi, Mwami Mwambutsa IV, confounded almost everybody by ordering the entire staff of the Chinese Communist embassy out of his kingdom without delay. And in the Belge, the African section of Bujumbura, the soldiers were making arrests, finding hidden supplies of arms, and shooting those who tried to crash their roadblocks. If the situation cried out for a curfew, it also called for an explanation. The explanation never came. I was told that the Mwami himself had tried to get the curfew lifted so that he could resume his tour of the kingdom's night clubs. The king was a great twister. They all said that about Mwambutsa IV. As a matter of fact, that's the first thing they always said about the Mwami, that he was a great twister. The second thing they told you was that he had a white girl friend. It was obvious that he had a way with women.

"C'est sure," said the proprietress of my favorite bar, her fingers fondling the orange spit curls at her temples, "qu'il est pas du tout pédérast."

Considerable as they were, the Mwami's powers were insufficient to the occasion on the night he sent his blonde companion looking for the minister in charge of curfews. She could not find him and returned to the palace. The curfew remained in effect. Her inability to find the minister jibed with my own experience in various government offices. Almost invariably the offices of those in command were empty, the explanation being that they were "en ville." In Bujumbura "en ville" meant "on the town." Having found so few of them in their offices during office hours, I asked one of the many Belgian advisers attached to the government what government officials did when they weren't behind their desks.

"They like to drive cars and have accidents," he said. He intimated that it could not go on like this forever. Recently, four out of five newly arrived Volkswagens, earmarked for government business, had been demolished on the day after their arrival, and it was only a question of time, he was sure, before the ministers went back to bicycles. What the adviser said was only partially true. Judging by the number of arrests (both announced and rumored) which followed the Prime Minister's assassination, it seemed clear that having accidents was not the sole occupation of government employees.

"We have," said Amadée Kabugubugu, the Minister for Information, Immigration and Security, "already discovered one large plot and at least two sub-plots."

By tradition and temperament, conspiracy was the national pastime. For the outsider it was a bewildering game. The Belgian ambassador started to explain.

"You see, monsieur," he said, "in Burundi there are many tendencies. . . ." Having said that, he stopped, looked at me with a smile, and spread his hands. He knew, and I knew, that it was just no good. Even if he could explain things to me (which was unlikely) I would never be able to explain them to anybody else. Sufficient to say that it was not a simple case of Tutsi versus Hutu (as seemed to be the situation in Rwanda) but of Tutsis and Hutus in alliance against other Tutsis and Hutus, a witch's brew of ancient feuds, curses and prophecies. The Mwami held the recipe. Only he knew which ingredients should go into the pot and at what stage. Being the sort of chef he was, he also realized that too many cooks would spoil the broth. Hence the expulsion of the Chinese—even before they had had a chance to open a restaurant.

Before coming to Burundi, I had heard and read much about the Chinese and their activities in the kingdom. If Zanzibar was their bridgehead into Africa, Burundi was their command post, their center of operations. Here it was that they were training Tutsi warriors to fight on the rebel side in the Congo and for an invasion of Rwanda. It was in Burundi that they were coaching Gaston Soumialot, the so-called Defense Minister of the Congolese rebels, in the techniques of revolution and guerrilla warfare, and it was from Bujumbura that Chinese arms were smuggled across the Ruzizi River into the Congo. In addition, the Chinese discovered what the Belgians had known all along—that the ruling circles of Burundi, being both aristocratic and sophisticated, were highly susceptible to bribery. Plain, unmarked envelopes from the Chinese embassy had become a staple of the capital's economy. All this I had heard before entering Burundi. What I learned after my arrival was largely in the nature of confirmation and amplification.

The curfew had not rung down on Bujumbura nor had the Chinese been expelled when I first arrived in the capital and I learned of these events not by receiving the information directly but through osmosis. Not any osmosis of mine—but other people's. At breakfast on the wide veranda of our hotel on Saturday morning, Jack announced that he didn't like this place. He could not explain why. It was just a feeling he had. I tried to cheer him up by offering him a bottle of Spit (a local carbonated beverage that comes in eight delicious flavors). He drank it gingerly and was not particularly amused. Later we ate lunch with Sylvain Gastellier in back of his night club, the Harlequin. Gastellier's girl, Jeannine, was fashioning bracelets and earrings out of bits of ceramic and copper wire in the corner of the porch, and from where we sat we could see across the northern tip of Lake Tanganyika to the mountains beyond. Occasionally we could hear the boom of a mortar shell coming from the Congolese side of the lake but the sky was blue, the drinks were cool, and the atmosphere was generally peaceful. Then Gastellier, who had apparently not been following the conversation, said out of the blue that something was afoot. Like Jack, he didn't know what it was. But various ministers had not been appearing in their usual haunts. Even the Mwami hadn't been around lately, either at the Harlequin or the Yacht Club. (Like all Belgians in Bujumbura, he pronounced it Yascht Clube.) He had not spent all his life in Africa not to feel certain things.

We met again for dinner and Gastellier said we had better order now because of the curfew. What curfew? He was astonished that we hadn't heard about the curfew at the hotel. No, it hadn't been announced over the radio and of course I couldn't have read about it in the newspapers because there were no newspapers, but it was all over town. Everybody knew. Halfway through dinner, Gastellier got up, wandered over to the bar and returned to report that the Mwami had just sent his troops to surround the Chinese embassy and that the Chinese were about to be kicked out of Bujumbura. There had been no announcement over the radio about that either, and it was not until Sunday evening that the government made its decision known to the public. The government, acting in the name of the Mwami, had the "regret to announce to the ambassador of the Popular Republic of China in Bujumbura that existing diplomatic relations between the two countries are momentarily suspended from this day. The government begs the ambassador of the

Popular Republic and Chinese diplomatic personnel accredited through the embassy of the Popular Republic of China in Bujumbura to return to their country as soon as possible." This being Burundi there was, of course, no official explanation for the move nor was one forthcoming during my stay in the country.

Having told the Chinese to get out of their country without delay, the Burundis kept them in their hilltop embassy until Tuesday (I suppose to give them the opportunity to distribute the last of their plain, unmarked envelopes). Then, flanked fore and aft by truckloads of armed soldiers, they were driven to the airport, where they waited for several hours in the hot sun for their chartered airplane to arrive. I drove to the airport with a reporter who had flown to Bujumbura from Leopoldville to witness their departure, but we were stopped at the entrance to the field by a man from Sabena Airlines who told us with obvious relish how sorry he was that there could be no witnesses to or photographs taken of the Chinese departure.

At the American embassy there were no signs of jubilation.

"We may be next," said one official gloomily. But why? Hadn't the ouster of the Chinese put the Western democracies one up in Burundi?

"Not necessarily," he replied. He did not know why not. It was just a feeling he had.

The Belgian ambassador seemed positively mandarin. He smiled a secret, inner smile when asked why it had happened, said "there are many tendencies" and then broke off. It had become a joke. Since I had presented the ambassador with a calling card bearing a London address, perhaps the ambassador thought I was British. He certainly made no bones about the fact that he did not think America's fortunes in Burundi had necessarily improved with the expulsion. Was this perhaps (the slow mandarin smile again) because the Americans were not quite . . . clever?

"What are they all doing in that big embassy of theirs?" he asked. "They certainly aren't contributing anything to the development of Burundi. And they are always so curious, always so terribly eager to know what is going on, always calling us up and asking whether we have heard such and such. . . ." I got the distinct impression that one of the foundation stones of Belgian foreign policy in Burundi was never to give the Americans the time of day.

Whatever the reason for the Chinese expulsion, I was pleased to see that the United States embassy did not view it in terms of a sudden awakening on the part of the Burundi government to the threat of World Communism or claim a triumph for the West. My own view was that the Chinese were asked to go because they had been caught meddling in the Mwami's brew—and because the Mwami discovered they were boors.

They were clods. They used the wrong forks. Worst of all they were pushy. At one diplomatic reception, the Chinese ambassador, Liu Yu Feng, kept sidling up to the Mwami with his interpreter and trying to start a conversation. A clear case of protocolar bad breath. The Chinese ambassador and his interpreter were so pushy, in fact, that the Mwami finally turned on them and said: "I only speak to ambassadors who know French." And on Sundays the Chinese would crowd into the front pew at the cathedral and hiss and giggle through the mass. Being the kind of Catholic he was the Mwami found it impossible to overlook this kind of behavior.

For Gastellier, the curfew was the final straw. It meant the closing of his night club, his last source of revenue in Bujumbura. Burundi was no longer for him. He would try Rwanda. There was going to be some construction work in Kigali and the Rwandese (because they had always been at the tail end of the Belgian administrative network which began in Leopoldville) hadn't yet learned about corruption. Unspoiled. Here in Bujumbura you could get nothing without bribing for it. Gastellier was sick of it, and now the curfew. No, it was too much. . . .

There were many Belgians in Bujumbura who did not agree with Gastellier, who argued, with considerable logic I thought, that the one thing which kept Burundi's head above water *was* corruption. It was corruption which oiled the wheels of commerce. Take away the lubricant and the wheels would stop. It was really quite simple, they said. The members of His Majesty's government did not care about the economic future of Burundi. What they cared about was getting their cut. To accommodate the steadily lengthening list of ministers on their payrolls, the importers of consumer goods (to take just one category) simply asked the manufacturers in Belgium or wherever to make out a bill for double the actual price of the goods. The importers in Bujumbura would make out a check for the inflated amount. The manufacturer would pocket half (or the true value of his merchandise), deposit the other half in the importer's European bank account, then send his products down to Burundi, where (depending on his governmental obligations) the importer would double and even triple the already inflated price on his merchandise.

Since everybody seemed to be in on the act, and each importer had already taken the precaution of ensuring that he was the sole agent for whatever it was he was importing, no harm was done—except, of course, that the price of everything kept going higher and higher. Even the Belgian technical advisers, paid by their government to run the various government departments while the Burundi ministers were "en ville," found they could do little to counteract the system. Whenever they remonstrated with their chiefs, they would be asked bluntly who they thought was running this department anyway? In case they hadn't heard, Burundi was independent now. The system bothered me not because of its immorality but because it hit me in my own pocketbook. During my stay in Bujumbura the price of cigarettes went up three times. Five days after I had moved into my hotel room, a mimeographed notice was pasted to my bathroom mirror informing the "chers clients" that room charges were being augmented 40 percent. Then, just as I had arranged with a black market contact for an exchange of some of my few remaining dollars into Burundi francs at a favorable rate, the banks closed and devaluation was announced. The black market, stunned, confused and in disarray, went into hiding. I took a terrible beating.

In following Stanley's trail through Africa, the countries I had visited thus far had all been infused with a certain idealism—however misplaced, chauvinistic or bigoted. Burundi set itself apart from the others by being at all times utterly cynical. Together the black ruling classes of the kingdom and the white *commerçants* formed an alliance of mutual corruption and the outsiders (the peasants and the foreign advisers and technicians) either fell in with the arrangement or did nothing about it. There was no one I met in Bujumbura who was not, in one way or another, cynical.

A member of the staff of the Belgian embassy, with whom I had a series of long conversations, said he had fought off the cynicism which had infected his colleagues as long as possible. But, like the others, he had been forced to give in to it.

"It is very sad," he told me one day. "I have had many Africans to my house. Once, twice, three times, four times, seven times and then, when everything is going well and I think they're truly my friends, they come for the eighth time and they ask me for money. I give them money. It isn't much but they never return the money. And what is really sad is that they too do not return. I invite them again. The money means little to me and I would prefer to forget about it. But I never see them again in my house."

Then he leaned forward and dropped his voice.

"Do not put this in your book," he said, "but it was the same with the late Prime Minister. He came, oh, ten times and the eleventh time he asked for money. It was about $200 in your money and I gave it to him. I never saw him again either. He was a good man, too. One of the best in Burundi."

At dinner one evening at the British ambassador's, the representative of a large petroleum company said he didn't mind bribing Africans, and that, as a matter of fact, he would be all for increasing the size of the bribes if it meant keeping them out of the management end of his business. But now, no longer satisfied with just taking their cut, they had got it into their heads that they could run things too. This caused him no end of problems. Under government pressure, he had brought several into his office and their presence meant that his own workload had increased to the point where he seriously wondered whether he could go on.

"They can't seem to tell the difference between what is important and what is not," he said of his Burundi executives. "They come in with the silliest and most inconsequential questions. What is more, they are incapable of any real sustained work. Some days they are in the office. On others they are simply not. One of them—and I am not exaggerating—has had his mother die eight times in the past year. This was his excuse for taking the day off. Every once in a while, I ask them to meet me in my office and I try to tell them the meaning, and the reward, of hard work. I tell them about how I myself rose to my present position, how I went to night school for fifteen years, paying for it out of the money I earned in the daytime. Now *we* pay *them* to go to night school but we're lucky if they appear two out of four evenings."

Variations were played against different backdrops but the theme was always the same. After giving me my first lesson in water skiing on Lake Tanganyika (the crocodiles stayed close to the banks so it was best to practice a certain distance from the shore) a friend told me of a European plantation which had been turned into an African cooperative after independence. Immediately, he said, there was an argument as to who should control the cooperative's finances and have physical possession of the keys to the safe. After much debate, it was decided that each member of the cooperative was to be allowed to carry the key for one day. It was to work on a rotating basis.

"You can be sure," said my friend, "that the third man in line never saw the money."

I asked what had happened and my friend began to choke with laughter.

"At last report," he said, "the Food and Agriculture Organization had sent in a team and do you know what they're doing? They're studying the constitution of the cooperative."

At the Circle Hyppique, where Belgians dressed in white jodhpurs and red hunting jackets jumped their horses around a floodlighted area, my host said that most Burundi politicians didn't give a damn about their constituents. All they cared was that things look right. Shortly after independence, he himself had attended the gala opening of a hoe factory at which one of the ministers had made a long speech hailing this enterprise as still another in a series of government-sponsored attacks on unemployment. The hoe factory employed exactly eight people but, still, it was a step in the right direction. However, when my Circle Hyppique host congratulated the factory's European manager on providing Burundi with eight new jobs, the manager laughed derisively.

"Do you think I would hire Burundis?" he asked. "Certainly not. All eight are from the Congo."

Even the Americans found their optimism withering in Burundi. At the United States Information Service library, I was told by a bitter public servant that as far as he was concerned all this talk about a worldwide "thirst for knowledge" was so much rot. Here in Bujumbura, he said, the most popular books were the large ones—fat, imposing volumes which they could take to their friends and say: "See how important I am. The Americans trust me with their most valuable books." Of course, he added, they never read these books. The first few pages were thumbed and greasy, but the rest were untouched and unread.

I suppose one of the reasons there was so much corruption in Burundi was that those involved knew it could not go on like this forever. This gave Bujumbura an eat-drink-and-be-merry-for-tomorrow-we-die atmosphere. The Tutsi feudal structure, already watered down with Hutus, would have to go someday. The question was not so much when but what—what would replace it? Would there be a proletarian revolution or would there be something else again?

The behavior of the Belgians in Burundi (when they were not bribing officials or fawning over the Mwami and his retinue) was certainly not designed to ingratiate the white community with the masses. At dinner one evening, Marie Jose, an attractive Belgian girl, talked about what it was like being the companion of an African. The man in question, sitting with us, was a tall, highly intelligent Tutsi named Didan Binagwaho, a physician. Being a Tutsi from Rwanda made him slightly suspect in the social circles of Bujumbura and now, because he had a white girl friend, life had become even more of a problem. Marie Jose said it was even worse for her. In Belgium, an association with an African was difficult but not impossible. Here, however, she was considered a traitor to her race.

The Belgians of Bujumbura, she said, were behaving as badly as possible, not only toward her but, more to the point, toward all Africans who, in their opinion, did not count. In Africa, the Belgians copied the English colonialists and called their African house servants "boys." Affluent Africans picked up the practice too—the only difference being that the Africans paid their "boys" less and treated them worse. In Bujumbura, Marie Jose said, "boys" are sent into town each morning armed with lists supplied by their mistresses to do the shopping and, since the "boys" tend to arrive at the shops at about the same time, long lines form before the counters.

"The shopkeepers," said Marie Jose, "always ask the boys whom they work for, and if they answer with the name of a white master they are served first. Those who work for African masters are served last."

She also remembered walking into a butcher shop and automatically taking her place in line behind six "boys."

"Come up here, my dear," the proprietress told her in a loud voice, "and let me serve you before these macaques." To Africans, the word *macaque* connotes something far more derogatory than "monkey." Marie Jose added that she guessed the proprietress of the meat market hadn't heard about her relationship with Dr. Binagwaho.

Listening to Marie Jose and others like her, it seemed logical to assume that there must surely follow a massive revulsion against this kind of behavior—a popular rising up of the people united, for the first time, by a common loathing of Europeans. But there was at least one individual in Bujumbura, a somewhat mysterious old white man who shuttled between government ministries and the Belge, speaking neither in French nor in Swahili but in all the local languages, who thought differently. Yes, he said, the Belgians were behaving with incredible stupidity. Being a Belgian himself, he knew how stupid Belgians could be. But by the time the phlegmatic Burundis got around to translating their resentment into action, there wouldn't be any Belgians left in Bujumbura to act against. The heady spiral of prices and profits which I saw about me in Bujumbura was a last-gasp effort to make hay before the sun sank (perhaps forever) behind the horizon. It could not last for much longer. One did not need to travel far beyond the city limits of Bujumbura to discover that the Belgians who really counted—the planters—had already left. Without them the economy was grinding to a halt. The explanation for this was, perhaps, unpleasant but it was simple, he said. Before independence, the whites had ruled Burundi by force. There was no other word for it. To get the ground cleared for coffee, or for tea or cotton, you had to employ vast hordes of natives. And to get them to work you had to beat them. You did not beat them all the time. You beat them only occasionally, when the situation warranted it, but often enough so that they knew they would be beaten if they did not work.

With independence, however, it was no longer possible to beat the natives. Consequently, it had become impossible to grow coffee profitably. The natives were still growing coffee but only enough to buy the necessities. With the Europeans pulling out, who was there to make the peasants prune the coffee trees and hold back the hungry jungle? The answer was no one. The chiefs had been stripped of their power and the *bourgomestres* installed in their place owed their positions to the people and, for that reason, did not dare make them work. What would happen next? Well, if the old white man could make a guess, it would be a return to tribalism. The passions which divided the Africans were far stronger than any which might unite them. They would break up into the old, the traditional tribal units. It would not be quite like the Africa which existed before the white man came. (He said that almost regretfully.) No, it would be something strange and ugly, like a defective child.

"It will be an Africa I hope I do not live to see. And yet I have already seen it," he said. "An Africa of fortified cities with roads between them on which only armed convoys will move. The rest will be tribalism, chaos, anarchy, banditry and disorganized, vicious rebel movements. . . . It has already happened . . . in the Congo."

I had, by this time, decided to travel alone into the Congo. When I told Jack that the time had come for us to part, he was delighted. Nairobi seemed to be the best place to sell the Land-Rover and, since Jack lived there anyway, we determined that he should drive it, together with our camping equipment and other odds and ends I had collected, back to Nairobi via Rwanda and Uganda. It was wise, we agreed, to avoid Tanzania. We spent the next two days gathering the appropriate government papers and were assured, finally, that Jack possessed everything required to recross the border into Rwanda. In a last-minute spur-of-the-moment decision, Gastellier agreed with Jeannine that it made good sense for her to accompany Jack to Nairobi. She might be able to sell her costume jewelry to one of the tourist shops and perhaps even make arrangements to furnish the shop with a continuing supply. The afternoon before their departure, Jeannine gave me lessons on her motor scooter. I could use it until her return. They left at dawn the following morning. I had put more than five thousand miles on the Land-Rover since Dar es Salaam without suffering so much as a flat tire. Feeling suddenly stranded and alone, I watched it drive away with genuine regret. A noble, uncomplaining and utterly dependable vehicle.

Late that afternoon, I returned to my hotel on Jeannine's motor scooter to find the Land-Rover parked in front and Jack slouched over a bottle of Spit on the veranda. He had been gone about eight hours and his language, as he told me what had happened, was foul. He and Jeannine had negotiated all the roadblocks on the road to the Rwanda frontier but at the Burundi side of the border they were told they lacked a permit to export the vehicle. Jack had pleaded; he had argued; he had tried bribery; but in the end there was nothing for it but to return to Bujumbura. He had left Jeannine at the border, he said—waiting for a lift to Kigali, where she had friends who could put her up for the night.

We had spent hours in government bureaus collecting every document known to Burundi officialdom—and now this! I exploded. With Jack, I went to every ministry I had been to before and, noisily and deliberately, lost my temper in each one of them. It was, I shouted, a shocking performance. Who was running the Kingdom of Burundi anyway—the government or a bunch of drunken louts on the border? We had come here as innocent and friendly tourists, only to be treated with suspicion and hostility. Our documents and our actions proved we were neither spies nor saboteurs. Why, we didn't even look like Chinese Communists! I produced consternation among the officials but no action. Then Jack took over and, through the deft intervention of the British ambassador, managed to secure the proper document in about fifteen minutes. I suggested to Jack that he spend the night in Bujumbura and try again the next morning but he said it would be better if he left immediately. He was, he said, worried about Jeannine.

My final days in Bujumbura were nerve-racking ones in which I did not know, from one moment to the next, whether I would get into the Congo or, indeed, whether I would be able to get out of Burundi.

The morning after Jack's second departure I received a telephone call at my hotel from the man from the USIS. He couldn't say what it was. He couldn't talk about it over the telephone but it was urgent. Would I come to the embassy as soon as possible? When we met, he was visibly agitated. A coded message had just arrived from the American embassy in Leopoldville pertaining to me. I asked whether I could read it. No, he replied, it was marked "Classified" but he would tell me roughly what it contained. With that, he disappeared into the embassy communications room and emerged a few moments later with a piece of paper in his hand. No, he wouldn't read it to me word for word but the gist of it, according to the notes I made as he paraphrased the message, was as follows:

"The American Embassy Leopoldville urgently requests that the Embassy Bujumbura dissuade Mr. Littell from taking the trip as advised in the telegram from Embassy Bujumbura. Leopoldville advises that any route from Kindu to Stanleyville is teeming with rebels. There is great danger of being made prisoner to the national detriment."

I asked what about my detriment if captured but the USIS man did not think that was in the least bit funny.

"And I must add," he said, "that if you leave here and travel on to Albertville the American consul in Elisabethville has instructions to stop you there."

The message worried me considerably. I had spent most of the week before in an elaborate and painstaking investigation of the ways and means of entering the Congo, settling finally on the weekly lake steamer from Bujumbura to Albertville—a voyage which included a one-day stopover at the Tanzanian port of Kigoma. Kigoma was just a few miles north of Ujiji where Stanley first met Livingstone and uttered history's prize-winning banality ("Dr. Livingstone, I presume?"). The boat was operated by the Compagnie des Chemins de Fer du Congo Supérieur aux Grands Lacs Africans, better known as the C.F.L., and from its representatives in Bujumbura I learned that "in principle" the company might (by lake steamer, rail and riverboat) get me all the way to Stanleyville. Of course progress would depend on the "situation" and how "normal" it was. Right now the situation was anything but normal but there was always a chance that it might become so. The C.F.L. would not sell me a ticket to Albertville until I obtained a military pass from the commander of the Albertville district. In the course of securing this permit, the Albertville commander changed from a French military adviser called Badoux to a Belgian called Badou to a Congolese who pronounced it the same way. Only he spelled it with an "M"—M'Badu.

Officially, the Americans could do nothing but try to talk me out of my proposed trip. Unofficially, however (and the Americans were doing many unofficial things in the Congo), there was much they could do. One word, for instance, to Major Badoux-Badou-M'Badu and my venture was over.

I sought out Thompson Buchanan, the embassy's second-in-command, and explained that it was not my intention to get myself captured. As a reporter with some experience in situations of this kind, I knew how to weigh the odds, when to go forward and when to take to my heels. I was cautious by nature, I told him, and would have no hesitation about turning back. But at the same time—as a reasonably responsible American citizen with a not entirely lunatic mission—I should be allowed to try. Buchanan said he would transmit my plea to Leopoldville.

I thought I had made a presentable case for myself. Overnight, however, the situation changed completely, and early the next morning Thompson called me back to the embassy. His expression as I entered his office was that of a truant officer confronting a particularly delinquent juvenile.

"What in God's name have you been up to in Bujumbura?" he asked. I said I didn't know what he was talking about.

"You seem to have insulted every minister in the kingdom," he said. Several heated complaints had been addressed personally to the ambassador.

"Apparently you said certain things," Buchanan was consulting some notes on his desk. "You said something about not being a Chinese Communist. . . ."

I admitted that perhaps this had been unfortunate.

"And it also says here," Buchanan continued, still studying his notes, "that you called one of them a 'sale nègre.' "

I told Buchanan that this was wholly untrue. I had never called anybody a "dirty nigger" before and it was unlikely, no matter how great the provocation, that I would start now. The words simply were not in my vocabulary. But it interested me that I should be accused of using this kind of language. It always came to the same thing, didn't it? White against black. Whatever I had or had not said, the fact remained that I had ruffled the feeling of several ministries at a time when even a slight ripple in the diplomatic pond could turn into a tidal wave. Would the government hold the American embassy responsible for my behavior? At Buchanan's strong suggestion, I drafted a long letter of apology to the ministers involved, saying that I had not meant to give offense and blaming my outburst on a congenital aversion to red tape—a distaste, I pointed out, acquired not in Burundi but in my own country. The letter was duly translated into French and copies distributed by embassy messenger. Buchanan said he thought we could consider the incident closed.

Three days before my scheduled departure for Albertville, Jeannine returned from Nairobi by plane and reported that Jack had behaved oddly on their overland trip back to Kenya. He had, she said, offered her one of my cameras "as a personal gift from him." Then, on reaching the outskirts of Nairobi, he had deposited her in one of the city's most inaccessible hotels with the promise that he would call for her that evening. That was the last she had seen of him. That evening, I wrote Jack a long letter reminding him of his promise to see to the sale of my Land-Rover and the return of my photographic equipment, my books and other paraphernalia to London.*

My last weekend in Bujumbura passed pleasantly enough—in water skiing on Lake Tanganyika and in a luxuriously long and liquory luncheon with Jeannine, Sylvain and a UN girl who held my hand, read the lines in my palm and said that I was about to go through a period of great danger. But, she added, I would survive. We all drank to that. On Monday, I got up early and gave my last suit to my room boy. Not only was it in tatters but I wanted to travel light.

At breakfast I was handed a note from the Immigration Department requesting me to report immediately. Boarding Jeannine's motor scooter, I rode over to the Immigration office, where an official asked me (ominously, I thought) what I had *really* been doing in Bujumbura. Even to my own ears, my recital of my efforts to retrace Stanley's steps through Africa sounded fraudulent. I ended by asking the official what he wished to see me about?

He replied by saying that it was not he, himself, who wished to see me but the minister, Monsieur Kabugubugu. What about? Ah, that was something he could not say. Would a rendezvous at 3 P.M. suit Monsieur? It would not, I said, because I was leaving that very day for Albertville and had been instructed by the C.F.L. to report to the pier for the necessary formalities no later than 3:30. We argued pleasantly and compromised on 2:30. Meanwhile, if Monsieur would be so kind, would he please hand over his passport? It

* Three months after he left Bujumbura, Jack surfaced again in Nairobi and was persuaded to turn in the Land-Rover. In that period he had added another five thousand miles and subtracted several hundred pounds sterling from its potential selling price. Then, according to the police, he disappeared completely—with my camera and much of my equipment. I have since heard that he made his way to South Africa, but the authorities there have written me to say that his whereabouts "cannot be established."

would, of course, be returned to Monsieur *after* his interview with the minister.

I spent the next hours in a deep and growing gloom. What *had* I really been doing in Burundi? I had done a little black marketing in currency. I had also been seen talking to a diamond smuggler who carried his wares in a matchbox. Although I hadn't bought his diamonds, I couldn't *prove* that I hadn't.

After lunch, Gastellier drove me to Immigration. It was 2:30. A messenger was sprawled in an easy chair in the anteroom, fast asleep.

"Africa at work," said Gastellier. He knocked at the door of the office. There was no response. He tried a second door and the clerk who appeared at the entrance said he did not know when his superior would return. We waited.

"You must accustom yourself to the rhythm of the country," said Gastellier.

"I can't," I said.

"Neither can I," he replied. Gastellier knocked again on the door to the main office.

"Monsieur Bernard," he shouted through the door. There was no response, but in the silence that followed we could hear a key turn. Gastellier tried the door handle. It was locked. For a few moments we stood there, looking at the door. Then Gastellier had an idea. Leaving the anteroom, he walked outside and around to the barred window of the locked office.

"Bonjour, Monsieur Bernard," I heard him say. Monsieur Bernard came to the window and the two men shook hands through the bars. Gastellier explained again that I had a boat to catch. Monsieur Bernard seemed astonished.

"But why are you here?" he asked. "Your rendezvous is with Monsieur Kabugubugu in his office in the Ministry of Information, Immigration and Security. It is not here."

Gastellier and I raced over to the ministry. There were several Africans in business suits outside the minister's office and I explained to them that I had an appointment with the minister for which I was, regretfully, already late. They disappeared into the minister's office, closing the door behind them. It was now after 3 P.M. I was alone with a tall secretary who was sticking Scotch tape onto the back of a loose-leaf calendar in an effort to bind the unattached pages into a book. Every time she opened the book, however, the pages fell apart. At 3:30 the minister's door opened and one of the men in a business suit motioned me inside. Kabugubugu was standing behind his desk. He was a tall man and his face was serious as he shook my hand and pointed out a chair for me. The men in the business suits were already seated in chairs on either side of me. Kabugubugu opened a manila folder on his desk and riffled through some typewritten pages. Then he looked up at me and said:

"You are well known to us."

My eyes dropped to the folder on his desk and I thought I recognized, upside down, the letter of apology I had written at the American embassy's request.

"Oh," I said. "I see that Monsieur le Ministre has received my letter."

Kabugubugu looked puzzled. No, he had received no letter from me. What he had before him was my dossier, a report on my distasteful behavior. Apparently I had menaced various members of his staff. Was this true? I replied that I certainly had lost my temper, and that I was deeply sorry for this, but that menacing people was not part of my character.

"But, monsieur," interjected the man on my left, "it seems in your character to get very angry."

"And is it true," said the man on my right, "that you said you would write against tourism in Burundi?"

The minister's eyes went back to the dossier and he shook his head. Had I, he asked, also made some remarks about spies and about Chinese Communists?

It had, indeed, been an unfortunate thing to say. I wished to apologize again. I had been very *stupide*. The heads around the room nodded in agreement. It was 4 P.M. I was sure that there was sweat on my forehead. Was there anything I could do to make amends, I asked the minister? In my mind, I could see the gangways of my ship being raised, the mooring lines unleashed . . .

"J'étais stupide," I said weakly. "Très, très stupide."

For a full minute Kabugubugu studied me in silence. Then he closed the dossier on his desk and stood up. He extended his hand and returned my passport.

"Au revoir, monsieur," he said. There was the faintest trace of a smile on his face. "I hope you have found that we are not all savages here."

Gastellier, who had been waiting for me in his car, had the motor going before my hand reached for the door handle.

"You were lucky," he said.

The ship was still at the pier when we arrived and I passed through the embarkation formalities without trouble. The captain showed me to my cabin and then disappeared into the pilot house. There were shouted commands; the ship's engines began to throb and we nosed out past the jetty into the lake just as the sun sank behind the hills on the Congo side.

I stood on the deck for a while, watching the lights of Bujumbura flicker on, one by one, and then went into my cabin and brought out a bottle of Scotch. I had just finished my first swallow when there was a knock on the door. I opened it to find an Arab wearing a striped nightshirt and a wide grin. He motioned me out onto the deck and pointed to the water below. There, standing up in the cockpit of their speedboat, were Jeannine and Gastellier. Their boat made a spanking noise as it hit the waves. Gastellier gave me a thumbs-up sign and I raised the bottle of Scotch and toasted them. They circled the steamer three times and then, in an arc of foam, roared away toward the lights of Bujumbura.

LAKE TRIP TO ALBERTVILLE

Here were a number of youths suffering under that strange disease peculiar to vain youth in all lands which Mirambo had called "big head." The manner in which they strutted about, their big looks and bold staring . . . were most offensive.

—H. M. Stanley

According to a bronze plaque mounted on her forward deck, the *Urundi* had been built in Belgium in 1926. Like Stanley's *Lady Alice*, she had been built in sections and then assembled in Africa. The *Lady Alice* was designed so that she could be dismantled easily, carried overland for long distances on the shoulders of the expedition's *pagazis*, and then put together again for use on Lakes Victoria and Tanganyika and on the Lualaba and Congo rivers. Once assembled at the C.F.L. boatyards in Albertville, the *Urundi* and her sister ship, the *Baron Dhanis*, were supposed to have stayed in one piece. Since the end of August, however, the *Baron Dhanis* had been sinking ever so slowly and gently into the mud of the Albertville harbor. The holes in her hull had been put there by exiles from Castro's Cuba piloting American fighter planes. The air raid took place on the final day of the rebel occupation of Albertville and even now, six months later, was a subject that the well-mannered personnel of the C.F.L. avoided when in the company of Americans.

Fifteen minutes after leaving Bujumbura, Captain Freddie Lallemand slowed the *Urundi* and took in tow two large barges which were anchored and waiting in the middle of the lake. The barges looked like freighters but they had no engines. There were women and children as well as crew members on board and the women had charcoal fires going under the cooking pots on deck. When the cables had been secured to the barges, Captain Lallemand came down from the pilot house and said I would be welcome to have beer in his cabin. We were joined by two ship's officers and my cabinmate, a lanky, elderly man who had decided to stay on in Africa after his retirement to serve as an adviser on economic affairs in the Burundi Prime Minister's office. He was on his way now to Dar es Salaam, where he planned to take a Polish freighter to Europe for a brief vacation before returning to Africa.

"I am a German," he told me in English. "From *West* Germany."

The captain's cabin was small but Lallemand had things organized. There was an icebox in the adjacent pantry filled with cold beer. Lallemand called it a "frigo." Next to the frigo was a closet which Lallemand kept locked. It contained the ship's arsenal—a machine gun, an automatic weapon or two, and some small arms and ammunition. One never knew when one might have to defend oneself, Lallemand said, although it had been more peaceful on board since the company had decided to close the ship's bar and restaurant. Before then, especially when the *Urundi* was docked in Albertville during the time of the rebels, everybody came on board, cadging drinks, ordering meals in the lounge and then not paying for them. It was better now but even so he always made sure his guns were cleaned and oiled.

Beer bottle in hand, the old German grew voluble. Beer was what made Africa go around, wasn't it? The others nodded. Without beer Africa would stop. The big *brasserie* in Bujumbura was the only thing in that country that worked any more. It worked night and day. Three hundred thousand bottles of beer a day, and still it wasn't enough. We all had another beer ourselves and the captain said the thirst for beer in Bujumbura was nothing compared to that in the Congo.

"Do you know why they have moved the government of North Katanga from Albertville to Kamina?" he asked. The others grinned knowingly but the Captain went on anyway. "In Kamina there is nothing. If you exclude the old Belgian air base, there is really nothing, monsieur, in Kamina—except the brasserie. The government in Albertville was not getting the beer from Kamina because the troops, the government troops, were taking it off the train at Kabonga and Kabalo. What could the government do? Stop the soldiers from stealing the beer? Impossible! So they moved the government to Kamina."

"Beer," he added, "is the only thing that marches in the Congo."

The beer we were drinking in the cabin came (as does all beer in the Congo) in liter-sized brown bottles. It was called "Simba," which is the word for "lion" in Swahili. The Simba bottle in his hand reminded one of the ship's officers that Simba was also what the rebel warriors had chosen to call themselves. Les Simbas. The whites called them Simbas too, but more often referred to the rebels as "Mulelistes" after Pierre Mulele, an obscure founder of the rebellion who no longer figured in the rebel hierarchy but whose name for some reason rang a mystical bell in the ranks of the faithful. The Simbas believed in Mulele, in the power of his name—believing that if they chanted "Mai, mai, Mulele" ("Water, water, Mulele") as they advanced, the bullets of their foes would turn to water.

The talk in the cabin was now entirely about the Congo, and the captain remembered the way it had been on August 28 when the American planes fired their rockets at the C.F.L.'s installations and the ANC's (the Congolese National Army) retook Albertville from the Mulelistes. It had not been a day of glory for either side. After the fighting was over, he remembered surveying the scene from the window of his ground-floor office in the C.F.L. building. Just outside, on the sidewalk, a rebel lay dying. Every once in a while his body would twitch and his face contort with pain. As the captain watched, two ANC's approached. After observing the dying man dispassionately for a few moments, one of the soldiers placed his rifle on the sidewalk and started flailing away at the man's innards with his *panga*. Eventually the two soldiers grew bored and wandered off. The rebel was not yet dead. Two more ANC's arrived and, with the captain unable to tear himself away from the window, went through a similar performance. This time, however, instead of using a *panga*, one of them produced a pocket knife and started sawing at the rebel's jugular. The knife was dull, the work arduous, and he soon gave way to his companion, who had in the meantime found a large rock. This he dropped twice on the rebel's head. By then, however, the rebel was dead and the two soldiers sauntered away.

It was now the chief engineer's turn. He said it was odd but at the very beginning, when the Mulelistes entered Albertville on June 18, they announced that they had come to stamp our corruption. For a short period it almost seemed as if they would achieve their goal.

"But then," Captain Lallemand interjected, "it went from bad to worse and in the end nothing worked. No mail, no police. Rien. Rien. Rien."

And with this general breakdown, a wildness, a brutality came over the Mulelistes and they began to kill. Usually, the captain said, they killed the intellectuals, those who had had a little schooling or some connection with the previous regime. The Mulelistes seldom killed mercifully. Sometimes they would force their captives to drink gasoline, then cut open their stomachs and set a match to their innards.

"It makes no difference whether they are Mulelistes or ANC's," Lallemand said. His French was very rapid now and he fired his words in short bursts. "They are all the same. They are neither human beings nor animals. Beasts!" Pause, and then a shake of his head. "No, they are not even beasts. They are *crapules*. I would not hesitate to kill them all.

"I have sixteen more months before I am fifty-five, before my retirement. I will leave here and return to Belgium and never think of it again. Not for one minute. I am happy here. I lead a pleasant life. I am the king of the lake. My own boat, and I like my crew. They are Congolese, but there is nothing that I would not do for them and there is nothing they would not do for me. But when I leave I will never come back. I will never think of the Congo again—not even for a second."

We had had enough beer for the time being and Captain Lallemand took me out on deck. In the distance, close to the western shore, we could see the lights of the fishing boats. The fish, like moths, were attracted to the lights and would run afoul of the nets strung between the boats. Lake Tanganyika was very deep, said the captain. Some people thought it was the deepest in the world. It was subject to storms so severe that sometimes even a ship the size of the *Urundi* had trouble riding them out. The lake was 450 miles long but narrow and these days its width presented problems. In normal times the captain would steer a course down the center of the lake so that he would be at least ten miles from either shore. But now that the rebels held most of the western shore—the Congolese side—from Uvira at the northern end of the lake down to a point just across the lake from Kigoma in Tanzania, it was considered safer to hug the Tanzanian coast, giving the rebels as wide a berth as possible. Right now, said the captain, we were at the narrowest part of the lake. To the west, a spit of land lunged out into the lake and behind this spit of land was an inlet called Burton's Bay. It had been named after the explorer Richard Francis Burton, who, with John Speke, had discovered Lake Tanganyika in 1858. But it was not the historical association that interested the captain now. On the far side of the inlet, on the mainland shore of Burton's Bay, the captain pointed out the lights of Baraka. Every night, he said, a boat or two carrying no lights of any kind, crossed the lake from Tanzania to Baraka with arms for the rebels. From Baraka, the arms were hauled overland to the rebel stronghold of Fizi, a few miles to the south. The captain had seen the boats used by the arms smugglers several times and had even toyed with the idea of ramming them with the *Urundi*. But the *Urundi*, despite the machine gun in the captain's cabin, was a noncombatant and it would be just his luck to ram a rebel boat carrying high explosives. The C.F.L. had already lost the *Baron Dhanis* to the Americans. It could not afford to lose the *Urundi* too. Flinching away from the Congo side of the lake, we were at this moment less than a mile from the eastern shore. A sudden squall could sever the cables to the two barges and send them both onto the rocks. But the night was starry and windless and the captain anticipated no trouble.

The German, who had been listening to all this, studied the lights on the Congo shore and breathed deeply.

"I like danger," he said. "My wife says the only time I shiver is when I am cold."

The captain looked at the German as if he had said something hopelessly stupid and, without a word, went up to the wheelhouse.

The German woke me at 6 A.M. Although the bunks were comfortable, I had slept badly and winced as he beamed down at me with his cruise-director smile and said: "Good morning, my American friend." He had already finished packing and his belongings were arranged in a neat row on one of the empty upper bunks. He would take the train here at Kigoma and travel overland to Dar es Salaam, but the train would not leave until the afternoon and he suggested that we go into town together. Having made certain that I was fully awake, he left me to shave alone. The sun, already pallid, had just appeared over the low emerald-green hills to the east, as I emerged on deck.

Captain Lallemand was wearing sandals and shorts and an unbuttoned shirt, and he said it would be hot today. We had anchored in a little bay surrounded by low and rounded hills. The two barges, detached again from the *Urundi*, were anchored side by side at some distance. Through a pair of binoculars the captain was surveying the port of Kigoma, with its cranes, its freight cars and its conglomeration of warehouses. There was no movement on the pier, no sign of life. We would just have to wait, the captain said. He would not move until he could see white men on the porch of the customs shed. If they did not appear, it would mean that there was trouble of some kind. If that were the case he would not bring the *Urundi* into port at all.

At about 7:30 a figure in a white uniform appeared on the porch of the main building. Lallemand studied him through his field glasses.

"Blanc," he said and gave the command to raise anchor. The engines rumbled again and the *Urundi* made for the pier. The lake had risen gradually over the past several years and much of the pier, including the spur of railroad track closest to the bank, was under water. We made fast to a barge which, tied to the pier, served as a temporary dock, and the gangplank was moved into place. The passengers on the deck below us—the African passengers—started filing off the *Urundi.*

"You had better leave that here," said a voice next to me. It was the engineering officer and he was pointing at the camera dangling around my neck. Just a few weeks ago, he said, they had arrested a young man from the Peace Corps for taking pictures of the Livingstone monument at Ujiji—"just to say they had arrested a white man." Captain Lallemand said he would lock the camera in the closet in which he kept the machine gun.

"That way," he said, "there will be no émerdements."

While the captain was locking up my camera, the engineering officer went on to say that he did not think it advisable for me to try to see Ujiji. Certainly there was ample time (we were to be in Kigoma until sunset) but Ujiji had become a gathering place for Mulelistes. Although he was not certain about this, he had also heard that the Chinese Communists were in Ujiji, running a training camp for Congolese rebels. I would only be asking for trouble if I went to Ujiji. The captain reappeared, armed with a fishing rod, and went to the prow of his ship. He nodded curtly at the engineer and myself, baited his hook with a wad of bread, turned his back and cast the line into the water. It was clear he wanted no further conversation with anyone.

I went ashore with the engineer. A Tanzanian guard at the gate that separated the port facilities from the town proper looked at my passport and said I should return to the immigration authorities before making any further moves. Immigration, he said, was located in an office in the police station. I followed the street uphill to a small traffic circle. The police station was on my right and an officer showed me to the rear and pointed to a small office. Inside, a young man in civilian dress looked at my passport and then said he would not have to stamp it because I would only be in Kigoma for the day and would, therefore, be classified as "in transit." I asked him whether I might have permission to visit Ujiji. No, he said, there was nothing to see in Ujiji. Why didn't I simply stay in Kigoma? We smiled at each other and the immigration official stood up and showed me to the door. If there was anything further he could do, I had only to drop by and ask.

Kigoma was small, dusty and hot. The main street, flanked by Indian stores, ran up from the lake to a large open-air market. The German was standing on the veranda of the Gold Lion Hotel and said he had just ordered breakfast. I joined him, and a waiter in a white shirt reaching to his knees served us passion fruit juice and ham and eggs. Afterward, the Indian proprietor told us that this was the only establishment in town where the food was decent and that he could give us a chicken curry lunch. But we would have to order it now. There were several printed notices on the hotel wall and, while the German covered for me, I tore one of them down and tucked it into my pocket. I thought I would mail it to Barbara Johannson in Mwanza and ask her if it was hers. Signed by M. A. Hassan, the commissioner for the Kigoma Region, it read:

> It has come to our notice that certain people, as well as Tourists, take Cinema Photography whenever they visit different areas of this Republic. Your attention is drawn to this effect that it is an offence when such pictures are taken without first obtaining the permission of the Ministry of Community Development and National Culture.
>
> 2. Therefore anyone found taking these pictures without permission his/her name shall be sent immediately to this office or the nearest Police Station for necessary prosecutions.

While the German went off to see about his train, I wandered around the market square, bought a two-day-old copy of *The Nationalist* and learned that Tanzania had decided to recognize both East and West Germany. Folding the paper under my arm, I walked back to the veranda of the hotel, sat down on one of the metal chairs, and started to read. I had not seen a newspaper since Kampala. I had gotten no further than the second page when I was interrupted by an African who strode up the steps of the Veranda and asked me—none too politely, I thought—just what I was doing here. He wore his sports shirt out over his trousers and his expression, cocky and aggressive, was that of a TANU man. Instead of answering, I asked him who *he* was and we decided, then and there, that we did not like each other.

"You have no permission to be here," he said.

"I do indeed," I replied. "If you'll walk down to the immigration people with me, I'll prove it to you."

"Yes," he said. "We will ride in my car." He pointed at a car which was parked, doors open, on the street in front of the hotel.

"I would just as soon walk," I said.

"We will ride," he answered. He was really angry now and took me by the arm and began to propel me toward his vehicle. The *Urundi's* engineer was passing on the other side of the street and I waved strenuously at him, hoping that he would see whom I was with and, in case I disappeared for too great a length of time, tell somebody about it. But the engineer suddenly became absorbed by something in a shop window. My captor spoke to his driver in Swahili and shoved me into the back seat of the car. Together we drove the short distance to the police station. In the immigration office again, the man in the sports shirt repeated loudly that I had no permission to be in Kigoma.

"Yes, I do," I said, looking pointedly at the immigration officer. He had stood up as we came in and appeared mortified by our presence. The man in the sports shirt said something sharply to the immigration official. Beckoning me to follow, he led us into an adjoining room. This chamber was dominated by a large wire cage which had been built, floor to ceiling, into one corner. The man in the sports shirt was still talking loudly in Swahili to the immigration official. I interrupted.

"What am I charged with?" I asked. The immigration official did not answer, but sports shirt turned on me with a sudden and evil smile.

"Ah," he said gleefully. "You are trying to make it appear that you have been arrested. Is that it?" I said it seemed to me that the position I was in could not be defined as liberty but he ignored that one. Turning back to the immigration official, he showered him once more with angry Swahili. At length he ended his harangue and, glaring at me, pointed imperiously at the immigration official.

"*He* will give you the final word," he said. Then he spun on his heels, and, without a backward glance, departed. The immigration official was staring hard at his shoes.

"What is the final word?" I asked him.

"You are to return to your ship," he replied. "Come, I will take you."

"I haven't had lunch," I said. The immigration man eyed me sadly.

"There is no food on board," I added.

"I am sorry," he said. He led me gently from the room with the wire cage and out onto the road leading to the harbor.

"But what have I done wrong?" I asked him.

"You have done nothing wrong," he said. We were walking side by side toward the lake.

"Have I violated any rules or regulations?"

"No," he said. "You have done nothing wrong. Goodbye."

Back on the *Urundi* Captain Lallemand had stripped down to an electric-blue bathing suit. The bucket at his feet was partially filled with small fish, most of them dead. He did not seem to be the least bit surprised to see me back so soon.

The sun rose slowly and steadily and then hung directly overhead, draining the hills of their color until they were an exhausted gray. On the barge to which the *Urundi* had been tied, the crew members were giving each other haircuts. A pretty African woman (whose husband, I was told, had been killed in the fighting around Stanleyville) walked slowly around the deck, her loose sandals making scuffing noises on the boards. Occasionally she would lean against the rail and spit into the water. She spat through her teeth without using her lips.

I typed notes for a while in the ship's saloon and then went back to sleep on the bunk in my cabin. When I awoke and came back on deck again, it was four o'clock and passengers were beginning to line up front of the gangplank. Captain Lallemand was still fishing and his bucket was almost full of small fish floating belly up in the hot water. I slumped down in a canvas deck chair under the wheel-house and was almost asleep again when two men appeared from the companionway. Both were bearded. One of them, the fatter of the two, hitched up his trousers and stared at me. The other, with his back to me, was looking at the captain.

"Bonjour," said the fat one. If he had been Tanzanian, he would have spoken in English. But this was French. I nodded at him.

"Feu?" He was holding an unlighted cigarette in his hand and pointing at it. I dug into my pocket and brought out a lighter. He came over, bent down and got his cigarette started. He never took his eyes off mine. Then he stepped back, hitched up his trousers again, and smiled. It was not a pleasant smile. Meanwhile, the other visitor had been walking around the deck. It was more of a swagger than a walk. The captain looked at me and shrugged his shoulders as if to say: "I don't know these people. Do you?" I shrugged back. They were staring now at the pretty widow leaning against the railing. She gave them an appraising glance, turned and spat into the water. The two men finished their cigarettes in silence. Then, abruptly, the fat one motioned to his companion.

"Au revoir, messieurs," he said and together they disappeared down the companionway.

"Crapules," the captain said. The engineering officer, who had been watching them from a distance, walked over.

"I know them," he told the captain. "Mulelistes, from Albertville."

I asked what they were doing here in Tanzania and why they had come aboard this way. The engineering officer replied that this happened fairly frequently. It was a form of control—the rebels and the Tanzanians joining together to prevent refugees from the Congo—those presumed to be loyal to the central government—from returning to Albertville. Most of the time it was the Tanzanian security people who boarded the *Urundi* when it docked at Kigoma. The fact that today's visitors were Congolese meant, perhaps, that they were looking for someone special.

"If I had my way," said the captain, "I would put them in the frigo and deliver them to Albertville personally."

That evening, with the barges in tow again, we sat on deck, finished a bottle of my Scotch, and ate the fish the captain had caught during the day. He called them "sardines." They had been fried and we ate them, head, tail and all. They were delicious.

CHAPTER 13

SEX AND THE SINGLE HINDU

A tramway is one thing that is needed for Africa.
—H. M. STANLEY

THE porch of my third-floor room in the Hôtel du Lac overlooked the tracks of the C.F.L.'s Albertville freight yards and beyond these, through the wire fence and the palms, the harbor itself. Every morning, soon after dawn, the street and the sidewalk would fill with school children, women with empty shopping baskets or vegetables and roots in platters on their heads, and men pushing bicycles. The human traffic moved from left to right, from the African quarter to the center of town. At about the same time work crews would appear on the tracks and begin shoveling sand under the rails. They were raising the tracks, trying to keep them above the level of the flooded lake. Between eleven in the morning and four in the afternoon the street would be almost empty and the gangs on the tracks would melt away until there were only one or two men with shovels and they were not working but just standing there. Then, shortly after 4 P.M., the tide came back again from the other direction, flowing this time from right to left.

The Greeks who ran the Hôtel du Lac served beer only in the dining room and then only with meals. They did not serve beer in the bar or on the terrace. This was to discourage the less affluent Africans and coerce the richer ones into buying their meals at the hotel. The management's policy had its desired effect and the hotel's clientele consisted in the main of white men and Congolese officers with their wives and mistresses. The men drank whisky, which the bar did serve, or cognac. The women usually drank orange Fanta, a non-alcoholic carbonated beverage. The terrace, especially at dusk, was a pleasant place to watch the world go by but the bar inside was the place for talk and information. It was here that the members of the *Equipe Polivalente*, the team of Europeans sent to Albertville at the expense of the Belgian government to put the town back on its feet, gathered to exchange acid comments on the nature of man in the tropics. The bar was also a meeting place for the three white mercenary soldiers assigned to Albertville to guard the civilian population. They were accustomed to having drinks bought for them and accepted my offer of a round as a matter of course.

"If it were not for us," said one of them, "the Europeans of Albertville would run away."

Had I been a European of Albertville, I would have started running immediately. None of the mercenaries had ever fired a shot in anger and none seemed in the least interested in doing so in the future. One of them was an Italian with the long, sad face of a bereaved bloodhound. He had come up from South Africa, lured by promises of money and adventure, but had found neither.

"I was in Johannesburg, in the bus traffic," he said by way of explanation. He would, he said, like to go to Canada because "Canada is rich." But any country, any continent, was preferable to the Congo, to Africa.

"The black man is no good," he said, wagging his finger slowly like a metronome keeping time to his words. "When I come South Africa from Italy, I say he no different. He like me only he have black skin. Only black skin difference. But he *not* like me. He different."

I asked what he thought the difference was.

"I don't know," he replied. "Is a difference is all. But I know how should be. Apartheid. Apartheid. Must be apartheid."

My first days in Albertville were spent in a state bordering on euphoria. The mere fact that I had managed to enter the Congo without trouble filled me with relief and gratitude. But there were other things about Albertville that contributed to my feeling of well being. To begin with, the hotel room was comfortable and hot water flowed from the hot water taps in the bathroom at any hour of the day or night. The hotel food was tasteless but adequate and the black market rate of exchange (350 Congolese francs to the dollar) was heavily in my favor. But most important, from my point of view, was the attitude of the natives. I was prepared for arrogance, suspicion and lawlessness. Instead I found them polite, friendly and apparently ready to do almost anything to make my stay a pleasant one. The day after my arrival, I reported to the Sûreté office to pick up the passport which had been taken from me when I landed. A long line had formed in front of the entrance, but instead of being told to take my place at the end of it I was whisked inside and introduced to the *Chef*. I said I had come for my passport.

"But of course, monsieur," he said, standing up and shaking my hand. "You must excuse me for asking you to come here, but you see, monsieur, I must look at you myself."

He had my passport on his desk top and it was obvious that he too had studied my visas, but instead of arousing suspicion in his mind they filled him with admiration. How he admired me. All those countries! The life of a journalist must be so very interesting. He himself, alas, had done little traveling. He had never been to Europe but, with luck, he would go to Israel shortly for a course in security. Had Monsieur ever visited Israel? Ah, that was too bad but perhaps that was for the future, no? In the meantime, if there was anything he could do for Monsieur le Journaliste while he was in Albertville . . . A drink with Monsieur at the Hôtel du Lac some evening? With the greatest of pleasure. Monsieur was really too kind.

After my friendly encounter with Security, I wandered further up the hill to military headquarters. Major M'Badu was due back in a matter of moments. In the meantime, would Monsieur care to wait? I sat on a bench outside the headquarters building, a private house which had once belonged to a Belgian family. The three soldiers doing guard duty let me examine their weapons and I was relieved to see that there were no bullets in their chambers. I had just finished inspecting the last of the three weapons when two small men carrying a large office desk came toward us along the road. They were dressed in ragged loin cloths and were surrounded by ANC's with rifles.

"Mulelistes," said one of the soldiers on guard duty. The two men carried the desk into the headquarters building and, when they emerged, I asked the guards whether I could take a picture. The guards pushed the prisoners up against the wall of the building and then, when they saw I was ready, pointed their rifles at the prisoners' heads. The prisoners' expressions did not change. Both had deep circular gashes above their elbows and, after I had finished taking their pictures, one of the soldiers twisted their arms behind their backs and bound them securely with cords. The rough cord tightening again over their open wounds must have hurt, but again their expressions did not change. I followed them and their guards down the road to another building. A cellar door was opened and the guards shoved the prisoners inside. As the second of the two stooped to enter, one of the guards gave him a savage kick in the backside. The cellar was dark and windowless and incredibly hot, and smelled foul. There were perhaps twelve other prisoners inside, squatting along the walls. Each had his arms tied behind his back. They were very thin. I asked a young lieutenant who seemed to be in command of the soldiers guarding the cellar what would become of the prisoners. He shrugged.

"We have no budget for the wounded or for prisoners," he said.

Major M'Badu was in his office when I returned to the headquarters building. He asked me to take a seat while he finished dealing with two other visitors. One was a young man in civilian clothes who stood at attention while speaking to the major. He was, the major explained, a refugee from Stanleyville who was seeking permission to board a military plane to Elisabethville.

"He would like to travel on a military plane to save money," Major M'Badu added. "But I will now tell him that he can only be classified as a refugee once. He has had free transport from Stanleyville to Albertville. He must travel the remaining distance by commercial transport."

The major then turned back to the young man and told him this in Swahili. He seemed to take the bad news well and did not argue. Instead, he thanked the major, saluted and did a smart about-face. Next the major turned his attention to a woman seated at the other side of his desk. She was nursing a baby, holding the child in the crook of her left arm. Her right arm was free and she used it to gesticulate to the major. After she had gone, the major told me that she was the widow of an army private and had not been receiving her pension. He wrote something out for her on a piece of paper.

"She has had no money for five months," M'Badu said. "Somebody—I do not know who—but somebody in the administration is cheating her of it. I would like to find him myself."

The major listened with apparent interest to my explanation of the purpose of my trip into the Congo and, when I had finished, walked over to one of the walls and parted a blue curtain to reveal a map of the Congo. There were arrows and symbols depicting military units. He said he could not speak with authority about any area other than Albertville. The Albertville operation, he said, would take time. It was aimed, as Monsieur was probably aware, at Fizi and Baraka, but there were escarpments on the road from Albertville north to those two rebel strongholds and the rebels were well entrenched. What was needed was planes—bombers to soften up the rebel positions. But Stanleyville, or maybe it was Leopoldville, controlled the planes and he was much afraid that the Albertville military area was considered of secondary importance by these other headquarters. Albertville would also like to cut off the flow of arms from Tanzania across the lake to Fizi and Baraka but perhaps it was best if he did not go into that aspect of the campaign since the plans were still secret. The major was pleased to say that there had been one notable success in the past few weeks. The ANC had managed to cut the road from Fizi to Kabambare in the interior, thus pinching off a major supply route. He said the ANC's would sit there for a while now and try to starve the rebels out. But this would be difficult, the major admitted, because the rebels lived off the land on practically nothing at all.

"As a unified military force," he said, "the Mulelistes are finished.

The movement is no longer run by Soumialot and Gbenye but has split up and consists of groups of bandits. It is difficult to fight a war against an enemy of this kind."

Not once during his briefing did Major M'Badu mention the white mercenaries and I thought it tactful not to bring them up either. At the bar of the Hôtel du Lac that evening, the mercenaries themselves were not loath to talk about the ANC's or, for that matter, Major M'Badu himself.

"He is always finding a reason for doing nothing," one of them said. I said the major had been most helpful to me, having gone so far as to write me a letter of introduction to the military commander of Stanleyville.

"If you wish to go anywhere in the Congo, or see the fighting, you must come to us," said another mercenary. "I don't care how many military passes you have—if we do not want you, you will get nowhere."

The speaker was new to me. He was not one of the home guard of Albertville and there was in his staring light-blue eyes the look of a man on drugs. He was short and powerfully built and the pockets of his camouflage jacket bulged with hand grenades. He seemed put on this earth to kill.

"I am called Christian," he said. "That is all you need to know about me."

Christian had returned that afternoon from the escarpments around Fizi. As usual, he said as the other mercenaries clucked in agreement, the danger had come from the rear. Ahead of you, there were only the Mulelistes shouting, "*Mai mai*, Mulele," and shooting wildly. They were improving but they could still hit nothing. To get the ANC's to advance, however, one had to be out in front, standing up in the middle of the road so the others could see that you were not getting hit. That was the time of real danger, Christian said, because then the ANC's would start firing (which was what you wanted them to do) but they would fire blindly, with their faces turned away. At that moment there was always the danger that they would shoot you down from behind. He had seen it happen, several times, to *copains* of his.

"You have to be crazy to be a mercenary," he said. He tapped his head. "You think I am crazy?"

"Yes," I said.

"You are right." Christian's dark, tanned face broke into a wide grin. He had found somebody who understood.

The following morning Christian took me around to his room. He wanted to show me some of his trophies—captured Chinese-made weapons, spears, poisoned arrows and the like. As we walked down the sidewalk leading to his hotel, Africans and Indian shopkeepers waved and smiled at him.

"You see," said Christian. "I am well known here. I am famous."

Christian posed on the porch outside his room with his weapons and a bottle of Simba beer, and I took some pictures.

"Do you know why I am fighting?" he asked me. I said I didn't.

"For the whites. Nothing more," he said. "And do you know why? Because the Congo is like the prodigal child. She has left Mother Belgium, no? But the child will return to the mother. You will see."

Rummaging around at the bottom of his green-painted tin box, he pulled out a wooden crucifix on which had been mounted a white plastic Christ.

"This is why I live today," he said. "It is always with me." He kissed the crucifix before returning it to the box, where it lay alongside an empty Simba beer bottle and the poison arrows he had taken from the rebels he had killed. Outside, on the street again, Christian hailed a passing car driven by one of Albertville's two doctors.

"You must give me a medical certificate saying my nerves are finished," Christian told the doctor. "I should go to Belgium for two weeks. Otherwise I will go crazy with all this killing."

The doctor promised to make out his medical excuse.

"I was not joking last night," Christian said, after the doctor had driven away in his car. "I am becoming mad. . . ."

From the terrace of the Hôtel du Lac, the engineering officer of the *Urundi* had been watching me talking to Christian. When Christian and I parted, the engineering officer waved me over to where he was seated. The *Urundi* had spent two days in port and the chief engineer was boarding the ship that afternoon for the return trip to Bujumbura.

"You must tell them," he said, lifting his eyebrows at the retreating figure of Christian, "to take Fizi and Baraka quickly. They are bringing in arms every night. And Chinese too."

I said it was my impression that the operation had been stalled because of the escarpments and maybe other things I knew nothing about.

"Then they will be too late," said the engineer. "See what you can do when you get to Leopoldville."

That was one of the odd aspects of my stay in Albertville—the widely shared assumption that I was something more than I was. For the white civilians, it was obvious that I had connections with the military. For the military, it was obvious that I knew people high up the political ladder in Leopoldville. For the Africans on the street, dressed as I was in khaki shirt and trousers, I was plainly the man with a gun, a professional soldier. It was best, therefore, to treat me with respect, to say "Bonjour, patron" and to make way for me on the sidewalk. Elsewhere in Africa, the white man could be a figure of fun, or someone to ridicule or hold in contempt. But in the Congo these days, because he carried a gun, he was a symbol of power. Better still, he *was* power.

I think that it was this recognition of the ultimate source of power that gave Albertville its strangely nostalgic charm. It was as if the clock had been turned back to the period long before independence, to the time perhaps just after the first white man arrived but *before* they put the black men to work. Albertville had been through much since those days but here it was again as it had been at the beginning—the amorphous black population and a handful of white men with guns. They were enough.

To Fernand van Vyve, the director of FILTISAF (Filatures et Tissages Africains) it was all quite simple and understandable—given the nature of Africans.

"They are born slaves," he said, and then added emphatically, "Not in the cruel and heartless Arab sense of slavery but in the old

Roman sense. They look for a master and when they find one then they wholly depend on him. They prefer life this way—relying completely on someone else, putting their lives and their futures in someone else's hands."

Examples? They were to be seen everywhere. For instance, FILTISAF had built a club for its fifteen hundred employees (there were not so many now—five hundred had been killed or driven into the bush by the Mulelistes) and, shortly after independence, had turned the club over to them. So many treasurers, however, absconded with the club dues and profits that the members came in a body to ask that a white man run the club again. "They felt I had stabbed them in the back when I said they were independent now and on their own," van Vyve said.

In the almost six months that had elapsed since the departure of the Mulelistes, the white man had restored calm but nothing else to Albertville. In itself, the restoration of calm—especially during the first few weeks—was no mean feat. The population was in a panicky mood, and, of necessity, there had to be an almost ritual period of bloodletting. The doctor who promised to give Christian a medical pass to Brussels told me (we were playing a rather phlegmatic game of water polo in the C.F.L. swimming pool at the time) that his primary mission had been to introduce some system into the carnage.

"I told the ANC's," he said, "that if they were going to shoot their prisoners not to shoot them here and there indiscriminately but to round them all up in one place. I explained it was bad for the *santé* to have to go around after the killing looking for bodies with one's nose."

Gradually the shooting had been brought under control. I suppose that the last time the inhabitants of Albertville heard firing was less than a month before my arrival, on the morning of January 23. But on that occasion, according to a yellowing notice on the hotel bulletin board, the population was asked not to allow itself to panic. It was only the Katangese police shooting stray dogs (*chiens errants*) within the city limits.

But Albertville, now that the shooting and terror had stopped, resembled not so much a patient on the mend, bandaged but ambulatory, as a sick man in a coma. Albertville's main streets had been cleared of the debris of war but her alleys were clogged with the skeletons of wheel-less cars. The harbor, with its sunken shipping and high waters lapping over the waterfront railroad tracks, looked like a sink full of dirty dishes.

There were basically two kinds of white people in Albertville: those who were paid to stay and would have left if the money hadn't been so good, and a much smaller group composed of older men and their wives who had spent most of their lives in the Congo and had grown to love it. Van Vyve was one of these as was Madame de Belder, who, with her husband, had lived through the rebel occupation of Albertville. The experience (its last visible reminder a bullet hole through Madame de Belder's living-room window) seemed to have left her unmarked. She loved Africa still, with a deep and almost mystical passion.

"When it rains," she said, in an effort to explain to me what it was she felt, "when it rains it rains so the roads are covered and you cannot move, and the bridges are washed out. And when the sun shines you cannot go out because if you do it will kill you. And when the wind blows on the lake ships are dashed to pieces. That is Africa—and the people are like that too. They are large people in a sense, and they live largely, unlike the people in Europe."

Madame de Belder seemed very much part of the vast and turbulent panorama of Africa. In Europe she would have been a caged bird and, slight as she was, too large for her cage.

The C.F.L. headquarters building dominated the harbor and the small railway station next to it. Much of the building's glass had been shattered during the recent fighting and many of the offices were empty, their floors littered with hunks of plaster and shards of glass. Marcel Cossaer was the man in charge of scheduling the rolling stock in and out of Albertville.

"They are looking for you," he said the first time I walked into his office. That morning, on the radio from Elisabethville, he had learned that three of the foreign consuls stationed there had chartered a plane and would be arriving in the afternoon. Arthur

Tienken, the American consul, was one of the group and had passed the word that he wanted to see me. My first reaction was to get out of Albertville before Tienken's arrival, but Cossaer said there would not be another train for Kabalo until the following Tuesday. From there, he explained, I could take a riverboat up the Lualaba to Kongolo. There was train service of sorts from Kongolo to Kindu but Cossaer said that no European had traveled along that section of track since the period of the Mulelistes.

"I would not advise you to be the first to try," he said. From Kindu on it was all rebel territory. I might manage to get as far as Kindu, he added, but there was no hope of getting any further.

Back in the Hôtel du Lac I waited nervously for Tienken's arrival. When we did meet in the lobby, it was obvious that he had been working on his opening line all the way from Elisabethville.

"Dr. Littell, I presume?" he said. Over drinks we established to our mutual relief and satisfaction that we were rational human beings. Tienken did his best to talk me out of any further travel in the Congo. Until a few months ago, a European, if captured by the rebels, stood a fair chance of coming out alive. But the odds had changed since Stanleyville, especially if you were an American, Tienken said. We talked, and out of the talk came compromise. Tienken would do nothing to stop me provided I wrote out and signed a piece of paper absolving the American government of all responsibility in the event of my capture and/or death.

On the morning of my departure, I settled my accounts with the Greek hotel proprietor. As a parting gesture of friendship, he let me have a bottle of water, charging me fifty francs for the bottle but nothing for the water. Cossaer picked me up in a truck at 3:15 with my bags and five cases of American army C-rations left over from the UN days. The train was not due to leave until 5 P.M. and would probably not leave even then, but it was best to get there early and install myself before the train ran out of seats. Tickets and reservations did not mean much any more and the two carloads of ANC's who accompanied each train into the interior and were supposed to keep order and protect the train against attack did not do much except drink and make trouble. We did not board the train at the station, which was flooded, but about a mile from the center of town where the tracks passed through a grove of trees. Cossaer forged ahead to find the *chef du train* while I stood guarding my baggage and watching the women lift suitcases through the open windows of the waiting train as the men talked and borrowed cigarettes from each other. Cossaer returned with the *chef du train*, a smiling Congolese with the stiff high-crowned cap you associate with the personnel of small railroad stations in the Swiss Alps. Followed by six young men carrying my things on their heads, we made for the train. The *chef* and Cossaer had found me a compartment. It contained two wicker bunks, top and bottom. There were no mattresses, no water and no lights but it was much better than I had expected. The *chef* said he would keep four of my ration boxes in the freight car, where, he assured me, they would be safe. The other I kept with me in case I got hungry. I thanked Cossaer profusely for all he had done, shaking hands with him through the open window, and then settled back to watch the crowd. About half an hour before train time, an Indian appeared outside my window with an African boy carrying a tin box on his head. The Indian pointed at my window and the African heaved the box inside.

"I am coming back," the Indian shouted at me and disappeared into the crowd.

I would have guessed he was in his early thirties. His face was pockmarked and dark and, on his return, he addressed me in English. He had learned the language in Tanzania as a youth and his name, according to a card which he pulled from an overstuffed wallet, was Sadrudin G. Jinah. He was, he said, a trader, a businessman, and proud to say that he was making a fortune in the Congo. All that was required was to find out what was needed, and where, and then get it there and charge the highest prices possible. On this particular trip to Kongolo, he was bringing cigarettes, twelve hundred bags of salt and two hundred bags of sugar.

"If you will permit me to say so," he added, "I have also an excellent shop in E'ville. It is called Au Bon Séjour. I named it myself, in French."

At 5:20—only twenty minutes late—the train's diesel engine gave a series of baritone blasts of its whistle. It was growing dark rapidly and most of the crowd in the grove next to the tracks had gone elsewhere when the train started to move. We traveled slowly, at fifteen miles an hour, the tracks cutting through tall reeds and elephant grass lining the banks on either side. Every two or three minutes, the grass would part like a curtain to reveal a group of African children sitting on the bank, with mothers with babies in their arms standing behind them, and all of them waving at the passengers on the train. Occasionally, one of the passengers would jump off the train, run up the bank, accept a parcel from one of the onlookers and dash back to the train. Usually the package contained food.

Jinah, in the meantime, had been charging in and out of the compartment, shouting and clapping his hands.

"Monsieur Pierre! Monsieur Giles," he bellowed. "Venez! Venez!" In a short while we had kerosene lantern, glasses, a bottle of Scotch, several bowls of curry and an admiring pair of Congolese Sûreté officials who toasted me with Jinah's Scotch and said they loved America. I offered to cut into my box of rations but Jinah made a sour face.

"Come," he said. "You are with me. You have nothing to worry about. More whisky? Come. Drink, drink, my friend."

It was all a matter of knowing whom to bribe and how much to bribe him, Jinah said as the Sûreté men nodded and smiled. They did not understand what he was saying but even if they had I am certain they would have agreed. The size of the bribes, Jinah continued, was determined by the bribee's salary. Small bribes for small functionaries and large bribes for people of real importance. That was the reason he always traveled with his goods. If he didn't, and without the bribes, the goods would never get to their destination.

The train moved slowly through the night, stopping every fifteen minutes or so at a station alive with the murmur of human voices and the firefly lights from hundreds of kerosene lanterns.

"Chef! Chef!" Jinah leaned out into the dark passageway, and when the *chef du train* appeared Jinah told him to make certain that he let no one else into our compartment. He poured the trainmaster another drink of whisky (the *chef* had appeared glass in hand) and waved him away. Then Jinah sat down and opened up the curry dishes and we ate the mouth-searing food with our fingers and drank more Scotch.

"You know," said Jinah, standing up, "I am growing fat." He stuck out his belly and slapped it with the palm of his hand.

"But it is better to drink than to gamble," he continued. "I was a very bad gambler. A terrible gambler."

But he had given up gambling when he had married, and now that his wife was pregnant again after two miscarriages he had promised her he would give up smoking too until the birth of his child.

"She is not young, you know," he said. "She is twenty-six. But I am very sexy. Did you know that? Yes, I am very sexy. I go to bed with my wife ten times a month, but she is very calm, you know, sir." He lapsed into silence, sat down and had some more curry, and then abruptly stood up again.

"Did you know," he said, "that we Indians have a certain exercise which we take if we are sexy when we are removed from our wives?"

Jinah began to demonstrate, folding his arms behind his back and then bending forward with a considerable effort until his nose touched his right knee. Then, his face flushed dark, he stood straight again.

"This exercise," he said, pointing to the area of his groin, "takes the blood away from here and moves it to other parts of the body. Are you sexy, sir?"

I said I didn't feel particularly sexy at the moment.

"Never mind," he said. "Some day you will feel sexy too, and then you will try the Indian exercise. It is very beneficial."

From somewhere, Jinah produced a set of sheets and a blanket and offered them to me, but I refused. I made a pillow of my bush jacket and lay down on the lower bunk and, listening to the clack of wheels on rails and the sudden, metallic whirring of cicadas as we passed through swampy ground, fell asleep.

I awoke at dawn with the train at a dead stop in the Kabalo station. It was a gray, dark day and I paced the tracks under a slight drizzle. The bodies piled on the platform under the station roof were beginning to come awake. The station was blackened and burned out and I heard later that this had been caused by soldiers who had lighted their cooking fires too close to a dynamite-filled freight car parked just in front of the station. Oil, kerosene or gasoline had caught fire and the freight car had exploded, killing more than a hundred people.

Jinah was awake when I returned to our compartment. He looked hung over and decidedly unsexy. We put our personal baggage on a freight car which we were assured would be shunted along the tracks to the dock and then walked across the tracks and down to the riverfront. The *Nicholas Cito*, an old and scabrous sternwheeler which was to carry us down the Lualaba to Kongolo, lay in what I judged to be about six inches of muddy water at the edge of the river. Her lower decks were packed with cords of wood to feed her ancient boilers. Sometime in the past her back must have been broken because she sagged in the middle. As we approached, stevedores were manhandling crates of beer aboard from a freight car, carrying the beer across the teetering planks which connected the ship with land and then down into the dark hold below the waterline. A bearded old Arab had turned part of the lower deck into a kitchen for himself and his friends and he gave Jinah and me sweet tea in tin cups. Jinah led me to the upper deck, shouting, "Capitaine! Capitaine!" as he went, and introduced me to Captain Ramazani, Charles. This is the way Congolese write their names and are introduced, and thus, during the course of the seven-hour trip to Kongolo, he was Capitaine Charles and I was Monsieur Blaine. Jinah left me with the captain while he went back to see about his goods, and the captain took me up another flight of stairs to the wheelhouse and said I was welcome to stay there as long as I wished. Capitaine Charles told me he was born in 1910 and that he had had his pilot's license since 1935. There were no chairs in the wheelhouse but there were on the first-class deck below, and I found one of these and pulled it close to the rail and watched the women squatting on their heels at the water's edge, scaling and cleaning fish rapidly and skillfully with their knives. Sometime later, Jinah appeared, followed by porters carrying our baggage, and this we put in one of the cabins on the first-class deck. But he was having trouble, he said, with his merchandise, and disappeared again among the tracks and freight cars on the bank above the river.

I opened one of my cartons of rations and found that some of the tin cans were bulging suspiciously; there were cigarettes, and packages containing fudge bars covered with white mold, and the toilet paper was packed with the chocolate powder. A small boy, who turned out to be the captain's son, stood next to me as I poked through the contents of the carton and I opened a tin of multicolored candies for him and gave him a handful. The bearded Arab and his friends had now mounted the upper deck too and I gave them some candy and cigarettes. The Arab, in turn, dug his hand into a bowl of rice, rolled it up into a hard and glistening ball, and handed it to me.

At noon two more freight cars were shunted down the spur of tracks that ran parallel to the *Nicholas Cito* and with them came Jinah. He said he had had much trouble that morning. The sugar had gone astray. It had not been lost. He was certain of that. It simply would not be found in time to get it aboard the boat before departure so he had arranged with another Indian to put it on the next boat bound for Kabalo. As for the cigarettes and the salt, that had been a simple matter of bribery. Of course there had been no intention of moving his goods from the freight cars to the boat until he had paid the *chef de la gare* 2,000 francs. Then it was discovered that one of his Congolese assistants (I presume he meant the boy who had carried his tin box aboard the train) had been arrested because his *carte civile* had been signed in red instead of black in Albertville. His release had cost Jinah 100 francs to each of two Sûreté officials and a policeman who had included himself in on the transaction at the last moment. Despite these setbacks, Jinah was in high spirits and, in the same mysterious manner as on the train, beer arrived. The beer, in turn, led to the appearance of several crew members and four Congolese army officers who shared in the beer and in the old Arab's rice and chicken curry.

At 1:15 Capitaine Charles yanked the cord which was attached to the boat's piercing whistle and gave three sharp blasts. He shouted at the people on the bank below and the planks leading to the ship were pulled on board. The *Nicholas Cito* began to drift away from the shore. Capitaine Charles ran from one end of the ship to the other, shouting commands and waving wildly and, after much jockeying back and forth, we had two barges attached by cable to our stern and were in midstream and heading downriver toward Kongolo. I moved myself and my carton of rations up to the wheel-house and made myself comfortable on top of a wooden box behind the helmsman.

Instead of steering a course down the middle of the river, we zigzagged from side to side. The helmsman's wheel was seldom stationary. Capitaine Charles said this was because the Lualaba was full of hazards—hidden shoals and mud banks—and it was all too easy to run aground or tear the bottom of your boat on a snag. You had to watch the signs on the banks carefully.

The Lualaba crept north (the river that Stanley had tried to call the Livingstone) like a flat, brown tapeworm. It divided the land-scape so that when there were hills on the right bank there were none on the left, and when there were high trees on the right the countryside to our left was barren savanna. Usually, the captain said, we would be seeing many hippopotamuses and crocodiles but the river was high, higher than it had been in many years, and the creatures had been flooded out of their usual haunts. They were probably back in behind the partially submerged trees and bushes. Then, as we passed the point where the Lukuga joins the Lualaba, we did see a hippo snorting and splashing in midstream, but he dived as we approached. Stanley had written extensively about the Lukuga. It was he who discovered that this major tributary originated in Lake Tanganyika, at Albertville, and that it flowed out of rather than into the lake. When, however, the time came for him to penetrate into the Congo itself, he went in north of Albertville and did not hit the Lualaba until a good many miles farther down-stream from our present position.

Although the sun came out in mid-afternoon, and the sky turned a brilliant blue, there was an eerie quality about the country through which we moved. Stanley had called it "the unspeakable majesty of silence." For miles on end, there were no signs of life. No birds overhead, no crocodiles or hippos on the banks, and, more troublesome still to the man from the cities, no people. We passed only two villages on that trip north to Kongolo and one fisherman in his hollow-log canoe. The rest was emptiness and, except for the sound of the ship's engines, silence.

I slept for an hour or so, reclining on the long box behind the ship's wheel, and when I awoke I was hungry and opened up a tin of crackers and an orange-colored cheese spread. The captain's son watched as I examined the moldy fudge bars. I thought of throwing them overboard but then, knowing that he would think I was insane if I did so and presupposing that his stomach was made of iron anyway, I gave them to him. We managed to speak together about various things—he in Swahili and I in French—acting the words out when language failed. He pointed at his father, who had lighted a pipe and was puffing on it as he surveyed the wide brown river. Yes, I said to him slowly in French, his father was smoking his pipe.

"Papa fume la pipe," the boy repeated happily. "Papa fume la pipe. Papa fume la pipe."

We made a song of it to the tune of the Volga Boatman.

"Papa fume la pipe. Ugh. Papa fume la pipe. Ugh."

Then we went belowdecks, singing our song, to where the women were drying the fish they had been cleaning on the riverbank at Kabalo. They were using the hot steam boilers of the *Nicholas Cito*. By now the fish were a yellow brown, glazed and thoroughly dry.

It was dusk when the white buildings of Kongolo appeared on the left bank around a gentle bend in the river. Capitaine Charles let the current carry his barges downstream until the *Nicholas Cito* and its charges pointed south and then approached the riverbank upstream. By the time we made fast, the passengers belowdecks were already struggling to get ashore, waving tickets and passes in their hands. But there was only one gangplank and gray-uniformed police formed a gauntlet and let the crowd through slowly, one at a time.

One tall policeman who seemed to be the leader of the group suddenly pulled several men out of the passenger line, punching them about their necks and faces as he pulled them away with his free hand. He concentrated on one passenger in particular, beating him about the face, then punching him repeatedly in the stomach and finally slapping his face so the sound could be heard above the babble of voices.

I was watching all this from the upper deck when I found myself surrounded by four white men. Two introduced themselves as members of the C.F.L.'s Kongolo contingent. The others were from the Cotonco station and together the five of us had a boisterous and amiable argument as to where I should stay. All had received instructions from their respective home offices in Albertville to put me up. Flipping a mental coin in my head and deciding that my future movements still depended to a large extent on the C.F.L., I chose Georges Van Clooster and Louis Van Buggenhaut. At this point, the tall policeman who had been beating the African passengers below emerged from the crowd.

"C'est l'Américain?" he asked the others. They nodded. He took my hand in his, smiled reassuringly, and led me down the stairs, past the gangplank and up to the bow of the ship. Three feet of water separated us from the shore.

"Sautez!" he said, and hand in hand we jumped to shore.

"Merci," I said.

"De rien, monsieur," he said. We shook hands and he returned to the boat. I caught a last glimpse of him as I walked inland toward a waiting car. He had two more male passengers off to one side and was beating them both savagely with his fists.

Chapter 14

MATATA

One really does not know whether to pity or to despise the natives of Manyema.

—H. M. Stanley

"Neffkewairee, neffkewairee, neffkewairee . . ." The voice at the head of my bed, an insistent monotone, the voice of a bored priest uttering a ritual incantation, balanced between dream and reality. For a while I kept my eyes closed, puzzling over the strange words, and then remembered gradually that I was in Kongolo and that the voice belonged to Georges Van Clooster and that there was a radio transmitter in my room and that what he was saying over and over again was "9-Q.R.I." in French. When I opened my eyes, Georges was seated in front of the transmitter and speaking into the microphone. He was wearing shorts and an undershirt and sandals. Louis Van Buggenhaut was in the next room slicing sausage meat and cheese for breakfast.

I found that 9-Q.R.I. were the call letters for the C.F.L. in Albertville. Kongolo's call sign was "Romeo Kilo," Kindu's was "Romeo Juliette" and the *comptabilité*'s (accounting) was "Caroline Chérie." The C.F.L.'s field stations checked in with the head office in Albertville twice a day, the conversations ranging from meticulous and lengthy recitations of what was being shipped where and when to requests for more cigars.

On my first morning, the talk was about 350 *dents d'éléphants*, destined for Albertville, which the Sûreté had blocked in Kongolo on the grounds that the Indian shipper had neglected to secure an export permit. The Sûreté in Kongolo had no right to ask for export permits (that was Albertville's job) and it was Georges's impression, as he outlined the case over the radio to Albertville, that the Sûreté was holding the ivory tusks in Kongolo either in the expectation of a substantial bribe from the Indian or in the hope that some of the ivory might just happen to disappear during the next few moonless nights. To keep the Sûreté's thieves away from the freight cars carrying the ivory, the C.F.L. had doubled its own guard. Meanwhile, Georges explained with some relish, the Indian had flown back to Leopoldville to straighten the whole business out and on his return there was sure to be a *matata*—trouble for the local officials. Perhaps Leopoldville might see to it that heads rolled in Kongolo.

"Très bien," said the voice from Albertville.

Both Georges and Louis used the word *matata* frequently. A day did not go by when they were not involved in some sort of *matata*—trouble with the local gendarmerie, trouble with their own workers, trouble with the home office in Albertville, which pretended not to understand why machinery broke down or why goods trains were delayed. Georges and Louis were always drafting devastating messages of resignation to the home office and then purposely forgetting to read them the next time they were on the radio. Perhaps, at the last moment, they remembered that they were on danger pay, which was more money than either of them had made before, and that their three refrigerators were stuffed with frozen turkeys, imported French cheeses, *pâté* and beer. It was, all in all, not a bad life if you did not mind being separated from your wife and children, and if you did not mind the constant *matatas*.

There was a *matata* under way on my first day in Kongolo—or rather a rumor of one—but it amounted to the same thing. The day before (or so the story went) there had been furious fighting on a tributary of the Lualaba some fifty kilometers north of Kongolo. The Luika River, it was called, and the Mulelistes were said to have fought their way across a bridge on the Luika, killing scores of ANC's in the process. Now, or so the story went, the Mulelistes were on their way to Kongolo in force. They would arrive in a matter of days and, as everyone knew, Kongolo could not be defended. All day long, C.F.L. workers, town officials and merchants would come up to the porch of the house in which Georges and Louis lived, to ask what they had heard. Should they make plans to evacuate? Georges and Louis, knowing nothing more of the fighting than anybody else, reassured the visitors. A fat young Pakistani with a high voice came by. He was extremely nervous, not so much for himself, he said, as for his goods.

"You will let me know if anything develops," he kept saying. "I must have warning in advance."

Georges and Louis promised that he would be the first to know.

You could not blame the inhabitants of Kongolo for being nervous. They had had nothing but *matatas* since independence. First there had been the fighting between the Lumumbiste followers of Gizenga and the Belgian troops after the ANC mutiny which followed independence. Then the Baluba tribal war. Then the fighting between Tshombe's mercenaries and the troops of the United Nations during the time of Katanga's secession. In July of the past year, three weeks before the Mulelistes took over Kongolo, the ANC's who were stationed in the town, and hadn't been paid for months, looted all the shops. Afterward they had packed off, leaving the civilian population to the mercy of the rebels. And now the *matata* just a few kilometers to the north, in the province of Maniema. Even in Stanley's time, *matatas* had a way of originating in Maniema and then spreading south.

"One really does not know whether to pity or to despise the natives of Manyema," Stanley wrote in *Through the Dark Continent*. "Many are amiable enough to deserve good and kind treatment, but others are hardly human. They fly to the woods upon the approach of strangers, leaving their granaries of Indian corn, erected like screens across the street, or just outside the villages, in tempting view of hungry people. If the strangers follow them into the woods to persuade them to return and sell food, the purpose of the visit is mistaken, and they are assailed from behind depths of bush and tall trees. They are humble and liberal to the strong-armed Arab, savage and murderous and cannibalistic to small bands, and every slain man provides a banquet of meat for the forest-natives of Manyema."

Even the monumentally patient Dr. Livingstone, who had preceded Stanley into the area by several years, took exception to the Maniema natives on their fourth attempt to take his life and ordered his followers to "fire upon them, these men are wicked."

Kongolo sprawled along the west bank of the Lualaba and, despite its raw nerves, was seductively somnolent in the heat of the tropical sun. It remains, for me, the most African town I have visited—not in the sense of straw-thatched native villages but in the way I always imagined it had been for white men who came to Africa at the turn of the century to carve a few acres of civilization out of the jungle, only to find in the end that the jungle has entered their souls. Conrad could have written about Kongolo, of the long grass weaving up through the bodies of the dead automobiles on the sides of the roads, of the grass growing on the floorboards of idled freight cars, and of the ghostly sternwheeler perched motionless amidstream in the rapids just north of the town. I think he would have understood why the handful of Europeans still remaining in Kongolo used almost as many Swahili as French words in talking to one another and why, when they were not working together, they often went their separate ways—one to fish by himself from a dead tree on the banks of the river and another to bargain for a woman in the African section of town.

What the jungle could not accomplish man took upon himself. The jungle was surer but man was quicker. Just before the departure of the Mulelistes, a riverfront warehouse loaded with dynamite had exploded, scarring brick walls and tearing the corrugated iron roofs off buildings for miles around. Since then, no one had tried to repair the roofs, even though people were still living in the houses. The failure to keep the elephant grass cut had meant more mosquitoes, and the dampness and the malaria, combined with a severe shortage of food, had brought much sickness and death.

Kabwa, Vincent, *administrateur territorial à Kongolo*, was a small man with glasses. When he took me into his office, the hangers-on in the anteroom stood up. Evidently he commanded respect even though he had only recently returned to Kongolo.

"If I hadn't left," he said, "the Mulelistes would have killed me." I did not ask Monsieur Kabwa what had taken him so long to get back. He said his area covered four hundred square kilometers and that he was responsible for a population of thirty thousand.

"Half the population is sick," he said, "and we have no doctor. There was an American doctor here for a while but he has gone home. He said he would return but I do not think he is coming back."

An Italian mechanic who had spent forty years in the Congo showed me, with what came close to pride, the destruction inflicted on the Cotonco cotton gin and seed press on the southern edge of Kongolo. Outside, in the yard, stood a row of tractors, each of them stripped of its tires. The doors on the workers' houses had been torn from their hinges. Machinery that could be broken was broken and it would be months, perhaps, before enough parts could be brought in from Europe to allow the establishment to start operating again. And none of this—the Italian mechanic was insistent on this point—none of this destruction had been caused by the Mulelistes. No, it had been done by the ordinary people of Kongolo during the period just after the Mulelistes and before the return of the whites. But why? The Italian spread his arms to signify utter bewilderment.

"The worst enemy of the black man," he said, "is the black man."

His companion and superior at Cotonco took up the theme. You could say without exaggeration that the people were starving, that never was their need for money to buy food and clothing more desperate. Remember, he said, the Muleliste invasion was only the most recent in a series of terrible calamities, coming at a time when the population was already on its knees. You would think that the people would be hungry for work, no?

"No," he said, answering his question. "Each year we would go out in our trucks and tell the village chiefs that now was the time to plant cotton. And then, later in the year, we would drive around again and tell them that now was the time to harvest their crop. But this year when we failed to drive around because of the trouble, do you think they went ahead and planted cotton without us? Certainly not. So we must begin all over again, from the beginning."

If Kongolo was the beginning then it would be a long way to the end. What energies were being expended to reopen the long road back (and they were few) were devoted almost exclusively to the military aspects of the problem. Kongolo was safe, or so they kept telling the populace. But just the other night the ANC's had shot two Mulelistes coming down the C.F.L. tracks from the north, and almost every night you could hear the drums beating across the river. Usually the drum beating meant nothing more than a village dance but sometimes the drums meant something else, and then, the next morning, there would be a wave of absenteeism in the ranks of the C.F.L. and those who did report for duty worked sluggishly and in fear. No, it was true, said the white men. There could not even be a beginning for Kongolo unless the fear was driven away.

There were never more than three or four white mercenaries in Kongolo during the time I was there and most of these came into town only to have a bath, eat a decent meal out of the C.F.L.'s three refrigerators, and get drunk on cold beer before heading out into the bush again. One of these came into Kongolo from the Luika. He told me later he had been prepared to tell the truth, to say there had been a minor attack on the ANC outpost there but that it had been driven off with no casualties. But when he had heard all the rumors of a large-scale *matata* he had dressed up his story considerably. It was, he confessed, the best way of getting more beer out of Charles and Louis. The mercenary's name was Henri Thiry. He held the rank of Adjudant Chef and, since he affected a pistol in a holster at his waist and was considerably bowlegged, his friends had given him the Wild West name of Cactus. The Africans, who could not pronounce Cactus and did not understand the significance of the name, called him Cartouche, which means cartridge in French. Small, wiry, balding and moustachioed, he had been a cab driver in Brussels and knew every way there was to gyp the company of its share of his fares.

"Never the passengers," he said. "Only the company."

I met Cactus on the evening he arrived in Kongolo. He was sharing a house with a fellow mercenary called Jean Paul Van den Brand and the latter's beautiful African wife. She was from Elisabethville and wore her hair differently each day. On the first evening she had braided two hanks of hair and then joined them in a graceful arch over the top of her head, like the handle of a palm-frond basket. She had done the same with the hair at her temples, joining the two braids in the middle so they bisected her forehead. Her eyes were large and oval and when she moved she was all hips and elbows, awkwardly graceful like a very young colt. Together Jean Paul Van den Brand and his African wife had produced a son, a blue-eyed child of about five months whom she called Petit. The mercenaries called him Le Capitaine and would dandle him on their knees until he wet on them. Then they would roar with laughter and ask each other whether that wasn't just like a captain to do a thing like that.

Cactus had been telling the story of the fight at the Luika River when Louis and I entered the room and after I had been introduced he began to tell it again, picking up his pistol off the table around which we were seated and flourishing it. There was ammunition scattered over the top of the table and Petit, seated on his mother's lap, had picked up the magazine of an automatic weapon and was chewing it with his toothless gums. There was no electricity in Kongolo other than that supplied by the C.F.L.'s generators and the room we were in was lighted by two kerosene lamps. Cactus had reached a climax in his story when another mercenary appeared in the doorway. Cactus stopped talking in mid-sentence. The newly arrived mercenary was tall and young and carried a full red beard, and he walked around the table shaking hands with everyone. Then he asked Jean Paul a question, received a monosyllabic answer, shook hands all around again and departed. The room remained silent for a while and then Cactus said that it was too bad about the mercenary with the beard but that these things sometimes happened and that when they did it was best to do what this particular man was doing and go away as quickly and as quietly as possible. The bearded mercenary had turned coward at Luika. He had turned his back on the enemy, and on his friends, and had run.

"It could happen to any man," said Jean Paul.

"Yes," said Cactus, "but if it should happen to me I would not let the blacks see what I am doing. That is unforgivable—to show the blacks that a white man can be a coward."

There was a murmur of assent around the room and Jean Paul started to laugh. After the mercenary had shown his cowardice, he said, the Africans in his platoon had gone into his tent and stolen all his beer. You could not blame them. It was simple justice.

They talked for a while about what makes a man a coward, or a hero, and Cactus said he was glad his assignment was to help build a new bridge across the Luika. It was like being in the army engineers in America, he explained. Sometimes you had to fight to defend yourself but most of the time you were working. Speaking for himself, he would not enjoy being a combat mercenary at the present time because you could not call what was going on now combat. Most of the real fighting was over—the capture of the large towns and the rebel strongholds—and what was taking place now was something called *ratissage*. Vast areas remained to be "pacified," he said—areas where the population's allegiance remained either doubtful or unknown. To secure these areas, a truckload or two of ANC's led by a jeepful of white mercenaries, would hurtle along the roads until they came to a native village. Then, unless the villagers demonstrated their fealty to the conquerers in some unmistakable way (and the tragedy was that they were often too frightened to do anything but run) they would be fired on indiscriminately. Of course, said Cactus, the ANC's did most of the shooting but still it was something he was glad he had no hand in. All those women and children. No, that was not warfare. That was no job for men.

Friday was payday for the C.F.L. It was the last Friday of the month of February and Louis had spent most of the preceding day arranging stacks of Congolese francs on the dining table according to their denomination. The paying of monthly wages to the workers was done from the C.F.L. office next to the railroad tracks by the Congolese paymaster and his assistants, but the beer ration was distributed from the house in which Georges and Louis lived, and either Georges or Louis did the distributing. Beer was more important than money. Each C.F.L. worker got five bottles of beer for which he was charged sixty-five francs a bottle. That was his monthly ration. He could double his money by selling his beer on the open market, but most of the employees drank it themselves. The employees' names were checked off on a master list as they appeared on the porch of the C.F.L. mess and, to obtain his five bottles, each of the workers had to produce five empty ones. It was no good arriving at the doorstep with two empties because that would lead either to confusion or cheating. It was five empties or no beer. A large number of town officials, gendarmes, ANC officers and the like also presented themselves at the C.F.L. mess that Friday. They would start off by asking Georges or Louis whether they had heard anything more about the fighting at Luika, or tell them about some other minor *matata*, and then they would ask whether the C.F.L. had any extra beer for sale. The answer was always in the negative. After all, it *was* beer that kept the C.F.L. going and it would be sheer stupidity to dilute its value by giving it away or selling it to outsiders.

That night, after the beer had been distributed, the sound of drums came from all directions. Cactus, who was having dinner with us, said it sounded peaceful enough to him but Louis said it made him nervous. He was going up the line tomorrow to pay off the workers who cut the wood for the wood-burning engines which ran between Kongolo and Kindu, and now, what with all this drum beating, he thought it was a good idea if Cactus came along to guard the payroll. Cactus said he would do anything for beer and had another on the spot. I said I would be glad to come along too and that that would make three of us. Louis looked happier.

We were scheduled to leave at 9 A.M., but when Louis and I arrived at the C.F.L. yards the small gasoline-engine handcar which was to carry us north had developed pump trouble and it was two hours before the mechanic-driver pronounced the engine fit to run. Louis put the cash box under the front seat next to the driver and climbed in. Between his knees he set a plastic sack containing three bottles of Simba beer, two bottles of soda water and a .45-caliber burp gun.

"Allez," he said.

Cactus, wearing an Anzac-style campaign hat with its brim turned up on one side, carried a Belgian-made F.A.L. automatic rifle on his shoulder and a .22-caliber target pistol in a holster at his waist. We shuddered forward, the clutch slipping badly—three whites, the Congolese paymaster and about ten Africans. We sat on wooden benches, facing backward, and rode this way to a switch about half a mile out of town. There the car was turned around and we started north facing frontward, the wind drying our sweating faces and arms and the tracks tunneling through the high elephant grass.

In almost no time, the driver started having difficulty changing gears, which he had to do frequently to climb the gentle grades. When the car stalled completely an examination of the fuel line showed that it was clogged with cotton waste. Sabotage? Louis thought it entirely possible. This was what was always happening to the Cotonco trucks. The driver-mechanic blew the cotton out of the fuel line and we started off again, the engine still sputtering and the clutch slipping so badly that Louis told the driver to keep it in one gear if he could. Cactus and I had hoped that we would travel fast because, if Louis finished paying off the workers in time, perhaps he could take us all the way up to the town of Samba, which marked the border between the province of North Katanga and Maniema. We had heard over the radio that a large group of mercenaries and ANC's had assembled there and were preparing to cross the Lualaba and attack Kasongo. Kasongo was the major Muleliste garrison in our area. Somehow it had been bypassed in the large-scale drive which liberated Kabalo, Kongolo and Kindu. But now the behavior of the handcar made it doubtful that we would finish in time to go on to Samba and return to Kongolo by nightfall.

Our first scheduled stop (we had stopped a dozen times on the way for repairs) was at the Lusindoi station, a collection of three buildings and a water tower at the side of the tracks. Louis and the paymaster sat themselves down behind a table which had been set up in the shade of one of the buildings and began to pay off the woodcutters. There was much argument between the paymaster and an old man who seemed to be the spokesman for the workers. It had to do with the C.F.L.'s policy of not paying in advance for wood to be cut. The old man said he understood the policy and that his men had cut wood in anticipation of payment. But the Mulelistes had come along and stolen the wood. He and the others had cut the wood in good faith. Was it *their* fault that the Mulelistes . . . Louis cut them off. They knew the rules. They knew the regulations. There was nothing he could do about it. The argument subsided and payday proceeded.

While this was going on another handcar—this one without engine—was pushed from a spur onto the main track and coupled to ours. Cactus, browsing around behind the buildings, found a pair of antelope horns which he bought for 350 francs and a skin, the stiffness of parchment, which he bought for 250. He said he wanted the horns for himself. The skin he would sell in Kongolo, certainly at a considerable profit.

It took Louis and the paymaster an hour to complete their work and then we were off again, this time towing the other handcar with ten additional Africans. Because of the added weight, we moved even more slowly now and it took us more than half an hour to travel the three miles to our next stop, a group of six or seven mud-and-grass huts in a clearing in the forest. While Louis and the paymaster did their paying from the handcar—this time there was no argument about payment in advance—the villagers made us sit in folding sling chairs produced for Cactus and myself, and then, with much laughter and considerable pride, introduced three shy and almost naked pygmoids. They seemed to be the village mascots and, with their eyes fastened on their own distended bellies, let me take their photographs. Payday here was a matter of minutes and Louis signaled to us to get back into the handcar. The driver started the engine and at the same moment that it sputtered to life, the floorboards of the car turned black with oil. Whatever the internal injuries, they were mortal and the engine died. We climbed out, wiped our oily shoes in the grass and then (it was the only decision possible) agreed to return to Lusindoi. Lusindoi was closer to Kongolo and it had a telephone.

The tracks pointed downhill and for a while we coasted south, traveling fast enough so that the driver had to apply the brakes on curves. We had enough momentum to take the first hill but on the second the car came to a stop well before the summit. The driver braked so that we would not roll back again and Cactus and I hopped out. Louis and the paymaster remained seated as did several Africans who, although they did not wear white collars, could be classified as intellectuals because they seemed to have come along to help the paymaster. The remaining Africans jumped off when Cactus and I did and started pushing the car up the hill. Cactus and I helped push too, and when the car reached the crest of the hill we got back on and rode until the car came to a halt again. Again the same Africans, Cactus, and I jumped off and started pushing. Under my breath, I asked Cactus why in hell the intellectuals didn't get off too.

"We and the others," he said, cocking his head in the direction of the Africans who were pushing, "are workers. The rest are administrators. They would lose face with the workers if they had to push also."

Louis sat in the front seat not looking at us but staring ahead down the tracks. I suppose Cactus and I embarrassed him. It was about two o'clock in the afternoon by the time we had pushed the car into Lusindoi. Cactus and I stretched ourselves out on the grass and Louis got on the telephone and started calling.

"Allô, Kongolo. Allô, Kongolo." There was no answer and after ten minutes of this his voice became hoarse, his tone irritated, and he turned the instrument over to one of the paymaster's assistants and sank down on the grass next to us. The sign on the tracks at Lusindoi said we were thirty-two kilometers from Kongolo. We moved into the little compound in back of the station house, where the women were pounding manioc into powder, straining it through sieves and then throwing the lumpy parts onto the ground, where the scrawny chickens pecked them up. Somebody produced a porridgelike substance, the consistency of plaster of Paris, which turned out to be a mixture of rice and manioc. We ate some of it with our fingers and finished what was left of Louis's beer and soda water. Through the walls we could hear the voice of the assistant paymaster calling Kongolo. Boredom. The chickens pecking at the manioc. The men recumbent under the trees. Boredom.

Cactus rose, picked up a large tin can and placed it at the far side of the compound. He backed away from it and then, raising his pistol until it was level with his eye, started shooting at it. He kept missing. The women went on pounding their manioc. Then Louis got out his little burp gun and started squeezing off single shots at the can. He missed too. I tried and also missed although the target was large and stationary. Finally Cactus picked up his automatic rifle, the F.A.L. He held the large weapon against his hip. With a series of blood-curdling yells he pranced toward the can, at the same time firing long bursts from the F.A.L. The bullets went all over. Some of them hit the can and it kicked backward, but many of them sprayed into the walls of the buildings in the compund. When he was satisfied that the tin can was dead, Cactus grinned hugely, went over and picked it up and held it above his head like a trophy. Several African men applauded but the women seemed not to have noticed. All except one. She came over to Cactus and asked what she was going to do now for a tin can. She needed the can for cooking and now it was full of holes. Cactus promised to give her a new can and a full one at that.

Boredom returned.

At about 5 P.M. the man on the telephone made contact with Kongolo. Since there were no more handcars in working order in the yards, they would have to fire up one of the locomotives and send that out. Although it was Saturday, the day after payday, they would see what they could do. Two hours later Kongolo got back on the line and announced that a crew had indeed been rounded up, that a locomotive—oh, miracle of miracles—had actually left Kongolo at 6:25. Louis looked at his watch and announced that, with luck, the train would arrive in Lusindoi around 8 P.M.

Night fell. We watched the women cook their manioc over a fire in the cookhouse. Heat lightning flashed in the sky. At 7:30 some of the Congolese thought they heard the hoot of a locomotive whistle. We assumed they had heard correctly because Africans have the reputation for hearing things long before a white man can hear them. But at 8 P.M. the same Africans announced that they could hear the whistle no longer. I walked out to the tracks and put my ear on the rails. I had read somewhere that this was the way the plains Indians detected the approach of an Iron Horse, but I could hear nothing. Most of the Africans were sleeping now. There was nothing to eat and, worse still, no beer. At 9 P.M., I asked Cactus how long he thought it would take us to walk from Lusindoi to Kongolo. Instead of answering he rose and hung his F.A.L. on his shoulder.

"Let's go," he said in English and added, in French, "Anything is better than this putain place."

Louis said he would stay behind with the others. He said something to Cactus about the darkness and the Mulelistes but Cactus laughed and we started off down the tracks toward Kongolo. Cactus walked ahead and I followed, keeping my eye on the vague blur which was the back of his shirt. We could see fairly well because lightning flashed frequently—at intervals of about five seconds—and illuminated the rails for some distance ahead. We did not walk on the ties but tried to follow a small footpath next to them. At one point Cactus stumbled on a loose stone and fell sideways into the steep ditch on our right. He scraped his leg and hand in the fall but otherwise was all right and we continued. It was still better to keep walking than to sit down and die gradually of a thirst for beer.

It was difficult to tell in the darkness but we guessed we had walked about three miles when suddenly, up ahead, there was a heavy, low-pitched noise followed by a shower of sparks. Cactus and I leaped to either side of the tracks just as the locomotive, thundering metallically and spewing sparks, lurched around a curve and bore down on us. Instinctively and simultaneously, Cactus and I hallooed and waved our arms as the cab of the engine drew abreast of us. For a moment I thought we had frightened the engineer into continuing but then there was the sound of escaping steam and the engine stopped about fifty yards down the tracks. Cactus and I swung aboard. The cab was lighted by roaring fire from the open door of the furnace and a taper which the engineer used to study the steam pressure gauge. The pressure must have been down because his two assistants climbed into the tender behind us and started pitching large logs onto the floor of the cab. When there was no room left to stand in the cab, they came down from the tender and pushed and jockeyed the logs into the furnace with the help of a long iron rod. Then they closed the door of the furnace and we waited. Gradually the water mounted in the tube of the gauge, and when it was sufficiently high the engineer pulled the throttle. In a bucket in one corner of the cab we found four bottles of beer. Cactus and I shared one, and then, knowing that Louis could not be nearly as thirsty as we were because he had not walked down the tracks with us, we polished off another.

At Lusindoi, we took on more wood, enough to fill the tender. The handcar and an empty freight car which happened to be sitting on a spur of track were coupled to the tender and then, with a decisive blast of the whistle, we began the return trip to Kongolo. Louis said he would ride in the freight car but Cactus and I elected to stay with the locomotive—a foolhardy decision as it started to rain heavily the moment we were under way and we had to huddle against the furnace, our backsides wet and our frontsides crisping like smoked bacon. But we felt fine. The beer had made us jubilant. The sparks from the locomotive's chimney flashed overhead like tracer bullets.

By the time we pulled into the yards of Kongolo, it was well past midnight. We had stopped several times to build up steam. The tender had been licked clean of wood and our faces were grimy with charcoal, soot and rain. Back in the C.F.L. mess, Louis could not seem to understand why Cactus and I kept laughing as we drank our beer.

CHAPTER 15

ALLONS, MES GUERRIERS

An internecine "war" in Manyema is exceedingly comical. Old Riba-Riba, a patriarch of eighty or thereabouts, who with his few villages guards the frontier on the range separating Uhombo from Manyema, told me he was at "war" with Mwana Buttu of Nyembu. The cause was the murder of a young man of Riba-Riba's by Mwana Buttu's people.

When the shocking affair became known there was great excitement, much manifestation of anger, loud talk, sharpening of broad-bladed spears, and industrious preparation of stacks of fire-hardened wooden assegais and other deadly war materiel. *All things being ready, Riba-Riba's people reluctantly set off to fight Mwana Buttu's villagers, not, however, without first communicating their intentions and publishing by criers a formal and fierce declaration of war.*

But Mwana Buttu is of a sterner nature than is common in Manyema; consequently, to Riba-Riba's surprise, he did not abscond for fear of the invading host, but calmly arrayed his warriors in order of battle on the opposite side of a stream that he might take advantage of the enemy's confusion while crossing.

Riba-Riba's warriors, on emerging from the depth of the forest, perceived the foe palisaded behind their tall door-like shields, and immediately formed themselves in like order on their own side of the stream. From this position they opened on the enemy volleys of tongue abuse, which lasted for hours; until at last both sides, fatigued with the wordy encounter and hoarse with the prolonged vituperative exercise, mutually consented to defer the battle until next day.

The morrow dawned, and both sides, vigilantly active after their night's rest, reformed themselves in the same positions which they had occupied on the previous day, and resumed the wordy war with all its fierce gestures, and a great clangor of wooden shields, until sunset, when both parties retired from the field with no decisive advantage to either side.

On the third day the wordy war was resumed, until both tribes, exhausted from the bloodless conflict, mutually agreed that they would postpone the war with spears to an indefinite period. Meanwhile they have left off visiting.

—H. M. STANLEY

THE time had come for Cactus and Jean Paul Van den Brand to leave Kongolo and return to the Luika River. Cactus said he would be able to find room for me at the forward camp and I joined him in the courtyard of the establishment he shared with Jean Paul.

Their official reason for having come back to Kongolo was to find a new cook for the camp and when I arrived the cook was seated on some bedsprings which had been placed in the back of a truck. Like most cooks, he felt himself unsuited for other work and sat on the springs with a dour and aloof expression on his face while the others helped load the truck.

The cargo included four cases of beer, which were the property of Jean Paul's African wife. She had bought them (I do not know how) from the C.F.L. at sixty-five francs a bottle and was taking them across the river to the town of Sola, where she would sell them for well over a hundred. When the truck was loaded, it contained, in addition to the beer and the bedsprings, several boxes of ammunition, blankets, bicycles, bananas, live chickens with their feet bound together, tenting equipment, a roll of heavy cable and about ten Africans.

With his wife holding Petit on her lap in the front seat and Cactus and me perched on boxes of ammunition just behind the hood, Jean Paul drove us down to the river and onto a ferry made of lashed-together American army pontoons. There were two outboard motors attached to the pontoons. Cactus could get only one of them started but it was powerful enough to get us across the river. Once on the far bank, we were joined by five more Africans and a goat, its feet bound like those of the chickens.

Cactus said it was about fifty kilometers to the Luika camp and that from here on he would have to pay attention. He placed his F.A.L. automatic rifle on the hood of the truck. The road, which had not been repaired since the summer before, was extremely rough, dotted with potholes and gnarled by the rains. Cactus and I, leaning forward over the cab, had to duck frequently to avoid low-hanging branches. The road followed the Lualaba for about seven miles and then wandered into the hills east of the river. Cactus said that the natives in this area were against the Mulelistes, which made them, if not exactly pro-white, at least not anti-white. We passed several broken-down trucks and I noticed that two of them belonged to the Cotonco people. We had started late and the sun now was directly overhead and very hot. The other passengers had managed to squeeze the new cook off the bedsprings and he appealed to Cactus for justice; Cactus told him he would have to learn to fend for himself and the cook, squatting uncomfortably on the handlebars of a bicycle, fell silent.

We deposited Jean Paul's wife and her baby at the empty mission station at Sola. Most of the other Africans got off with her, emptying the truck of everything except the ammunition boxes and the steel cables. Le Capitaine, true to his name, drenched the arms of one of the Africans who had been holding him while Jean Paul's wife supervised the unloading of the beer, and everyone laughed. From Sola it was ten kilometers further north to the Luika camp. We arrived at dusk.

The camp consisted of six large army tents, several grass-walled huts and a grass roof erected over a long dining table. The area around the tents, long since denuded of grass, was surrounded by a rail fence. Sentinels had been placed at intervals around the fence and the guards at the gates, carrying bows and arrows, saluted as we drove inside. Cactus said he and I would sleep in the tent usually occupied by a Belgian captain who had left the week before and would not be returning from leave until some weeks later. The tent was crammed with boxes of ammunition and dynamite but Cactus said that there was nothing to worry about because the fuses were kept in another tent.

Jean Paul and the other mercenaries were drinking beer at the dining table when Cactus and I joined them. Like Cactus and Jean Paul, Yves Corroy was a nonfighting mercenary and held the rank of Adjudant Chef. Shorter but stockier than Cactus, he had covered his upper lip with a drooping blond mustache. The two others were fighting mercenaries. One, a huge and taciturn young man, they called Yeng. I suppose that it was spelled "Jeng" but I never did find out and he seemed satisfied that I should know as little about him as possible. The other was called Freddy. My appearance at the camp was excuse enough for Corroy to produce a bottle of Scotch. We drank it down rapidly and I contributed another I had bought from Georges and Louis in Kongolo. We drank that too. By now, Cactus had pumped a Coleman lamp into life and the mess boys served us soup and then meat and potatoes. I thought it was delicious but Jeng pushed it away with a curse and glared at Cactus.

There had been some chivvying back and forth between Cactus and the two fighting mercenaries, much of which I did not understand, but now the fight began to clarify itself. Jeng and Freddy, it seemed, had been left in charge of the *guerriers* by the departed captain. The *guerriers*, or warriors, were some forty local tribesmen whose duty it was to guard the camp and go out on occasional reconnaissance patrols with the mercenaries. Their training, Freddy was saying now, was his and Jeng's responsibility, and he did not want Cactus interfering in any way. Cactus' job was the mess. He could do what he liked there. Freddy and Jeng would not interfere with the mess except, of course, to serve notice that the food was inedible. But the point was not the mess but the *guerriers*, and

Freddy wished Cactus to know that he had seen Cactus give one of the *guerriers* a bottle of beer. Cactus was incensed. He had not given a *guerrier* a bottle of beer and if he had he had forgotten it.

"Our job is the bridge," said Corroy, including Cactus and Jean Paul in a wave of his hand. "And your job," he added, pointing at Freddy and the silent Jeng, "is to fight. Tout le monde fait son boulot. Everybody has his work."

Freddy was not mollified. Again he accused Cactus of giving beer to a *guerrier*, thus undermining his authority, and again Cactus denied it.

"So you say," Freddy snarled. "We'll see. We'll see."

His tone of voice was nasty. Jean Paul, who had said nothing thus far, stood up and announced that he was driving the truck back to Sola. He would return the following morning with the *ouvriers*—the Congolese workers who spent their nights in Sola and their days at the bridge three miles to our north.

After Jean Paul's departure, it was Jeng's turn. As the officer in charge of the mess, Cactus held one of the two keys to the hut in which the food and beer was kept. Was this not so? Yes, that was so, said Cactus. Jeng started to grin. It was a lethal grin. Cactus rose to his feet unsteadily. He was trembling.

"What do you mean by that?" he shouted. "I demand that you say what you mean."

"We'll see. We'll see," said Freddy. Corroy banged his fist on the table so that the dishes rattled. I noticed that Freddy's eyes did not blink.

"But listen," said Corroy. "Listen. This is stupid. We are all buddies . . . copains, aren't we?" Sleepily Freddy's eyes moved from Cactus to Corroy.

"We'll see. We'll see."

Jeng had a portable radio next to him on the table and started to play it loudly. He kept twisting the dials in an infuriating way so that no piece of music lasted longer than a few seconds, so that no sentence spoken by an announcer was ever complete. I said good night and went back to the captain's tent and lay down on one of the two canvas cots. I do not know what time it was when I was awakened by the sound of raised voices and the radio playing louder than ever.

"You go fifteen kilometers in one direction, and I'll go fifteen in the other direction," I heard Cactus shout, "and you'll see. I'll find the Mulelistes first."

I did not understand what that meant, nor did I hear Freddy's response, but I imagined he was still egging Cactus on and saying something like "We'll see." I dropped off to sleep again only to be aroused a few minutes later by Cactus stumbling into the tent. He muttered something I could not understand and stumbled out again. Then, from outside, there were loud cries of "That's enough," and "What have you done?" from Corroy, followed by comparative silence.

I slept fitfully that night, waking several times to the music from Jeng's radio. Cactus was already seated at the table when I got up next morning. He was removing a long bandage wrapped around his head and a Congolese medical orderly was seated next to him. The medical orderly had a high voice and wore a Red Cross armband. There was an open metal box on the table containing socks, dust, shoelaces and a motley and filthy collection of medical equipment. The bandage which Cactus was unwinding from his head was bloodstained but after it had been taken off and the medical orderly had sponged his forehead, using water from a tin can, there remained only a small cut on Cactus' forehead. The medical orderly made a smaller bandage and fixed it to Cactus' forehead with two strips of flesh-colored adhesive tape. Cactus looked pale.

In answer to my questions, he said there had been a fight with that *crapule* Freddy and that Freddy had thrown two beer bottles at him. Only one of them had connected. Cactus said he thought he had hit Freddy with something, too, but he couldn't remember with what. The medical orderly, having finished with Cactus, washed a syringe in the can of bloody water he had been using to sponge Cactus' forehead and offered to inject Cactus with penicillin. Cactus looked at the needle, turned even paler, and refused. The medical orderly put the used bandages into his kit, closed the lid, and walked away. Cactus and I ate cornflakes with powdered milk. There were large black flies all over the table and we had to eat rapidly to keep them out of the cornflakes. Cactus said he had seen them empty a bowl of powdered sugar in less than half an hour.

Corroy seemed pale too when he appeared but he was nothing compared with Jeng and Freddy. They approached the breakfast table with that painfully stiff walk men have when they are violently hungover. Apparently the medical orderly had been with Freddy because a cut under his eye had been painted red with Mercurochrome. Neither Jeng nor Freddy spoke, and when Corroy suggested that Freddy and Cactus shake hands Freddy did not answer.

While the others were getting ready to go down to the bridge (Jean Paul had by now arrived with a truckload of *ouvriers* from Sola), Jeng took me to a corner of the camp, next to the fence, to show me his eagle. It was a young bird and Jeng had built it a perch and a small house on stilts. The bird was still too young to fly and uttered piteous peeps as we drew close, but it must have acquired something from its keeper because it glared at us balefully and lashed at Jeng with his beak. Later in the day, Jeng said, he would go down to the swamp and catch some frogs for the bird. He said it was interesting the way the eagle ate the live frogs. He always took out their eyeballs first. Jeng said he wouldn't be going down to the bridge that morning.

"Let the others," he said. "I've had enough."

Cactus, Jean Paul, Corroy and I drove in the truck with the *ouvriers* to the Luika, passing Freddy and his *guerriers* on the way. Freddy did not return our waves. Just before reaching the Luika, we slowed down so as not to run over several members of the Congolese National Army who were lying in the ditches on either side, their backs against the bank and their feet in the road. They were part of the ANC company assigned to guard the bridge against rebels. And then the Luika itself—a gray-brown stream flowing swiftly from east to west past high banks choked with lush green foliage and tall, overhanging trees with trunks the color of old bones. The stream was about thirty yards wide at this point and the road led down to the approaches of a reinforced steel and concrete bridge. But the bridge itself had been blown up by Belgian paratroopers in 1960, ostensibly to hamper the Lumumbistes but more likely to see how well they could do it. A few yards farther downstream someone had constructed a floating bridge made of boards and cables and fifty-gallon gasoline drums but the drums were beginning to fill with water and this bridge could no longer be used by vehicles. And so Corroy, Cactus and the others had rigged up a ferry which was wired to an overhead cable and could be pulled back and forth across the Luika by hand. They hoped to go to work soon on a more permanent structure, using what was left of the original bridge to support the new one, but too much equipment and material were missing to make much of a start and Corroy had most of the *ouvriers* working on entrenchments and machine-gun nests instead.

A group of ANC's were drinking something out of a canteen and when I asked what it was they offered me some. It was harsh but not unpleasant, like some of the corn likker that is brewed in South Carolina. I, in turn, offered to take their pictures. Lying down in a row, they waited until I was ready and then smilingly pointed their rifles at my head.

The *ouvriers* went to work on the trenches and Freddy, who had arrived at the bridge by this time, led a squad of his *guerriers* across the gasoline-drum bridge to the far side of the stream. He had his hands in his trousers pockets and did not seem to care where he was going as he disappeared down the road and into the trees. Ten minutes later he was back, his hands still in his pockets, and told Corroy that was enough patrolling for one day. Besides, he said, there was no sense taking risks so close to his departure. Corroy arched an eyebrow. What departure? Oh, hadn't Jeng told him? Yes, he and Jeng were taking the second truck back to Kongolo that afternoon. It needed a part. Freddy waited for Corroy to challenge his authority to go off with the spare truck but was disappointed. Corroy merely turned and went back to supervising the *ouvriers* in the trenches. But for Cactus, who had heard what had passed between Freddy and Corroy, it was too much.

"Then you are finished here?" he asked. Freddy replied that he was indeed finished here.

"Then if you have no objections," Cactus said acidly, "I will take the guerriers on a real patrol. What you have done with them today is nothing."

Freddy shrugged his shoulders.

"As you wish, mon commandant," he said.

Freddy had left his squad of *guerriers* on the banks of the river and when Cactus and I arrived several of them had started washing themselves in the stream. I noticed that they kept themselves apart from the ANC's and Cactus said this was because they were Bahembas and the ANC's were from the South. It was a tribal matter, he said, and therefore it was difficult to say at any given moment which they hated more—the Mulelistes across the Luika or the ANC's presently encamped on their home ground. If it weren't for the whites, he added, they would be at each other's throats in a minute.

Cactus got the *guerriers* lined up on either side of the road on the far side of the bridge. We were now, officially, standing on rebel territory and Cactus told the *guerriers* to keep five meters' distance between each other. There were fourteen *guerriers* in all. Three carried rifles and the rest carried spears and bows and arrows. In most cases the arrows had been dipped in poison. If the poison was fresh, the slightest wound would cause death. Cactus sent two *guerriers* ahead as scouts and when they had gone about fifteen yards he motioned the rest to follow.

Cactus pointed out several places along the side of the road where the grass had been beaten flat. These, he said, were where the Mulelistes had made their beds on the night before their dawn attack on the bridge. There had been much firing, he said, but no wounded on the ANC side. Later on the same morning they had searched the area on the rebel side of the river for bodies but had found none. Perhaps the Mulelistes had suffered no casualties either, but one could not be certain. Of late, the Mulelistes had taken to carrying their dead away with them. Cactus said he thought they had been taught this by the Chinese.

We walked down the road for about two miles until Cactus, apparently satisfied that the enemy was elsewhere, about-faced the *guerriers* and led them back toward the Luika. At least he had gone further than Freddy.

Because of the amount of drink the night before, Corroy, Jean Paul and Cactus decided there was no real reason for prolonging the agony any longer and agreed to call it a day. We drove back to camp and after lunch the three nonfighting mercenaries retired to their tents. Jeng went off to feed his eagle and pack the things he needed for his trip to Kongolo and Freddy and I sat at the table and drank beer. Freddy's spirits seemed to have been restored. Compared with last night's performance, his behavior was downright engaging.

The difficulty, he said, was that Jeng and he were fighters. The others were workers. There was bound to be a conflict especially now that the captain had gone and there was no one in command.

"I am not here in this life to work," he said. "I am a fighter. It's true that I do not like to patrol. Cactus was right. But when the bullets start to fly, ça c'est mon métier."

He took off his beret and showed me a scar high on his forehead. A bullet had entered there, he said, and had departed just behind his ear.

"If I die," he said, "what does it matter? No wife, no children . . ."

He had been in the fighting business most of his adult life. Morocco, Indo-China, Algeria. Seven years in the Foreign Legion. Then for a while there had been no place for him to fight and he had gone back to Belgium. Civilian life, however, was not made for Freddy. Not long after his return, he was arrested and sentenced to fifteen months for having five girls working for him. He served ten months of his sentence and then was released on parole. The conditions of his parole were such that life on the outside was almost worse than life behind bars. For two years he would be forbidden to visit a race track or see a football match, nor would he be allowed to see his Polish girl or appear in a public place such as a bar or a restaurant. And (the unkindest cut of all) he was supposed to go to work. Casting about for some way out, he found his way to the

Congolese embassy, where a recruiter signed him on as a mercenary with the rank of Adjudant Chef. For five more years, he said, he would not be allowed to return to Belgium. He doubted that his lawyer, who was appealing the case, would be able to do much to shorten this period of banishment.

Jeng was now ready to go and he and Freddy started walking toward their truck. Freddy gave me his address and asked whether I would write him. He was receiving no mail from anyone, he said, and an occasional letter would be appreciated. I said I was a terrible letter writer but that I knew a girl or two who might welcome the chance to correspond with a bona fide mercenary.

"Bien," he said. "But get me a girl who will work for me. Otherwise, ça ne va pas."

After their naps, conscience drove Corroy and Jean Paul back down to the bridge and their *ouvriers*. Cactus and I wandered a short way down the road to a small stream and found a place where the stream widened to form a pool. Cactus said he thought the stream flowed fast enough so that there was no danger of bilharzia, a debilitating disease which is carried by minuscule fresh-water mollusks, and we took off our clothes and plunged in. The water was beautifully cold. Cactus had brought a bar of soap with him and afterward we washed ourselves and our clothes and placed them on the flat rocks next to the stream.

When we got back to the camp, Corroy and Jean Paul were standing next to one of the tents listening to a voluble and agitated African. When he had finished, Corroy replied in Swahili. The African nodded several times and then turned and jogged out of camp and down the road toward the Luika. Corroy waved us over. The African, he said, was a runner from a village on the other side of the Luika in rebel territory. The name of the village was Mukwanga. The day before, said Corroy, the Mulelistes had walked into the village and demanded that the village chief give them eighteen goats and several women. The Mulelistes said they would be back in a few days to collect the ransom. If the goats and the women were not forthcoming, they would burn the village and slaughter the inhabitants. Corroy said it was important that something be done to protect the villagers and, at the same time, show the rebels that the forces of law and order meant business.

It was agreed that a large patrol, led by the white men present and consisting of a platoon of ANC's and an equal number of *guerriers*, cross the Luika early the following morning, march across country to Mukwanga and reassure the village chief. Cactus would be in charge of the *guerriers*. Corroy would return now to the Luika and talk to the ANC commander. It would then be up to the commander to talk his troops into going. That was the commander's problem but Corroy was reasonably certain that he would succeed, not so much because the troops wanted to fight the rebels but because, after a week of inactivity at the bridge, they were bored.

While Corroy occupied himself with ANC's, Cactus checked the *guerrier* guards stationed at various places around the camp. He told each of them to be particularly alert and sent one up a tree to get a better view of the terrain to the north. Then, having satisfied himself that the camp was secure, he started bargaining with a group of natives who had gathered around the mess table. They had with them various kinds of fruit—mostly bananas and mangos—and scrawny chickens. Cactus bought five chickens at two hundred francs apiece and an incredibly thin young goat for eight hundred. He had almost completed these transactions when Corroy reappeared and said that the ANC commander had guaranteed him a platoon of soldiers for the following day. Then he looked at Cactus and at the traders.

"They should not be allowed in the camp," he said angrily. "They should not be allowed past the gate. How do we know what they are? They could all be spies."

Cactus looked abashed and the color rose to his cheeks.

"You are right," he said and ordered the civilians out of the camp. Then he sent one of the *guerriers* for the leader of the warriors, and when he arrived Cactus told him that henceforth no unauthorized personnel—and that included villagers, friends, wives and even ANC's—would be allowed past the gate without the express permission of Corroy, Jean Paul or himself. The leader of the *guerriers* was an old man with gray hair, a lesser tribal chief, and he saluted smartly after Cactus had given him the instructions. Then he said there was another matter which he would like to bring up as long as he had Commandant Cartouche's attention. A few hours earlier, seven dried fish had been stolen from the *guerriers'* mess. If Commandant Cartouche was interested, he had the names of the three guilty men. The old man dug into the pocket of his khaki shorts and produced a crumpled piece of paper on which he had written the names of the guilty men.

I think Cactus would have dealt differently with the matter if Corroy hadn't been there, but with Corroy present and listening with interest Cactus would have to be severe. It was a terrible crime, Cactus told the old man, and the men responsible must be dealt with harshly. The sentence would be three days' pay. Three days' pay forfeited. The old man bowed, saluted and walked back toward the *guerriers'* section of camp. Corroy pursed his lips.

"It is your decision," he said, examining his nails. "I will naturally do nothing to interfere. Nevertheless, I myself would not have punished the men at this time. Not just before a patrol."

The truck carrying the *ouvriers* drove into the camp. Jean Paul was in the cab and he shouted at Corroy that they were finished for the day and that he would be going back to Sola for the night with the workers. Corroy walked over to the truck. It was not right, he said, for Jean Paul to go back and leave only three white men in the camp. Jean Paul said he realized that the departure of Freddy and Jeng posed a problem but that he had his wife to think about.

"You should not have brought her to Sola," Corroy said. But Jean Paul, in his quiet way, was insistent and two minutes later he and the *ouvriers* were rolling down the road back to Sola.

That evening, Cactus was troubled by a headache and went to bed early, leaving Corroy and me at the dining table with two bottles of beer and the key to the food locker in case we should want more. We talked for a while about the problems of command and Corroy noted that each of the whites at the Luika River camp was there for a different reason—Jeng because he enjoyed killing, Freddy because he could not go back to Belgium, Jean Paul because of his African wife. If the motives did not coincide there was bound to be conflict.

He himself was there because he believed in a way of life which could only be found in Africa. Until the troubles had started after independence, he had been a *colon*, running a coffee plantation east of Stanleyville. Now that was all finished. The forest had come back and the coffee plants had shriveled and died. Perhaps it was too late but as long as there was the slightest chance that he could live that kind of life again—a simple life, mind you, with just enough food, no frills—he would fight for it. I asked Corroy whether he liked Africans and he replied that he did, that he felt closer to many Africans than he did to many whites, but that this did not mean he understood them. One should not even try to understand the Africans, he said.

"Africa is like a great river," he added. "It is a great undiscovered river. You should not try to swim against the current but with it. Here and there, on the banks, there are places for Europeans. You can if you want, and if you try, find a place for yourself on the bank. And from the bank you can watch the river go by, as I did. Or, as in your case, you can float down the river and watch the whites on the shore. But, whatever you do, do not try to swim upstream. If you do, you will get nowhere, or drown."

Corroy and I were about ready to call it a night when one of the *guerriers* at the gate came running over and told Corroy that he had heard the sound of a truck. He said it was about fifteen minutes away. Corroy and I could hear nothing but in ten minutes we did hear the sound of a motor, and in another five a truck, moving fast, came down the Sola road, swerved through the gate and into the camp. The back of the truck was filled with Africans, many of them carrying bows and spears. Jean Paul jumped out of the cab, holding a rifle in his hand. Were we all right? Corroy said of course we were all right. Had there been any trouble back in Sola? Jean Paul looked puzzled. Hadn't we heard the mortars? It was odd. In Sola they had distinctly heard what must have been the sound of mortar shells exploding and they had all agreed that the sound came from the Luika camp. Of course their first thought had been that we were under attack and so they had come up to join us and help us fight off the invaders.

Corroy and Jean Paul spread a map on a dining table and tested the wind with their fingers. It was just possible, they agreed, that the sound came from Kabambare fifty-odd miles northeast of the Luika camp. A group of white mercenaries and a company or so of Congolese soldiers, surrounded by rebels, had been holed up there for more than two weeks. Or could the sound conceivably have come from the Luika bridge? Joined now by Cactus, we ran to Jean Paul's truck, climbed aboard and roared toward the Luika. But at the Luika it was the same story. The ANC's huddled close to their fires had heard nothing.

It had been decided to start off on the first leg of the patrol at dawn but neither Corroy nor Cactus was much surprised when the truck from Sola with Jean Paul failed to arrive until 9 A.M. Jean Paul was not asked for an explanation nor did he volunteer one. While Corroy took the truck to the Luika to pick up the ANC's, Cactus lined up his *guerriers* for an inspection. Fifteen had been chosen for the patrol and, of these, six carried firearms. The rest were equipped with spears and bows and arrows. Cactus walked through the ranks, examining the weapons. He found grease on one of the rifles, wiped it off with his finger and smeared it on the *guerrier's* cheek. The *guerrier* said nothing but he looked as if he could have killed Cactus on the spot. Fifteen minutes later Corroy came back with twenty-five ANC's. Somehow Cactus and the fifteen *guerriers* also found places in the back of the truck and, with Corroy driving and Jean Paul and me riding in the cab with him, we headed south, away from the Luika, toward Sola.

The plan was to execute a wide flanking movement and come on the village of Mukwanga from behind. If the Mulelistes had prepared an ambush (it was always possible that the chief's messenger was a rebel agent) they would be expecting us to come from the east, from the road down which Cactus and I had walked the day before. Instead we would cross the Luika several miles downstream and then, marching northeast, approach Mukwanga from an unexpected direction.

At Sola Corroy changed course and followed a small road which ran northwest. The closer we got to the Luika, the narrower the road became and it finally petered out completely at a small village. Cactus handed me a burp gun and told me to carry it. I reminded him that I was a noncombatant and pointed to my heavy camera bag to indicate that I already had enough to carry.

"Give the cameras to one of the guerriers," he said. "You carry the gun."

With Corroy in the lead, we walked for about two miles along a trail that led to the river. It was a narrow trail, flanked by elephant grass and dense jungle growth, and we walked single file. The women returning from the Luika with jugs of water on their heads had to stand aside to let us pass. They looked frightened and when I said "Jambo" to one of them she turned and fled into the underbrush.

At the Luika Corroy was discouraged to find only one hollow-log pirogue to take us across the stream. He had asked for many. Corroy made some rapid calculations in his head and said it would take us over two hours to cross the river if everyone rode in the canoe. The Luika at this point was wide and shallower than it had been farther upstream and, after a short exploration of its banks, Corroy decided that the stream could be forded. He, Jean Paul and Cactus immediately stripped, made a bundle of their clothes and waded into the water. They held their clothing and their weapons over their heads.

"*Allons, mes guerriers*," Cactus shouted and the *guerriers*, to a man, plunged into the stream after him. From the bank the ANC's stared sullenly at the men splashing across the Luika and decided they would have none of this. Two of them got into the pirogue and the fisherman in the stern started paddling toward the far shore. The other ANC's sat down on the bank to await his return. Feeling slightly traitorous, I took the pirogue across too, telling myself that getting my cameras across was more important than joining Cactus and the others in trying to shame the ANC's. Besides, it would take more than this to shame the ANC's. They did not shame easily.

The three mercenaries were dressed and waiting by the time I reached the other side of the Luika and, followed by the *guerriers*, we struggled up the steep and slippery bank and emerged on a grassy hillside dotted with acacias. At the crest of the hill, Corroy called a halt and sent three *guerriers* forward to scout the terrain ahead. Then we sat down under the acacias to wait for the ANC's. We opened up some vintage American C-rations and ate pork and beans and drank the juice from a can of stewed tomatoes. I took off my shoes and socks, thoroughly soaked during the trip across the Luika, and tried to dry them in the sun. It was terribly hot and there was no wind. After about an hour, the ANC's started struggling up the hillside. We could see them coming from quite a distance because each wore a strip of bright red cloth around his helmet or shoulder strap. They did this so that they would not mistake each other for Mulelistes, but it also served to make them highly visible in the open countryside. The ANC's were talking loudly and carrying their rifles upside down on their shoulders and they kept talking even after Corroy told them in a fierce whisper to shut up because this was rebel country. When all the ANC's were present and accounted for Corroy said he would take them forward and told Jean Paul and Cactus to split the *guerriers* into two squads and follow the ANC's–one squad of *guerriers* to the left and the other to the right.

We set off at a fast pace but after two minutes Corroy signaled us to stop in our tracks and crouch down in the grass. Cactus, who was just ahead of me, put a bullet in the chamber of his F.A.L. But then Corroy passed the word back that it was a false alarm. They had simply came upon the three *guerriers* he had sent ahead and momentarily mistaken them for rebels. We moved off again.

The trail took us through swamps, open savanna and dense jungle. The carrying straps of my camera case and the burp gun began to saw into my shoulders and any fear I might have had of a rebel ambush was soon supplanted by a fear that I simply would not be able to keep up. Out in the open, the sun was ferociously hot but I remembered something about "water discipline" from my army days and did not drink when Cactus offered me his canteen. Five miles, ten miles, then fifteen . . . It became a matter of putting one foot forward, then the other. It took enormous concentration. Left foot, right foot. Keep the breathing regular. Rhythm is important.

Inhale . . . one two. Exhale . . . three four. One, two, three, four . . .

At about four o'clock we halted and Corroy came back to tell us that we were now very close to Mukwanga. The ground here was covered with dense undergrowth and tall trees. Instead of walking straight into the village, we would surround it and then come in from all sides. This way any Mulelistes found in the village would have trouble escaping. While Corroy spread his ANC's on either side in a long line, Jean Paul took his *guerriers* to the left and I followed Cactus to the right. I doubted that we would surprise anybody because we made a fearful racket as we struggled through the jungle of vines and dead leaves. When at last the ground cleared and we saw huts to our left and walked toward them, the villagers looked at us not with terror or surprise but quizzically as if we had gone out of our minds.

There were no Mulelistes in the village. The ANC's searched all the huts and found nothing, and the village chief, whose name was that of the village, said they hadn't been back since the day they had come to demand the goats and women. The chief offered us sling chairs made of animal skins and we sat in a circle while the chief, using a pointed stick, scratched a map on the ground. Since independence, he had kept his village on the move, changing its location every year or so. He had done this for varying reasons, sometimes to avoid trouble with one of the neighboring tribes, sometimes in an effort to hide from the troops of the central government or from Lumumbistes or the Mulelistes, but more often simply to find better soil in which to grow corn and manioc. The earth in these parts was not particularly rich and since it was never plowed or fertilized it soon became exhausted. Or it washed away during the rains. Before independence, the Belgians had made the villages stay where they were and tried to teach the natives something about soil conservation, but now they were gone and the villages had taken to wandering around again. The chief drew a road on his map and said his village had been there (he dug into the ground) next to the road, but now it was here (another hole) in the bush. The rebels, he said, were strung out along the road, and to the north, here (he bisected the line he had drawn on the ground with another), they had established a roadblock. Corroy asked how far that was from Mukwanga and the chief said it was about ten kilometers across country. He said the Mulelistes were guarding the roadblock with eight men. The rest, the main rebel force in the area, were some distance behind the roadblock in a village they had commandeered.

Corroy looked at the sun and at his wrist watch and consulted with Jean Paul and Cactus. They agreed that there was not enough daylight left in this day to march to the roadblock, engage the guards and perhaps the main force of rebels as well, and return to the Luika bridge by nightfall. Corroy relayed this information to the chief in Swahili. The chief seemed terribly disappointed at first but then brightened. He had an idea. Would Corroy tell his troops to fire several rounds in the direction of the rebels? Corroy replied that it was a great distance and that the bullets would fall far short of their target. The chief said he understood that but added that he wanted the shots fired so that the rebels would hear the noise. Hearing the noise, the rebels would become afraid and the villagers of Mukwanga could celebrate a victory. As a matter of fact, said the chief, the village would be honored if Corroy and the others would stay on and join in the celebration. The chief would order a goat or two to be killed to mark the great victory over the Mulelistes. It would be a joyous occasion. Corroy, however, was adamant. He told the chief it would take more than noise to defeat the rebels and, standing up and shaking the chief's hand, promised that he would return soon.

It was time to go for another reason. The ANC's had started a little gentle looting around the village. Nothing big as yet. No chickens—only stalks of sugar cane and a mango or two—but it was best to pull them out quickly before they got serious about it.

We walked another five miles through bush and jungle before we reached the road which led back to the Luika. We passed through three more villages on the way and, while the ANC's looked for things to steal (one of them now had a chicken) Corroy told the village elders that he had come to protect them from the

Mulelistes. The elders, eying the ANC's with some alarm, did not seem to be particularly grateful to Corroy for this information.

It was dusk before we reached the bridge over the Luika. The ANC's straggled across. Cactus, who was in the rear with his *guerriers*, watched them with disgust and then halted his warriors. He formed them up in a column of twos and then, counting cadence briskly, marched them across the bridge. The *guerriers* were grinning proudly but the ANC's, for whom this performance had been staged, looked away and pretended not to notice.

Then, bilharzia or no bilharzia, Corroy, Jean Paul, Cactus and I and most of the *guerriers* tore off our clothes and drove off the bridge into the brown current.

The truck from Sola was to have been waiting for us at the far side of the Luika and carry us back to camp. But when, after waiting for another half an hour, it had still failed to appear there was disappointment but no surprise. While we were waiting for the truck I asked Corroy whether he planned to attack the rebel roadblock on the following day. If this was the case, I would be grateful if he would let me come along. If not, I would return to Kongolo.

"I would like nothing better," Corroy said. "And the guerriers would enjoy it too. But it depends on the ANC's. Why don't you ask them? I know what they will say, but ask them anyway."

I turned to one of the Congolese soldiers and put the question to him. He consulted the man next to him.

"No," he said, without turning back to face me. "No, not tomorrow. Tomorrow we are on guard duty."

We lost the beneficial effects of our plunge into the Luika on the long walk back to camp. I was exhausted but immensely pleased with myself. We had walked twenty-five miles that day—something I hadn't tried in twenty years. Jean Paul, who had done his walking in a pair of loose sandals, had acquired two large and painful blisters, but his wife was there and she gave him Petit to hold and this seemed to take his mind off the pain. For a while we sat numbly around the dining table, without speaking or thinking. Then, at precisely the right moment, Jean Paul's wife shuffled away from the table and came back with five bottles of beer. She opened them with her teeth and handed them to us, solemnly, ceremoniously, one at a time, like a geisha.

At noon the next day in Kongolo, Georges and Louis said it was too bad I'd gone to the Luika because I had missed all the fun. While I was gone, some gendarmes had shot two *chefs de cabinet* on the main street–one in the arm and the other in the leg. They had been *soignéed* by a former medical assistant who was now the director of the hospital and flown out in a special plane from Kamina. Just after the takeoff the pilot radioed back that one of the *chefs de cabinet* had died. . . .

I could not help thinking of the medical orderly and his filthy syringe back at the Luika camp, and I still do not know whether the *chef de cabinet* died of his wounds or from a dose of penicillin.

CHAPTER 16

WAZUNGU! WAZUNGU!

Through a fine rolling country, but depopulated, with every mile marked by ruined villages, we marched. . . .
—H. M. STANLEY

THE passenger cars of the Friday train from Kongolo to Kindu, scheduled to leave at noon, were already full to overflowing when Georges, Louis and I walked down to the station. The two C.F.L. men consulted with the stationmaster, who shrugged his shoulders. He had not expected this sort of problem. It had been—he had forgotten how many months now—since a white man had taken the train to Kindu. Was Monsieur certain that there was not some mistake? Perhaps next week . . .

"My friend! My friend!" The voice came from the end of the train, from the platform of a wooden *train de service*, a caboose built for the train crew. I recognized the figure as that of the Pakistani who had been so worried about the attack on the Luika. As we walked toward the caboose, the voice continued:

"Everything is arranged. Come. Come! I have bought the train de service. It is mine. For five thousand francs. Now it is yours. You are my guest. I have beer. I have everything. . . ."

The rear third of the *train de service* was equipped with wooden benches and a table. The remainder of the car had been divided into cubicles furnished with sleeping pallets and closets. The Pakistani, who introduced himself as Mr. Nathu, led me to one of the compartments and told me it was mine. He said his traveling companion

—"we are cousins but he is like a brother to me"—would take the other two. I offered to share in the cost of the caboose but Mr. Nathu would not hear of it.

"Jinah took you to Kongolo. I will take you to Kindu. When you are with us, you have nothing to worry about," he said. Like Jinah, he spoke to me in English and, like Jinah, he played the role of *grand seigneur* with flair and conviction. It was all done with boyish humor so that his cousin-brother actually seemed to enjoy acting out the part of an obsequious body servant. One snap of Mr. Nathu's fingers meant beer. Another snap indicated that the beer bottles should be opened. A third snap called for glasses. All this was accompanied by shouts and curses from Mr. Nathu and mock groans from his young companion. The charade was interrupted momentarily when the stationmaster came to the platform to report that one of Mr. Nathu's goods cars had been taken off to make room for a car carrying beer for the troops in Kindu. Mr. Nathu exploded with wrath. He had paid five thousand francs for that car. The stationmaster appeared crestfallen. It was not his fault, he pleaded. It was just that the engine could not pull all that weight.

"Where are my five thousand francs?" Nathu demanded. It was a rhetorical question. Mr. Nathu knew as well as the stationmaster that he would never see the five thousand francs again.

The train left the station at 1:20. Georges and Louis had warned me that the engine was a wood burner and that it would travel slowly but that, judging by recent past performance, it would arrive in Kindu on the following morning. Searching for a way to repay Mr. Nathu for his hospitality, I bet him a bottle of Scotch that we would not be in Kindu by 10 A.M. He shook hands on it enthusiastically and, when the train stopped at Lusindoi for wood and water, sent his cousin-brother up to the front of the train with a small wad of bills and a bottle of beer for the engineer as insurance for his bet.

At dusk, the train came to a stop at Samba on the border between the provinces of North Katanga and Maniema. The space between the train and the station was marked by a line of police in blue uniforms. All of them carried rifles and as the train came to a halt they started shouting instructions at each other. Then, having reached some sort of agreement among themselves, they advanced on the train. Mr. Nathu motioned to me to keep my cameras out of sight, and leaned out the window.

"They are controlling," he observed. Even as he said this, a knot of policemen spun off the platform of the car ahead of ours. The remaining policemen on the ground were drawn irresistibly into the vortex and it was some seconds before the whirling tornado of blue broke apart sufficiently to reveal the civilian at its center. One of the policemen had the man's left arm pinioned behind his back while two of his colleagues jabbed him in the area of his kidneys with the butts of their rifles. In this fashion, they controlled him, stumbling, through the crowd behind the station barrier and out of sight. The passengers on the train appeared not to notice.

The car behind ours—the last in the train—contained about ten ANC's and a handful of officers, and these had by now climbed down from their car and were mingling with the blue-uniformed policemen on the tracks. Suddenly, without warning, they were having an argument. One of the policemen, a voluble and highly excited man wearing glasses, started pushing an ANC officer in the chest. The officer fell back but his companions pushed him forward. This went on for several minutes—the officer, like a spinning top, bouncing first off the policeman and then off his companions. Weapons were brandished and pointed and it seemed that firing would break out at any moment. But, as suddenly as it began, it ended. Hands were shaken all around and the ANC officers, wreathed in smiles, turned back toward their car. They were, I noticed, accompanied by a woman. When they reached the platform of their car the officers helped her up onto the platform and then spirited her inside. Mr. Nathu and I asked one of the officers what had happened. He said they had intervened because the police had found a woman without papers and were about to take her away. The captain, he said (pointing back to the interior of the ANC car) had told the police that the woman was his wife. She was not his wife, we were told, but she was known in Kongolo and was too good a woman to be allowed to fall into the hands of the border police.

After leaving the North Katanga–Maniema border the train stopped often to pick up small loads of wood that individual woodcutters had stacked in small clearings next to the tracks. At one of these, an old woman, naked to the waist, came out of the bush and walked up and down the train, haranguing the passengers. Mr. Nathu explained that she was complaining about the woodcutters who had trampled on her small plot of rice. Mr. Nathu said he remembered her from previous trips. She was always out on the line when the train went by, demanding indemnity.

"I think she has lost her mind," he said.

At ten P.M., at the town of Lubao, Mr. Nathu gave me one of his blankets and I stretched out on the pallet in my cubicle. The compartment smelled of vomit but I consoled myself with the knowledge that it was not vomit but the smell of a liquor made from the sap of palm trees which a previous occupant had spilled on the floor. I awoke several times during the night, noticed that the train was not moving, and fell asleep again. In the morning we were still in Lubao. Many of the passengers in the cars ahead of ours were seated on the tracks cooking over charcoal braziers as Mr. Nathu and I walked to the head of the train. The reason for this overnight halt was obvious. We had run out of wood. The platforms at the side of the tracks on which the large logs should have been piled was empty, as was the engine's tender. Mr. Nathu snooped around and learned that the truck which was normally used to haul the logs from the forest to the tracks had broken down. The C.F.L. in Kindu had telephoned Lubao to say that it was sending a mechanic down the tracks by handcar. In the meantime the woodcutters were to take their wheelbarrows into the forest and bring back as much wood as they were able. But the woodcutters had decided that they would wait instead for the mechanic to come and fix the truck.

At mid-morning, the C.F.L. in Kindu must have said something threatening over the telephone, or offered some financial inducement, because a line of men with wheelbarrows materialized from behind the station and marched down a path leading into the woods. An hour later they began to reappear, their wheelbarrows filled with large logs, which were heaved onto the platform and then into the tender. It was a slow process and the locomotive, although stationary, seemed to consume the logs almost as fast as they were wheeled in from the forest. As the embers from the fire in the locomotive dropped through the grate and onto the tracks, they were scooped up by the passengers and poured into the cooking braziers. There was also a brass faucet protruding from the engine. Mr. Nathu snapped his fingers and his cousin-brother filled a pot with boiling water. We poured part of it into an empty beer bottle and made instant coffee and I used the rest to shave. Then, since it was well after 10 A.M. and he had lost his bottle of Scotch, I bet Mr. Nathu double or nothing that we would not arrive in Kindu before midnight. This time Mr. Nathu bribed the engineer personally and came back to our *train de service* saying we would arrive well before nightfall.

At noon, we started off again. At every stop now, we took on not only wood but goats. Bleating in terror, the goats were packed into small compartments which had been built for this purpose into the ends of the freight cars. When these were filled, the overflow goats, one man holding the front legs and the other the hind legs, were flung into a flat car containing machinery. In most cases, the goats landed on their heads or their backs. I suppose if they had landed on their legs they would have broken them.

Kibombo was the largest town between Kongolo and Kindu and the crush of goats and people to board the train rivaled a New York City subway stop during rush hour. Mr. Nathu and I sat side by side on the platform steps of our *train de service.*

"I have said you are a mercenary," Mr. Nathu told me. "I hope you do not mind but it is the best way of keeping the people out of our car."

I nodded absent-mindedly, unable to take my eyes off a scene which was unfolding in front of me. An ANC adjutant (I was beginning to be able to identify the insignia of rank) was saying goodbye to his brother. The adjutant was an extremely muscular man with a spade beard. He was wearing shorts and his left knee was bandaged. His brother, the younger of the two and a civilian, was weeping copiously but noiselessly, the tears coursing down his cheeks like two spring freshets. The adjutant reached into his pocket, found a handkerchief, and daubed at his brother's cheeks. The brother's eyes filled up again and, still without a sound, he began to shake convulsively. I was so immersed in the brother that it was some moments before I noticed that the adjutant was dead drunk. The second time he reached over to wipe his brother's face, he missed and lost his balance. Immediately his two wives (Mr. Nathu told me they were his wives) stepped in and propped him up. The adjutant shrugged them away. Then he started to cry too and, as if on signal, the two brothers fell into each other's arms, sobbing and teetering like two exhausted prizefighters in the twelfth round.

Mr. Nathu, too, had become immersed in the activities of the two brothers, and when he reentered the *train de service* he found three Arabs occupying the bench in the dining area. One of them had already fallen asleep with his head on the table. While Mr. Nathu was trying (unsuccessfully) to persuade the Arabs that this was his car and that they had no place in it, one of the adjutant's wives flung two suitcases, several bundles, a portable radio and a wooden folding chair onto the platform outside and then climbed up after them. Before Mr. Nathu had a chance to remonstrate with her, she had unfolded the chair and, seating herself on it, turned on the radio so that it was louder than Mr. Nathu's voice. Mr. Nathu looked at me reproachfully and then cuffed his cousin-brother behind the ear.

At nightfall the train whistle cut loose with a series of staccato blasts. The ANC's separated the adjutant from his brother and boosted him onto our platform. When the train gave its first lurch forward the adjutant lost his footing and almost fell over backward and onto the tracks, but he recovered his balance and, laughing demoniacally, took his pistol out of its holster and entered Mr. Nathu's *train de service*.

"Ah! Ah!" he said, pointing the pistol at Mr. Nathu and then at me. Mr. Nathu froze and turned pale. Something happened to me, too, and I heard my voice (it seemed to be coming from somewhere else) saying something to the adjutant. The voice was telling the adjutant that he should not do this. The words should have been in French, or Swahili but—for reasons I cannot fathom to this day—they came out in German.

"Nein, nein. Das muss man nicht machen!"

The adjutant stared at me. His eyebrows lowered in concentration and then he answered—not in French, Swahili or even German—but in English.

"Not good," he said. He pushed his pistol back into his holster and smiled.

"Bière?" he inquired hopefully. With that, the tension evaporated and, with Mr. Nathu snapping his fingers like castanets, beer was produced in abundance.

Mr. Nathu had by now exhausted his supply of chicken and fish curries and we dug into my army rations for dinner. Mr. Nathu managed to push the Arabs off the bench and onto the floor and the cousin-brother set the table for us by the light of a kerosene lantern. We had been aboard the train to Kindu for thirty hours and I was beginning to feel tired, dirty and bored. The enchantment of being a trail-blazing white man had long since worn off. I felt no pity for the tired and hungry Arabs at my feet or the desperately uncomfortable Africans crowded into the cars ahead of ours. All I could think of was a bathtub filled with hot water and clean, unwrinkled sheets stretched over a soft, wide bed. Midnight went by (Mr. Nathu now owed me two bottles of Scotch) and it was not until two o'clock in the morning that the train pulled into Kindu. Kindu was lighted by electricity but the station seemed ominously empty. Mr. Nathu and I, leaning out of one of the windows, noticed that none of the passengers was getting off. A soldier holding a flashlight came toward us from the station and, in answer to a question from Mr. Nathu, said we would have to spend the night on the train. Nobody could descend until the Commissaire de Police gave his permission. Where was the Commissaire? The soldier turned away without answering. Angry and fed up, I started to get off the train but Mr. Nathu held me back.

"I think," he said, "they will shoot you."

Now that the train had stopped, we could hear the goats again. At previous stops they had bleated piteously. Now, however, jammed together and unwatered, they were screaming with the agony of it all.

A voice was calling down the tracks:

"Le journaliste. Le journaliste." Mr. Nathu nudged me.

"I think they are calling for you," he said.

I got off the train and walked toward the lighted station house.

"Le journaliste?" It was one of the soldiers and, when I had identified myself to his satisfaction, he led me into a room and to a telephone. There were several soldiers asleep on the floor, their heads under their blankets. I picked up the receiver and a Belgian voice at the other end said its name was Hauwaert of the C.F.L. and bade me welcome to Kindu.

"Our apologies," said Hauwaert, "but there is a curfew. I will drive to the station at six in the morning to pick you up. In the meantime, have a pleasant night."

What with the smell of vomit in my compartment and the screaming of the goats, it was not a pleasant night. At dawn the soldiers let the Africans out of the cars and they began to line up with their baggage and their goats in front of a breach in the fence which ran parallel to the tracks. A white man dressed in shorts and sandals came out of the station house. It was Hauwaert. His hair was curly and gray, and in a quietly authoritative way he had me and my baggage on the other side of the fence and in his Volkswagen in less than two minutes. I turned for a last look at the train on which I had spent the past forty hours and at the hundreds of passengers struggling through the needle's eye formed by the policemen at the breach in the fence, and I asked Hauwaert why there was a control here so far from any provincial border.

"Ah, control," Hauwaert replied. "It is the occupation of young nations."

Kindu had always been a company town, dominated by the C.F.L. The C.F.L. hill, dotted with comfortable houses (most of them were now empty and I was given one of them to myself), was higher than the others and the C.F.L. mess, presided over by Hauwaert, served as the social center for the town's remaining Belgians—company men like Hauwaert, Catholic missionaries and mercenaries—and the Greek *commerçants* who had survived the Mulelistes' occupation. It was a motley group, held together, like the alumni of some particularly harsh and uncomfortable boarding school, by their common experience under the rebels. Like most recent graduates, when together they talked about nothing but the grim old days. It started on my first morning in Kindu, at breakfast in the C.F.L. mess, a dining room in a house occupied by Hauwaert's affable and enterprising two assistants, Bourloo and Daeman. Food was not *repas* or *nourriture* in the C.F.L. mess. It was "chop." Hauwaert guessed the word had originated with the English military, but it had been adopted by the Belgians and Gallicized.

"Tu veux du chop?" I was asked when I arrived for that first breakfast, to which (I learned later) my answer should have been: "Oui. J'ai pas encore chopper."

Breakfast was served at eight, by which time three C.F.L. men had been up and at work for two hours. It did not take them long (between mouthfuls of cheese and liverwurst) to get to the subject closest to their hearts. Did I know much about Kindu, they asked? When I replied in the negative, I was told with considerable enthusiasm that Kindu, next to Stanleyville, was the most bestial town in the Congo. Did I remember what had happened to the thirteen Italian airmen? I said I had been in Leopoldville at the time, so they told me again. It was during the period when the United Nations was trying to end the Katanga secession. When a plane carrying the Italians landed at Kindu to refuel, the ANC's at the airport got it into their heads that the Italians were Belgians on their way to Katanga to help Tshombe. The ANC's shot two of the Italians right there at the airport and killed the remaining eleven in town. They dismembered the corpses, ate parts of them and threw what was left into the Lualaba. For days afterward, Hauwaert added, bits and pieces of Italian flesh kept turning up at the meat stalls in the market place.

Bourloo had been in Kindu during the time of the Mulelistes, sometimes at liberty and sometimes under arrest. He was beaten several times. On one occasion he was beaten and told to say, "Thank you." He refused and was beaten again. Again he refused. The third time, as he lay on the floor with the rebel *gendarmes* standing over him, his thoughts turned to his children, sent home to the safety of Belgium some months before.

"It seemed stupid to die and leave them without a father," he recalled. "So I said 'thank you.' But I will never forget that. A beating, yes. That you can forget. But to have to say, 'Thank you!' That is something else again."

As breakfast ended, we were joined by a bearded young man called Paul Schipper, who ran a sawmill for the Société Foncière des Grands Lacs (SOFOLACS), and a Catholic priest from the Holy Ghost Mission in Kindu. Father Thones was dressed in a dirty white cassock and he held in the palm of his hand the sound head of the mission school's motion picture projector. Could the C.F.L. fix the sound head? He had just received a film from the United States Information Service—the first in many months—about the late President Kennedy, and wished to show it to his students. Daeman said he had an excellent Congolese electrician and would put him to work on it immediately. Father Thones sank back onto a sofa at the other side of the room, accepted a cigarette gracefully, and began talking about *his* experiences under the Mulelistes.

On the day of the rebel entry into Kindu, three separate contingents of Mulelistes had come to the mission. The first two assured the fathers that they would not be molested. The third, however, decided that Father Thones would be shot. One of the Mulelistes raised his rifle (Father Thones remembered that it was an old German Mauser), aimed and pulled the trigger. But the gun did not go off. On examining his weapon, the rebel discovered that he had neglected to put a bullet in the chamber. He rectified this omission, aimed and pulled the trigger again. This time the gun fired and the bullet struck Father Thones between the neck and the shoulder. It was a grazing wound but the force of the bullet hurled him to the ground and knocked him unconscious. He awoke and found himself on his back, staring up at the sky.

"Do you know what my first thought was?" Father Thones asked the group. We shook our heads.

"I thought: the sky in heaven is as blue as the sky on earth."

Daeman snorted. "You drink and you swear," he said. "The Bon Dieu would not have received you." Father Thones laughed.

"No," he said, "at that moment he could have received me, but he was not ready."

It was Sunday. The C.F.L. yards were closed and Bourloo said he had time to drive me around Kindu in his car. The corpses of cars, looking like creatures that have been left at the bottom of a suddenly emptied pond, lined the empty streets. Most of the store windows were broken. We drove under a large banner that had been strung across the road leading to the market place; it honored Godefroid Munongo, the Minister of the Interior, who had visited Kindu the week before.

"Bienvenue," the sign read. "The Population is Starving, needs food."

It was true, Bourloo said. The usual sources of food in the gardens and the plantations of the surrounding countryside were still in the hands of the Mulelistes. I asked about the recent shipments of American wheat and flour to the Congo and Bourloo said that these shipments had indeed arrived but that Maniema Province, having always had the reputation of being a pro-Lumumba, anti-Central Government stronghold, had received short shrift from Leopoldville. We drove past what had been the Lumumba monument. The ANC's had blown it to pieces after Kindu's liberation from the Mulelistes, and the weeds were now creeping in over the pile of rubble that remained. This had been the Mulelistes' favorite execution ground, Bourloo said, adding that no one knew how many had died. All that was known was that the executions took place almost daily. After Kindu's recapture, there had been many bodies in the streets. Despite pleas from doctors, the ANC commanders refused (or were powerless) to order burial parties and the bodies stayed where they were for days. Bourloo said the smell was almost unbearable. There were also many bodies in the Lualaba and some wedged themselves between the tied-up river barges and the wharfs of the C.F.L. Men with gaffs and long poles were assigned by the C.F.L. to push the corpses out into the current, where they could be eaten by crocodiles. Bourloo added that during the months of the Muleliste occupation a day seldom went by when you could not walk down the banks of the Lualaba and see a body floating downstream toward Stanleyville.

At the C.F.L. installations on the riverfront, we rejoined Daeman, who took me into the repair shed and showed me two locomotives with broken boilers. Daeman said the Mulelistes had fired them up without bothering about the water. Crossing the freight yards, we boarded a paddlewheel riverboat tied to the dock. Plates of quarter-inch steel had been riveted to the ship's sides so that they protected the engine, and a sign had been hung from the upper deck proclaiming that the vessel and those on board came in peace and friendship, and asking those on shore to lay down their arms. But the paddlewheeler had not left Kindu since its conversion into a gunboat and Daeman said he wondered whether it would ever be put to use.

"From here to Stanleyville," he said, looking north down the wide, brown river, "the Mulelistes own the Lualaba."

The ship's captain, an elderly Congolese, had seen us board his boat and was waiting for us when we crossed back to the shore.

"You have done no work in months," Daeman said, pointing an accusing finger at the captain. "Therefore you show lack of initiative." The captain grinned broadly.

Just then we heard the sound of a plane and a few seconds later a twin-engine Aztec flew overhead, dipped its wings and then banked toward the airfield.

The pilot and its three passengers turned up for lunch at the C.F.L. mess. They were from Cobelmin, the Belgian mining concern, and had come to Kindu to welcome back to civilization three of their white employees who had spent the past seven months as prisoners of the rebels in Kampene. Kampene lay on the other side of the Lualaba and about one hundred miles southeast of Kindu. Just before landing at Kindu, the Cobelmin plane had flown over the road leading north from Kampene and had spotted the rescue party—two jeeps and four trucks—some forty kilometers from Kindu. It would take them a while to cross the river because there was only one ferry capable of carrying vehicles. But they should be in Kindu (here the Cobelmin chief, Alfred Brys consulted his wristwatch) by 3:15. Brys was a very precise man. He did not speak often and when he did it was usually to announce a decision he had taken. The others in the Cobelmin party held him in considerable awe and called him Monsieur Brys.

The last of the vehicles from Kampene was bouncing off the ferry as we arrived at the bank of the river. It was 3:15. Each of the jeeps was driven by a white mercenary and there was another mercenary perched behind a .50-caliber machine gun mounted just in back of the hood of one of the trucks. The mercenaries and the three men who had been rescued were haggard and unshaven. Brys walked forward and shook the rescued men's hands and gave them the letters which had been accumulating for them at the company's headquarters in Bukavu. The men did not say much but the eldest of the group, a Greek chemical engineer called Basil Loucaitis, thanked Brys for the letters. The others—Gert Hans Spät, a twenty-six-year-old German, and Ivan Ribic, a twenty-three-year-old Yugoslav mechanic—thumbed through their letters slowly, stopping occasionally to stare at the stamps, but they did not open any of the envelopes.

The jeeps and the trucks contained about fifty ANC's in camouflaged jungle fatigues. Some of them wore monkey-skin headdresses which they had taken from the bodies of Mulelistes they had killed —or who had been killed for them by the mercenaries—and they were jubilant. Somebody suggested that the jeeps and the trucks be driven through Kindu to show the inhabitants that a victory had been won over the rebels, and the jeeps set off, followed by the trucks and then cars containing Brys, Schipper, Hauwaert, Bourloo and Daeman. It was a colorful and noisy parade. The military vehicles flew yellow and orange banners. Artificial roses had been entwined around the machine-gun mount on one of the jeeps and, as the convoy entered the African quarter, the ANC's on the trucks started firing their rifles. I was in one of the trucks and the ANC's, instead of shooting straight up into the air, fired past my head at the tops of the palm trees. Often when they fired they looked away from their weapons, or closed their eyes. Amazingly, no one was hit and the crowds on the street waved and shouted with delight.

The parade finally came to rest in front of the ANC barracks at the edge of the C.F.L. football field. As those who had stayed home rushed out of their barracks to greet the conquering heroes, they were met with a fusillade of shots from the trucks. Crouching down as low as I could in the truck, I noticed that the bullets were chipping the tiled roofs of the barracks. On the ground below, a woman suddenly screamed and fell writhing to the earth. I was certain she had been hit and that the incident would develop swiftly into a fire fight, but it turned out that the woman had simply been told that her ANC husband had been left behind to hold Kampene against a possible counterattack.

At the C.F.L. mess, food and drink in large quantities were produced for the mercenaries and the refugees. I think it was only then that the three men from Kampene began to realize that they had really been liberated. And, as they did, they began to talk and the room reverberated with shouts, the sounds of backs being slapped, and laughter. Loucaitis drew me aside. He had heard I was a journalist. Perhaps I would write in my newspaper what it had been like during the seven months he and the others had been held captive. There was something about the way he said this that was not so much a suggestion as a plea. It was his way of building a bridge back to civilization. I am sure Loucaitis is still working on that bridge but that day he was throwng out the first, tenuous strand.

The experience, he said, had been something he would never forget. No, it had not been so much what the rebels had done to him and the other white men. It was what they had done to his African workers. Where could he begin? It was such a difficult story to tell because what the rebels did was always so chaotic, so lacking in rhyme or reason. There had been Christmas, for instance. On Christmas the Mulelistes had shot eight of his workers simply to mark the day. Two of those singled out for execution were six- and seven-year-old boys. Loucaitis had pleaded with the rebel commander, and the commander had agreed with Loucaitis that it would be criminal to kill such young children and he let them go. He asked Loucaitis afterward whether this did not prove he was civilized—letting the children go. On the lawn in front of his office, the Mulelistes speared a number of men through the back. The men were kneeling down, their hands trussed behind them, and they were killed one at a time. Loucaitis said he had some money hidden which he used to ransom some of his personnel. He always withheld this money until the final moment—until he was absolutely certain that the rebels were about to kill. You never knew what they would do. Sometimes they said they would execute somebody and then change their minds and walk away. Loucaitis remembered particularly a rebel lieutenant who went by the name of Issa. On one occasion, Issa, calmly playing high-life music on his portable radio, ordered his men to shoot a group of Cobelmin workers in the back.

"Kupiga, 'piga," he said. "Fire, fire."

His soldiers fired. Some of the prisoners fell but others remained standing.

"No," Loucaitis remembered Issa as saying. "No, that was not good enough. Again. 'Piga!"

Only when all the prisoners were dead did Issa shut off the music on his radio.

Loucaitis and the two others were being flown back in the Aztec to Bukavu the following morning and thence, as rapidly as possible, back to Europe. I asked Loucaitis whether he had any thoughts about returning to the Congo.

"To the Congo, yes," he said. "But to Kampene, never. Do not misunderstand. It is not the memory of the Mulelistes that would keep me away but the memory of my workers. They have nothing, the poor ones. They are dressed in grain sacks and they are eating dirt from the ground. I could not support it."

One of the white mercenaries, a man in his very early thirties with an undershot jaw and a mouth full of broken teeth, had been listening to Loucaitis, and when the Greek was finished and had moved away the mercenary looked after him and said that he would not have gone on this mission (there were only ten more days to go until his leave) if it hadn't been to rescue these Europeans. They had set out the Sunday before and on the road to Kampene he had fired twelve hundred rounds from his .50-caliber machine gun. Not long bursts, mind you, but two or three shots at a time, and then only when he had something in his sights. That was too much firing, he said. Now his nerves were shot and his hands were trembling. He had been in the Korean War but this was far worse than that. In Korea you knew your objective was only six or eight kilometers. Here it was two hundred or three hundred, and you had to be ready for anything every inch of the way. I said that was probably true but was it not also true that the casualty figures in the Congo were comparatively light—certainly far lighter than those of the Korean War? The mercenary said this was so.

"But in Korea," he said (he was deadly serious now), "they did not cut off your testicles and eat them before your eyes."

It was almost too easy to collect horror stories in Kindu. I did not have to ask for them; they were thrust upon me. But in a curious way even those who had suffered personally at the hands of the Mulelistes did not seem to feel much resentment. The terror, the inhuman slaughter, the almost casual torturings, were simply manifestations of the Congolese character. The character could not be molded or changed. At best it could be suppressed. That was what they, the Belgians, had done. Suppressed it. But of course it had come straight to the surface again with independence when the Belgians had lost their grip on the people and their leaders.

"Look at my house boy." It was Paul Schipper speaking and he pointed at the barefoot and beaming African carrying drinks to us on a tray. "I like him. He likes me. I treat him very well and I think there is nothing that he would not do for me. When times were normal he was alone, sometimes for days, with my wife and children. I had nothing to fear. But the Mulelistes are coming back into Kindu—the politicians, even some of the murderers. I remember their faces. It is election time and we can do nothing. So one day they will be in control again and then it is quite possible that my house boy will kill me. He won't kill me because he hates me. In fact he will still like me when he does it. Can I explain this to you? Of course I can't. All I can tell you is that he does not think as I do, he does not feel as I do. . . ."

Even if he did not understand them, Schipper, along with many of his compatriots in the Congo, accepted the Africans as they were. The British might see them as noble savages or near apes, to be loved or hated depending on their principles or prejudices. But for Schipper they were simply part of the landscape, part of the African way of life. You accepted the Africans as you did the heat, the brilliant sunsets and the sudden rains, the green mold that grew on the shoes in your closet, the cacophonous chorus of birdsong at dawn, and the periodic bouts of malaria. Either you learned to live with these things (and the Africans with them) or you got out of Africa.

What disturbed Schipper was that the Congolese had been in contact with the Belgians only long enough to achieve the most superficial understanding of Western civilization. And what they had learned from the white men was most often those things of which the white man was least proud—his acquisitiveness, his venality. . . . For some reason these were the characteristics that came to the surface in the Congo. For the black man, European civilization was a giant cornucopia, a heavenly vending machine everlastingly pouring forth the shiniest, newest automobiles, radios, university degrees and first-class airline tickets. The white man always got what he wanted simply by putting coins in the machine. Africans did not realize that it had taken much work to build the machine, that it had to be refilled when empty, and that it would not operate at all if the plug was taken out of the socket. The poor Africans could not be blamed for this but what infuriated Schipper was that the politicians, who should have known better, were going around telling the people that the reason the machine didn't work any more was that the white men had been furnishing them with the wrong sort of coins.

Only the week before, Schipper said, he had received a notice from the provincial government of Maniema charging that his company was in arrears on its taxes and demanding the immediate payment of an "astronomical sum." Considering the fact that SOFOLACS had not been able to harvest a square foot of timber during the period of the Mulelistes; considering the fact that half its work force had either been killed or driven into the forest by the rebels, and considering the fact that the government itself had not as yet seen fit to pay the company for the houses it rented from SOFOLACS, Schipper refused. He coupled his refusal with the threat to close down operations and dismiss the five hundred workers remaining on the payroll. Of course, Schipper added, the tax revenues the government had been seeking would not have gone into public services but into the pockets of those who collected them. Proof of this, he said, came in the form of a delegation which assembled in his office to suggest that the matter of taxes could be dropped in return for a case of beer.

It would take the Congolese a long time to realize that the plug had been pulled on the vending machine. And, by the time they realized that, the machine itself (like the tireless cars with the elephant grass growing up through their broken windshields) would be past repair. This was the way the C.F.L. men in Kindu saw it as happening. It had been years since the C.F.L. had put any money into repairs and replacement. The rolling stock, by European standards, belonged either in a scrap heap or in a museum and the tracks were in a parlous state. The wooden ties were rotting. One of these days there would be an accident and, with six or seven hundred Africans on board, perhaps two hundred would die. Of course the Africans would blame the whites (probably with some justice) but it would end, not in the massive infusion of new capital which was required to ensure some degree of safety, but in the swift disintegration and eventual disappearance of the entire railway system.

The big companies like the C.F.L. or SOFOLACS or corporate Goliaths like the Société Générale insisted on being able to see ahead for five, maybe ten years, before carrying out any investment plans. The Africans, on the other hand, would not think even as far ahead as tomorrow. Invariably, the C.F.L.'s African employees spent their monthly wages during the first three days. The Lord only knew what they lived on for the rest of the month. Schipper said it was the same with his lumbermill workers. The African merchants, too, could not seem to plan ahead. They waited until their stores were depleted and then ordered by cable and had the merchandise shipped by airplane, which was, of course, much more expensive than by train or riverboat. They passed the higher costs on to their customers and *they* didn't seem to mind. Schipper and the others had never seen African women shopping for bargains or haggling with the merchants. Like their husbands, they too did not plan ahead or know what it was to save. When it was there, they bought it—whatever it was and whatever the price. When it was not there, they went without.

Most of the whites who came to the Congo were engaged, in one way or the other, in the care and feeding of that giant vending machine, and the Africans who came in contact with them worshiped at its shrine. But there were other whites who brought to the Congo an alternate deity which, if not as popular with the Congolese as the vending machine, was equally misunderstood. When I called on Les Pères de Saint Esprit, they were gathered in the refectory for mid-morning coffee. Father Thones introduced me to four of his colleagues and Monsignor Pierre Shandano, their spiritual leader. Monsignor Shandano was an elderly Congolese with a beatific smile who insisted that I wait until he had put on his crimson stole before taking his picture. He excused himself afterward and it was only after he had gone that the white fathers who remained in the refectory began to talk. I think they liked the old African Monsignor, and addressed him with deference, but it seemed obvious that he was not one of them.

The Christian religion had never really penetrated the Congolese soul, the fathers said almost the moment the Monsignor had left the room. They had gone along with the Catholic theology because it was the white man's religion and since the white man was powerful it stood to reason that his god too was powerful. But, while paying lip service to the white man's god, most Congolese continued to worship their own gods, sometimes covertly (because it made the white fathers angry) but more often quite openly. Even during the time of the Mulelistes, when the white man's stock was at its lowest ebb, there were Africans who attended services. Often they would come to the fathers and give money so that the fathers would say mass for one of their deceased relatives, but they would not attend the mass personally. One Muleliste asked for a mass for his dead brother. Since the rebel knew that the spell cast by his witch doctor to guard him against enemy bullets would be broken if he touched anyone, he dropped his offering at the feet of one of the missionaries. He was not being disrespectful. He was simply being sensible about the matter.

If there was one thing that the Congolese lacked, the fathers agreed (they disagreed with one another only over the most minor points), it was a sense of personal responsibility. They never blamed themselves for their trouble.

Perhaps the fathers had done some good before independence but, ever since, their influence and their effectiveness had been on the decline. It was all the fault of the politicians, said one of the missionaries. The politicians had ruined an entire generation of Congolese by telling the young people that they were no longer to believe their teachers, their priests and even their elders. All were agents of the imperialists.

I asked the white fathers what they thought of their African colleagues in the mission and African priests in general. I expected a spirited defense or an evasive answer. Instead the white fathers quickly agreed that African priests lacked initiative. Oh, they had learned what had to be learned, and, with some exceptions did what had to be done, but they seldom went any further. For them the teachings and precepts of the Church were like the vestments worn during the mass: they could be removed afterward. Even in this mission it was known that several of the black fathers had accepted bribes from their primary school students for passing grades. In one instance, the white fathers' suspicions were aroused when a notoriously weak student received an 80 percent average on leaving primary school. The white fathers tested him again when he entered secondary school. He received 30 percent the second time around.

It would become harder now, the task of educating the young, of bringing God into the lives of the inhabitants of Kindu, not so much because of what the politicians had been saying but because the Mulelistes had made a point of executing so many of the men who had exerted, or might now be expected to exert, some moral influence on the population. The rebels, the father said, had gone about this work in a diabolical way. They did not kill these leaders—in most cases they were the tribal elders or those who could read and write—outright and thus risk turning them into martyrs. Instead, they humiliated them first so that in the eyes of the people they were as nothing when the time came for them to die. The elders, the notables, the chiefs, were starved, stripped of their clothing, driven about the streets naked, and spat upon. Only when they were as nothing in the eyes of their people were they finally dispatched by the rebels.

While I wandered about Kindu, Brys, the Cobelmin chief, had been organizing a return to Kampene. His Europeans were out and safely on their way back to Europe, but there remained several tons of cassiterite, one of the ores used in making tin, which would have to be brought out before the liberation of Kampene could be called complete. Brys was methodical and insistent and three mornings after his arrival in Kindu we found ourselves gathered on the far bank of the Lualaba—Brys, his two assistants, sixteen Congolese gendarmes, myself and Marcel Lardinois, a soft-spoken Belgian who served as the technical adviser to the Kindu police. He was, in effect, the police commissioner. The convoy consisted of seven diesel trucks, two small pickup trucks and Lardinois's Land-Rover truck which he had equipped with a .30-caliber machine gun. Lardinois said I should ride with him, that we would head the column. He gave me an F.A.L. automatic rifle to hold and told me to sit next to him while he drove. He put three of his gendarmes in the back of his Land-Rover, two of them armed with rifles and the third standing behind the machine gun.

For the first 40 of the 149 kilometers to Kampene we drove through friendly territory dominated by a tribe called the Warega. Stanley had described them as cannibals, noting that "unless force is very strong they never let strangers pass." But the Waregas had not been pro-rebel during the time of the Mulelistes and they let us pass by their villages with no difficulty. Then, after driving about 30 kilometers along the road which led southeast from Kindu, the villages abruptly became deserted. It was obvious that they had been empty for some time. Most of them had been burned, either by the rebels or by ANC raiding parties. The occasional dog, ribs sawing through its mangy coat, slunk away into the underbrush as we approached.

It was eerie and unsettling, and Lardinois did not help much by slapping the roof of the Land-Rover without warning from time to time to alert his gendarmes to what he considered a particularly appropriate spot for an ambush. His hand always banged on the roof when I least expected it and the sound made me jump. We drove very slowly past a large, empty village. Lardinois said it had been the headquarters of a notoriously murderous rebel called Stanislaus, who was probably even now watching us from a secret observation post in the top of one of the tall trees that dominated the landscape.

Often, when the road dipped into a pocket between the hills, we breathed the sweet-sour smell of death. At one bend in the road Lardinois turned the wheels of his vehicle to avoid running over a skull. The skull lay in the middle of the road. The man's femurs, both of them, were in the ditch to our left, still covered with gelatinous green flesh. Lardinois wrinkled his nose. The dead were seldom buried, he said. Instead, the villagers hacked the corpses to pieces, eating parts of them and scattering the rest about so that the victims' spirits could not rest in peace.

We approached a hill and Lardinois's hand smacked the roof of the Land-Rover. On the crest of the hill we could see several buildings which once belonged to a Catholic mission. As Lardinois started to explain that the rebels had used the mission as a command post, firing suddenly broke out. I ducked instinctively, not knowing from which direction the shots were coming. I raised my head only when Lardinois started to laugh. He stopped the Land-Rover and got out. Behind us, Brys and company and the several gendarmes were blazing away at the crest of the hill.

"We are testing our weapons," said Brys. I did not test mine. The humor of the situation had eluded me.

There was a fork in the road at the village of Lumuna and, before taking the road that led to the left, we stopped and counted trucks. Three of them were now missing and it was presumed they had fallen apart some way back. Brys did not seem concerned. Even before we had started, he had estimated the vehicular casualty rate at about 50 percent.

From Lumuna onward, the villages were populated again. The inhabitants wore white headbands. Lardinois said this was a symbol of peace and also of fealty to the central government. As we drew near, they ran into their huts and women clutched their babies to their breasts and turned their backs. Then, as it dawned on them that we had not come to shoot them down, the atmosphere changed electrically from one of fear and suspicion to wild jubilation. First the women, then the children, stormed out of their huts and ran toward the convoy. They were followed by the men. They held their hands high, palms outward, in the traditional sign of welcome. The women clapped their hands rapidly over their mouths, making a warbling, high-pitched "yu-yu-yu-yu" sound.

"Wazungu! Wazungu!" they shouted, which meant "the white men." Seven months under the rebels had taken their toll. What clothing they wore consisted in the main of bits of burlap bags. The women's breasts were flat. Lardinois said most of the young girls had been kidnaped by the Wazimba during the Muleliste period. The Wazimba, he said, were a bad bunch—*très Arabisée*, he said, by which he meant that they had developed a propensity for murder and pillage under the tutelage of the old Arab slavers. The Wazimba lived to the south but, under the Mulelistes, they had been given free reign again to conduct their depredations over a wide area.

In each of the villages, Lardinois stopped and made a little speech. He said that the war was now finished and that he and the others had come in peace. Soon there would be work again, and money with which to buy food and clothing. The white man was returning to reopen his plantations and help the inhabitants plant cotton. In the meantime the people must come out of the forests and back to their villages. If they did this, the white man could help them by bringing salt and whatever else they needed immediately. Lardinois made his speech a sentence at a time, and each time he stopped his listeners would cheer. And at the end the women would go "yu-yu-yu" again and start to dance, and the men would shout "Wazungu! Wazungu!" and crowd up to the trucks to shake hands with the white men and Congolese gendarmes.

In this fashion we proceeded to Kampene, where, in the compound formed by the Cobelmin administration buildings, there was another wild scene of jubilation, this time focused on Brys. He stood there for a while and then, looking both pleased and embarrassed, turned his back suddenly and disappeared into one of the offices.

We spent the night in the house once occupied by Loucaitis, the Greek in charge of Cobelmin's Kampene operation, and the next morning, while the Cobelmin people went about the business of loading the cassiterite ingots onto the trucks, Lardinois and I, followed by a truck carrying a handful of gendarmes, struck out for Lumuna. At Lumuna we took the road which led to Kunda. Lardinois had a coffee plantation at Kunda which he had not even seen since the rebels moved in seven months ago. His mission was also to reassure villagers along the way that the white man had returned for good and also, he warned, to do a little *nettoyage* if that became necessary. *Nettoyage* meant "cleaning up"—a gentler form of *ratissage*.

The villages were depopulated as we drove away from Lumuna. Lardinois's hand thumped the metal roof of the Land-Rover again and he told me to take my F.A.L., which I had between my knees, and rest it on my lap. We would have to be extremely alert now, he said, because we were entering the territory of the Wazimba. He himself reached into a canvas bag behind him and extracted three grenades, which he placed in the glove compartment under the windshield.

As we drew near Kunda, Lardinois slowed down and peered ahead intently. Kunda had only recently been occupied by a company of ANC's and Lardinois was worried that the ANC's, seeing an unknown vehicle approaching from Wazimba territory, would open fire on us. We crossed a bridge arching over a small and sluggish stream and then waved strenuously at a group of about twenty ANC's crouched behind a bank with their weapons leveled at us. The ANC's did not wave back, nor did they lower their rifles. But they did not fire and we drove into Kunda and found the lieutenant in charge playing a game of checkers with one of his sergeants. His men, listless and bored, sprawled in the grass about him.

Lardinois asked the lieutenant whether he had seen any Mulelistes in the vicinity. No, the lieutenant replied, there had been nothing to report for several days, not since the day after the ANC's had taken the town. The day after they had moved in, the lieutenant said, three Mulelistes had walked into Kunda. Apparently they had spent the previous day in the forest and did not know what had happened because they were much surprised to find themselves surrounded by ANC's. Two of them were young boys—the lieutenant said he thought they were eleven or twelve—and their leader was a very old man with a *poo-poo,* a home-made muzzle-loading blunderbuss. I asked what had happened to the prisoners, whether they were still alive.

"Oh, no. We cut their throats," said the lieutenant, making a sawing motion with his hand against his windpipe. "Comme ça, c'est fini."

Lardinois found his home a shambles. Most of the furniture had been broken up and used as firewood and the walls were pockmarked with bullet holes. There were monkey-skin headdresses scattered about and the toilet had been used until it could be used no more and then abandoned. But in the sheds there were several tons of dried coffee beans, and two of his trucks appeared to be in working order although he could not start them because the batteries were dead. We drove along a small dirt road into the plantation. Grass and weeds choked the coffee trees. There was a small pond which Lardinois said contained many fish. He took a grenade out of the Land-Rover, pulled the pin and threw it into the water. We waited and nothing happened. He threw another grenade and it, too, did not go off. The third one, however, exploded with a muffled thump, but no fish floated to the surface.

The ANC's had been in Kunda for more than a week but, as yet, none of the inhabitants had returned to their village. Back at the ANC headquarters, Lardinois asked the lieutenant to see what he could do about passing the word into the bush that it was safe to return. The thought had not occurred to the lieutenant and he seemed puzzled when Lardinois said it was important that the villagers come back and get the economy moving again. Lardinois also asked the lieutenant how far he had sent his patrols down the road toward Kasongo. The lieutenant replied that he had received no orders to send any patrols anywhere. Lardinois did not show his irritation. Instead he called together the three gendarmes who had been riding in his Land-Rover and told them to climb aboard. He himself, he said to them (loudly, so that the lieutenant would overhear), would see what lay down the road to Kasongo.

We drove slowly. I had my F.A.L. on my lap. Lardinois took his pistol from its holster and held it in his right hand, driving with his left.

"Take the F.A.L. off safety," he said. I did as I was told. Our eyes searched the jungle on either side of the road.

"Now put your finger on the trigger, and if anything moves you shoot."

My hands were covered with sweat. I noticed that Lardinois had cocked his pistol and that he had taken a grenade in his other hand and was steering the vehicle with the heel of his hand. Suddenly, about fifty yards down the road ahead I saw a flash of white—the figure of a man dressed in white shorts and a white shirt. Simultaneously, the machine gunner behind us opened up. The figure bounded across the road and disappeared into the jungle. The machine gunner fired another short burst. Lardinois brought the Land-Rover to a stop and jumped out. He climbed up beside the machine gun, pushed the gunner aside, and sprayed the road ahead.

"It must have been a Muleliste," he said. "He was too well dressed to be anything else."

He climbed back down and we drove on, even more slowly now, and passed the spot where the figure had vanished. There was nothing to see but broad leaves and the dark shadows behind them. I had told Lardinois about my experiences with the Americans in Bujumbura and Albertville and I said now that I did not think the embassy in Leopoldville would approve of my present whereabouts. Lardinois laughed. We drove on for another mile, and then he stopped. This was far enough, he said. We were driving into a trap. It was too easy to ambush us here. The rebels had obviously heard us firing and in another ten minutes they would have us cut off from the rear. We turned around and started back. Lardinois drove faster now. At a small deserted village he stopped quickly and got out. Two goats were staring at us from the side of the road—as surprised to see us as we were to see them. Lardinois raised his own F.A.L. and brought them down in sudden heaps with two single shots. They were incredibly thin and small. The gendarmes tied them with wire to the front bumper. One goat would be for them. The other would be given to the ANC lieutenant.

As we re-entered Kunda I switched the F.A.L. back to the safety position and pulled the bolt to eject the shell from its chamber. But there was no shell in the chamber. There never had been. It was only then that my hands began to tremble.

On the way back to Kindu, this time with the springs of the trucks flat with the weight of cassiterite, we stopped at the village which had served as the headquarters of the rebel leader Stanislaus and burned it to the ground. The gendarmes found a dozen mattresses which they loaded onto the trucks and a few bicycles which only needed tires to make them serviceable again.

The morning after we crossed the Lualaba back to Kindu, the ferry which had carried us sank suddenly and silently into the river. On the following day, Schipper received a written order requisitioning his two bulldozers to help pull the ferry out of the mud.

"If they had asked me politely, perhaps I would have said 'yes,' " he fumed. "But this—no! They can go to hell."

Bourloo and Daeman thought it was pretty funny. Eventually they would have to step in, pull the ferry out and patch it up in the

C.F.L. yards. But, in the meantime, they would wait. It was odd, they agreed, how efficiently the ferry had run during the seven months of rebel occupation. But that could be explained. If the ferry hadn't operated to the complete satisfaction of the Mulelistes, they would simply have taken the captain and his crew and cut their heads off.

CHAPTER 17

END OF THE ROAD

I am conscious that I have not penetrated to the depths. . . .

—H. M. STANLEY

KINDU was, for me, the end of the line. I had been warned that this was as far as I could go, as far as anybody went, and in Kindu the prophecy came true. The ironclad paddlewheeler, its bow pointing toward Stanleyville, rested and rusted at its moorings. The rain forest and the rebels had closed in again over the road the mercenaries had used as recently as November, when they rushed north from Kindu to free the white hostages in Stanleyville. Someday the road and the river would have to be reopened. But no one knew when that would be. In the meantime, for the traveler still determined to see Stanleyville, there was of course the airplane. . . .

I kept my bags packed and, hearing the drone of motors overhead, raced often to the airport, hoping to catch a ride to Stanleyville. Sometimes they were military planes, piloted by Americans. Sometimes they were cargo planes, chartered by the Tshombe government and piloted by Rhodesians or South Africans. But they were always on their way elsewhere—to Kamina, Leopoldville, Elisabethville or to little towns in the northeast called Paulis, Buta and Watsa. Never to Stanleyville. One never knew when a plane would come or where it would go afterward and I spent long hours waiting on the roof of the airport terminal. A white mercenary with the enviable sinecure of airport security maintained his quarters on the second floor of the terminal building. He kept parrots and monkeys on the roof, and I suppose it was he who made me realize that I had always wanted a parrot. I bought a young gray one with red tail feathers from Marcel Lardinois, who already had four, and fed him peanuts from my hand. In two hours he thought I was his mother and was tame.

Somehow, having a parrot who thought I was his mother helped dissipate the frustration, the disappointment I felt now that I knew I could follow Stanley's trail no longer. He, of course, had gone on from here, following "the hateful, murderous river" in its great arc to the sea. Had I been Stanley, I might have done the same and with a well-armed band of mercenaries fought my way through the savages, the jungle and the rapids. But I was no Stanley. I had no money to pay mercenaries and no stomach for risking their lives—or mine. In comparison to Stanley's voyage, my trip was no more than an escapade, a whim. One does not risk lives for a whim.

Kindu was the end of the line in another sense too. It was in Kindu that I realized I had had enough. I tried to keep listening, to keep asking questions, but my mind was beginning to wander. It seemed that nothing new was being said, that I had heard it all before. Was it in Uganda, or in the highlands of Kenya? Did repetition mean I was approaching the truth or had I been led to the ultimate roadblock on the path to understanding? I suppose I was tired too. Five months of looking and listening, of trying to understand, of never knowing for certain what would happen next, of anticipating danger (and anticipating was always far worse than the danger itself)—all this had worn me down. Finally, one morning, I grew weary of the fruitless trips to the Kindu airport and bought a ticket on the next Air Congo flight to Leopoldville. There would always be planes flying between Leopoldville and Stanleyville. Having made that decision, I felt not so much discouraged (although I *was* discouraged) as relieved. I was like the losing poker player who drops out of the game with just enough money to get home. I had tried, and failed, but at least I hadn't been a fool.

As it always had in the past, Leopoldville reminded me of a gasoline station which, impregnated by a cash register, has spawned a city. It was a marriage of convenience, not of affection, and its issue, although efficient, is totally lacking in charm. Leopoldville is both pretentious and pugnacious, ignoring rather than blending with the countryside on which it is built. I never liked Leopoldville and I liked it even less now, largely because my old friends and associates from the United Nations and the press corps had been driven out and supplanted by Belgians. There were more Belgians in Leopoldville now than I had ever seen before and they, together with the cars on the streets and the new refrigerators in the shop windows, gave the city an atmosphere of prosperity. But it was, I soon learned, an artificial prosperity which derived not from the Congo itself but from aid from abroad. And the aid—whether it came in the form of cash or consumer goods—did not go to the rest of the Congo. It stopped in Leopoldville. I was also told that the government was spending 80 percent of its national budget not on schools or reconstruction programs and the like but on salaries for politicians and civil servants. Since the civil servants I had encountered in the hinterlands seemed to be paid late, spasmodically or not at all, I assumed that most of the national budget, too, stopped at Leopoldville.

Most of the people in the American embassy were strangers to me. But my name was known to them, and when I walked in unannounced shortly after my arrival I was treated something like a conquering hero. The fact that I had conquered nothing, that I had retreated to rather than advanced on Leopoldville merely added to my discomfort.

In my search for familiar faces, I walked into the Memling Hotel and noticed that the birds in the glass cage behind the bar had died off since my time and been replaced by monkeys. When I asked the desk where I could find *les journalistes* I was informed that there was only one of them in the hotel now. The few others who remained in Leopoldville (once there had been as many as fifty) had found places to live in houses with gardens on the edge of the city. I did, however, run across Lloyd Garrison of the *New York Times*, who was an old friend.

"I'm awfully glad you're alive," he said. I did not have the heart to tell him that I had never been in much danger. From Garrison and John Bulloch of the London *Daily Telegraph* I learned that the Congolese military authorities had placed Stanleyville off limits to reporters. Apparently there had been too many newspaper stories about the victories being won by Colonel Mike Hoare's white mercenaries and too little mention of the role played by the Congolese National Army in these encounters. The fact that most reporters thought they were practicing discretion by withholding the activities of the ANC's from their dispatches had not been understood by the Congolese high command, and journalists were now thoroughly *persona non grata* with the military.

With the connivance of the army attaché in the American embassy, I managed to persuade a Congolese army major at army headquarters (the building overlooked Stanley's statue on a bluff above the Congo River) that I was a publisher's representative, and he gave me a military pass to Stanleyville. When we were clear of his office, the American said I had better get on the next plane before the major changed his mind. A day later the major did change his mind (or it was changed for him) and revoked my pass, but by then I was aboard an American Air Force C-130, its cavernous belly filled with jeeps, bound for Kamina and thence to Stanleyville. At Kamina, the Congolese bystanders were impressed by the size of the plane, the Belgians were impressed by the loadmaster's command of four-letter words, and I (having just emerged from a land where cooking fires always seemed to be lighted as close as possible to the nearest gasoline and ammunition depot) was impressed when the American Negro sergeant in charge of the guard detail told me to take my cigarette the hell out from under that wing. There was something else about the sergeant that impressed me and it took me a moment to realize what it was. He was the first soldier I had seen since setting foot in Africa whose uniform was clean and did not look as if it belonged to someone else.

Stanleyville would be my last stop, my final effort, before returning to London and I wanted to get it over with quickly. I had read and heard so much about the horror of the place that I was quite ready to spend my few days there in a nightmarish investigation into the depravity of man. I was prepared to feel revulsion, perhaps even hatred, for the executioners, for those responsible for so much tragedy and sheer misery. And at the beginning, as Fritz Scheller, the UN representative in Stanleyville, told me some of the things that had happened, I did experience a numbing feeling of futility. During the period in which they occupied Stanleyville, the rebels killed 10,000 Congolese. That was Scheller's estimate. Then, to balance the scales, the white mercenaries who followed the Belgian paratroopers into town—and the execution squads and the ANC's who followed them—killed another 2,500. Where once there had been an adult male work force of 25,000 now there were 5,000. Scheller guessed that of all those killed perhaps only 1,000 had been killed for what might logically be called a reason. The rest had died because they belonged to the wrong tribe, or because they wore a clean shirt, or because (as one particularly ghastly day) they happened to live in houses which contained telephones which might have been used to send surreptitious messages to Leopoldville. The mercenaries were no better. According to Scheller, they shot at everything that was black and moved. And what the mercenaries, in their haste to loot the shops and blow open the bank vaults, failed to do, the ANC's did for them later. Scheller remembered the rebel brought to the hospital with the badly lacerated eyes. The doctors worked on him for hours. A delicate piece of surgery. With luck and care the man would see again. When the operation was completed, the ANC's, who had been waiting patiently and politely in the vestibule, took the man outside and clubbed him to death.

Scheller went on. He was outspoken, he had humor, and he saw things from all sides with just the right combination of cynicism and idealism. He seemed the perfect man for Stanleyville and I liked him. But after a while my questions came mechanically. I stopped taking notes and, when he came to the end of one of his stories, I thanked him, said I would see him later, and walked out into the street. I had had enough.

I do not know why it was but suddenly, as I left Scheller's office and emerged into the sunshine, Stanleyville took on a different quality. The horror had gone and in its place came a sadness—the kind of gentle, quiet sadness that permeates graveyards where the stones are covered with moss and the grass is thick and soft underfoot. Reverie replaced the nightmare.

I walked the streets of Stanleyville with a Congolese called Juma as my guide. Like the other Africans in the city, he wore a strip of white cloth around his head to denote his allegiance to the central government in Leopoldville. He had started wearing the white headband the moment the Belgian paratroopers began dropping from the sky, as had most of the citizens of Stanleyville. Even so, many of his friends had been killed by the white invaders. But Juma bore the killers no malice, nor did he seem to mourn his friends.

The Congo buries its memories with its dead. The rains fall, the rivers flow and the sun rises after a night of carnage to shine down on new leaves glistening green in the heat of morning. Yesterday did not happen. Tomorrow will never come. There is only today.

Has it always been thus? I am certain only that this was the way it was with Juma on the day of our walk through Stanleyville. We walked, we drank beer, and we talked, but when we talked about the past or the future Juma became vague. It was not that he was trying to avoid talking about them, although the memories must have been painful and assuredly the future was bleak. No, it was simply that he had not been thinking about these things or talking about them with his friends. After we had finished our beer, I asked Juma to take me to the place where the rebels had shot down Paul Carlson. I had read that he had met his death near the Residence Victoria while trying to scale a wall. Juma said he knew the place well. He himself had seen the medical missionary's body. But when we arrived in the area Juma became confused. It had all happened so long ago . . . in November.

For the whites of Stanleyville it was, of course, different. They remembered. They *had* to remember if only to assure themselves that what they had been through meant something, and those who perished had not died in vain. The blacks might be content to have Stanleyville mean nothing—nothing at all—but for whites such a course was unthinkable. So it was that on Saturday morning a requiem mass was celebrated in the Cathedral of Notre Dame for the victims of the rebellion. I do not know whether the prayers uttered silently by the whites at that mass elevated the victims into the ranks of Christian martyrs or consigned the savage executioners to the everlasting fires. Perhaps both. However they prayed, I am sure their prayers were selective and that the souls that rose to heaven because of them were white and those that sank to hell were black.

I would not pretend to know how the black men prayed on that Saturday morning, but afterward many of them assembled at a bar which had the day before run the following half-page advertisement in the Stanleyville *Gazette:*

> PROSABEL wishes to inform its honorable clientele that its bar is being placed entirely at their disposition to serve them refreshing bottles at the end of the requiem mass.

The whites would say that was "very African." They would say so disparagingly or with affection, but, in either case, using it to illustrate the African's inability to feel deeply, his tendency to leap without apparent rhyme or reason from tears to laughter. Perhaps I had been in Africa too long, or just long enough, because the advertisement and its response struck me as neither frivolous nor disrespectful. It merely reflected the African desire to make each day, if not pleasant, at least bearable.

Today. To live for the day, for the hour. It is both a weakness and a strength. In Stanleyville it was a strength because it preserved sanity. A man could not be expected to live with a remembrance of hell and a foretaste of doom and remain sane.

In back of the American consulate in Stanleyville there is a patio. It is a curiously American patio with a wading pool, flagstones, a green lawn and a barbecue pit. During the time of the rebels, the consulate was used as their headquarters and the patio as a torture chamber for prisoners. A week or so before I arrived, Scheller, who had taken over the consulate until such time as the Americans returned, was sunning himself by the wading pool in the patio and watching his Congolese gardener cutting the grass with his *panga.* Suddenly the gardener stopped swinging his *panga* and, bending down, began pulling at something buried in the turf. The UN man watched in horror as the object revealed itself as a man's thighbone. What added to Scheller's horror was his growing awareness that the African was laughing. He tugged at the thighbone, laughed, and tugged some more.

My God, Scheller thought, it could have been his brother.

Perhaps the bone was his brother's and perhaps, for an instant, the gardener's mind had come unhinged. It is more likely, however, that he had long since relegated his brother to the past so that now neither the past nor his brother impinged on the present. The thighbone, instead of serving as a grisly reminder, became an unexpected and welcome surprise in an otherwise uneventful day. It was something he could tell his friends about. His friends would listen and appreciate the story.

The whites would say that this too was "very African." They would say that if learning was the accumulation of experience the African would never learn anything as long as he forgot what had happened to him the day before. Over the centuries, what had the African accumulated? Nothing. Where were his cities, his museums, his libraries? There were none. Having accumulated nothing from the past how could he be expected to move into the future, to progress? All this, the whites would say, was further proof of his inherent inferiority.

The more thoughtful whites would say that it went deeper than this. The mystery must lie deep because, try as they would, they had never succeeded in understanding the African. Challenge and response, cause and effect . . . somehow the African eluded the fundamental principles.

It is natural for the whites to judge the African by white standards, using their strengths to demonstrate his shortcomings. Technologically he *is* inferior; politically he *is* embryonic; he *does* lack energy, drive and ambition.

True. And yet, when I upend the yardstick and measure the African against my weaknesses, he becomes something else again. It is his turn now to ask why I grow nervous among the silences of the Serengeti, why I jump at sudden noises in the dark, why I recoil from the unseen things that make the leaves twitch underfoot, why

I flinch from pain . . . why I fear death. If I tell him that it is not so, that I fear none of these things, he will know I am lying.

That is where he has it over me—this ability to penetrate to the essence of a man, to feel deep down into the essential truth of a matter. He does not listen to my words but stalks my conscience as he might an animal or a bird—not by following its footprints but simply by *knowing* where it will go. Where does he get this extra sense, and with it his acceptance of what it tells him is so? He cannot explain it to me (or even to himself) in language because it is something far beyond the scope of vocabulary. Whatever it may be, it has its roots in his long and intimate association with nature and the land.

Nature can be bountiful, but more often she is harsh and cruel. Above all she is irrational. Floods follow droughts, the locusts ravage what is saved, and disease lurks in the life-giving pool of water. Yet her brutality is strangely compassionate. The zebra grazes peacefully a stone's throw from where the lions rend the bloody carcass of its mate. The zebra does not hate the predator any more than the lion hates its prey.

The African, too, has made his accommodation to nature's irrational design. Shoeless, he feels her pulse through the red earth underfoot. Her rhythm is his rhythm. He walks in time with the elements. The white men who came to Africa wore shoes on their feet and never felt the rhythm. Is this why they cannot understand the African—because the African, walking in step with nature's erratic rhythm, is irrational too?

I am not persuaded that the white men came to Africa to commit a rape upon the continent. True, they did envisage profits and there were some who beat their servants or participated joyfully in punitive expeditions against recalcitrant tribes. But for every one of these there were ten others who cleared land, planted coconut palms, built little schools in the bush and brick churches amidst the mud and wattle huts of primitive villages. If the Baptist missionary bickered over territorial rights with his Catholic counterpart, he was simply obeying the instructions of his superiors. And if the statesmen of Europe carved Africa up to suit themselves (in a way that bore no relation to the natural terrain or the tribes which found themselves arbitrarily and irrevocably divided by new borders) they could be forgiven. Not only did they not know better but never in their wildest dreams did they think that the backward savages of the dark continent would ever achieve independence.

The white men came to Africa blessed by church, state, crown and commerce. Because theirs was a *civilizing* mission it would not fail. But it did fail. Had the colonizers held on for another one hundred, five hundred or a thousand years it might have been another story. But they departed, less than a century after their arrival, and what they left behind—their legacy for their black brother—was a taste for the unattainable and a gnawing sense of his own inferiority.

It was easy to make the African feel inferior and the white men, sometimes maliciously but more often unwittingly, did so every day—by living apart in houses that were clearly superior to those of the African, by driving cars where the African walked and by having more money in their weekly pay envelopes than an entire African village would see in a year. In case he missed the point they also *told* the African he was inferior by informing him that virtually every last one of his habits, customs and beliefs was wrong, or ridiculous or both. His body could cry out for protein, but he was no longer to hunt elephants. Even though the parasites in his system made him reel with the effort, he was to work hard. Though it humiliated him in the eyes of his peers and elders, he was forbidden to circumcise his daughters or make war on his traditional enemies. Be like us, said the white men. Learn from our example. If you want what we have, you must become as we are.

I am quite convinced that a vast majority of the white men who came to Africa were themselves convinced that they were helping the African. If they could not make over the African into their own image at least they would implant in him the desire for the tangible assets of civilization—power over other men, suits hanging in closets and mixed drinks in air-conditioned bars. Give him a hunger for *things* and the rest (democracy, hard work, the rule of law, monotheism, etc.) would follow.

The hunger was there but the *things* were not, and the African awoke on the day of his independence to discover that the wealth of his continent was largely a mirage. Perhaps, deep down, he had known this all along, but for a while the white men had led him to believe otherwise. After all, they *had* found copper in Katanga and diamonds in Kasai. They *had* planted coffee in the highlands and bananas on the coast, and some of them *had* grown rich doing so. But most of Africa wore erosion's leprous skin. Her soil was thin and her bones as brittle as the gnarled gray bush that sheltered the killer tsetse fly. Large as it was, Africa never supported more than a relative handful of whites and these managed to turn a profit only because they worked terribly hard, because the labor they employed was so terribly cheap and because that part of the profit which was diverted to schools, hospitals, government salaries and public services was held to an absolute minimum. Upset that formula in the smallest degree and there would be no further profits, let alone enough money to provide the continent and its people with even the sleaziest of cornerstones on which to build a modern civilization.

The immediate impact of black Africa on the visitor today is one of bitterness, hatred and frustration. Even the mildest and most enlightened of the leaders feels he must rail against the whites, or the Asians, and blame them for the lack of *things*.

The white men would say that all this was foolish and futile, a cynical diversionary exercise on the part of the leaders designed to take the people's minds off their own shortcomings and postpone the inevitable moment of truth. The sooner the Africans get over their foolish tantrums the better.

I think it is far more than this. I do not think it is a passing phase at all but a manifestation of something very deep indeed, something which is going on—noisily in the cities but quietly and without rancor in the countryside—throughout black Africa, in each and every one of the newly independent states south of the Sahara. What is happening is a steady, inexorable return to the bush. It derives, I believe, from the African's knowledge, deeply felt, that nothing that has occurred since the arrival of the white man has made him happy or done him any good. He does not like to be reminded, even by implication, that he is inferior. As for the *things*, he does not want to be reminded of them either. He never wanted them as badly as we thought he did and, now that he knows he cannot have them, he is prepared to see them go.

It is an almost imperceptible movement, this return to the past, and those who are looking for masses of marching men accompanied by martial music and ringing proclamations will never see it. Rather, it is a quiet drift, but the trail is clear, marked as it is by abandoned cars which need only gasoline to make them run again, by discarded radios requiring only batteries to bring them back to life, and by vanishing roads and crumbling, vine-choked plantation homes. It will not take nature long to obliterate these final reminders of the white men's occupation of this land.

The jungle; the bush; the open savanna. It was here, where he was born, that the black man would return to slough off the imperfectly grafted skin of civilization, to regain his sense of superiority. Yes, here *he* was superior—to the animals he stalked and to the white men who had stalked him.

I do not see anything on the horizon, I can imagine nothing which will halt or even slow this return to the bush. The African leaders in the cities, preoccupied with the increasingly difficult task of protecting their own interests, will be able to do little. Neither will their successors—the indignant generals and the angry young men with educations who rise up in a puritanical reaction against inefficiency and corruption—be able to do much. The power they seek is largely illusory. Power was one of the things the white men *did* take with them when they left Africa and it has not been replaced. In Africa today there are no armies, no forces of persuasion worthy of the name. Nor will the African be lured back by outsiders. That was tried once before and, for the African, it ended in disaster and disillusionment. Perhaps—but only perhaps—it could be done through aid and assistance from overseas. But the gigantic sums required, far more than the niggling amount sent to Africa today, are not forthcoming. In fact it seems more likely that, as the African turns his back on the outside world, the outside world will respond by turning its back on him. Civilization and its advantages are a lure only so long as they are attainable. Now that the African knows that they are not, they are no lure at all.

I think it was this return to the ancient verities that gave Stanleyville its dreamlike atmosphere of tranquillity. Its inhabitants had been through all the hells that could be devised for Africa—the hell of colonialism, the hell of Patrice Lumumba's broken promises, the hell inflicted on them by a vengeful and corrupt central government and, finally, the hell under the rebels. Stanleyville had tried everything and had failed at everything. Now, at long last, it was going back to the only way of life that made sense or had ever made sense. It was the only way.

> South of the moon, where man was born, all values and all symbols seem upside down,

Robert Ardrey wrote in the final pages of his *African Genesis.*

> There are the smiles, broad and white. But what lies behind the smile? I do not know. There is laughter, like small old cymbals ringing. But what lies behind the laughter? . . . The conscience I face in the African street bears no resemblance to my own.
>
> I am alone in the African street, lost, afraid and without allies. I understand nothing. Yet this is the street where I was born.

Ardrey was right. I cannot continue my search for answers by following the African into the bush. Unless I wrap myself in the cocoon of civilization—my pills and serums, the generator for my lights, my radio—I will fall sick and die. Wrapped in them I remain isolated, as cut off from the truth as I am in the African cities. So I will never know what he sees in the jungle, what meaning he draws from the shape of a cloud, the quiver of a leaf or the sounds of distant drums.

In the meantime the gulf between us widens. We draw apart. My thoughts are not his thoughts, nor are his mine. I fear what he embraces and when he laughs I cry. There was a time when we might have met and talked and agreed that we were different, that each of us possessed a secret which was ours and ours alone. The African was willing but I and my kind, in our arrogant assumption that all God's children are cast in our image, insisted that he learn to become one of us. But the time for understanding—or at least an agreement that we do not understand—is long since past.

Of the African mind and personality, of the African heart and soul, I know no more now than when I started. But the beginnings of wisdom are sometimes found after the light goes out . . . in the darkness. There is a secret in the African bush. I have not found it. And if it is found I am not sure it will have meaning for me. All I know is that it is there. For the time being, simply knowing that it is there is enough for me.

INDEX

Set in Linotype Janson
Composed, printed and bound by The Haddon Craftsmen, Inc.
HARPER & ROW, PUBLISHERS, INCORPORATED